DESCRIPTIVE PSYCHOLOGY AND THE PERSON CONCEPT

DESCRIPTIVE PSYCHOLOGY AND THE PERSON CONCEPT

Essential Attributes of Persons and Behavior

WYNN SCHWARTZ

ACADEMIC PRESS

An imprint of Elsevier

Academic Press is an imprint of Elsevier
125 London Wall, London EC2Y 5AS, United Kingdom
525 B Street, Suite 1650, San Diego, CA 92101, United States
50 Hampshire Street, 5th Floor, Cambridge, MA 02139, United States
The Boulevard, Langford Lane, Kidlington, Oxford OX5 1GB, United Kingdom

Notices
Knowledge and best practice in this field are constantly changing. As new research
and experience broaden our understanding, changes in research methods, professional
practices, or medical treatment may become necessary.

Practitioners and researchers must always rely on their own experience and knowledge
in evaluating and using any information, methods, compounds, or experiments described
herein. In using such information or methods they should be mindful of their own safety
and the safety of others, including parties for whom they have a professional responsibility.

To the fullest extent of the law, neither the Publisher nor the authors, contributors, or
editors, assume any liability for any injury and/or damage to persons or property as a
matter of products liability, negligence or otherwise, or from any use or operation of any
methods, products, instructions, or ideas contained in the material herein.

Library of Congress Cataloging-in-Publication Data
A catalog record for this book is available from the Library of Congress

British Library Cataloguing-in-Publication Data
A catalogue record for this book is available from the British Library

ISBN 978-0-12-813985-1

For information on all Academic Press publications
visit our website at https://www.elsevier.com/books-and-journals

Publisher: Nikki Levy
Acquisition Editor: Emily Ekle
Editorial Project Manager: Barbara Makinster
Production Project Manager:
  Prem Kumar Kaliamoorthi
Cover Designer: Matthew Limbert

Typeset by SPi Global, India

Working together
to grow libraries in
developing countries

www.elsevier.com • www.bookaid.org

Contents

4. The Judgment Diagram, Some Categories of Cognizance, and the Unconscious

5. Relationships, the Relationship Formula, and Emotional Competence

6. Verbal Behavior, Language, and Linguistic Self-Regulation

7. Community and Culture

8. Reality and the Worlds

9. Empathy in Practice: A Demonstration of Some Person Concepts

Preface

Inauspiciously, I started graduate school skeptical about my field of study—clinical and experimental psychology. As an undergraduate, I was impressed by the reasonably designed experiments described in my psychology classes, but the personality theories taught read like warring theologies. And what made it worse, the more scientific they sounded, the less I recognized anyone I knew. Where was the person in the theory? Not alone, I remember one of my professors saying, "with so much horseshit around, there must be a pony in there somewhere."

Other than refinements in experimentation and the acknowledgment of failures to replicate classic studies, not much has changed—except, too often, rebranding practices with the prefix "neuro." Clinicians, when they bother with theory at all, still align as partisans of faith. Even today, when my students interview for training sites they're asked if their orientation is psychodynamic, cognitive-behavioral, or humanistic. To quell their anxiety, I suggest they answer they've a psychodynamic and social-learning appreciation of relationships, and a set of cognitive-behavioral tools they empathically apply. Some hear this and relax, intuitively feeling it expresses what they actually try to do. I'd like to offer their intuition explicit coherence.

What gives a subject matter coherence and integrity? Once a subject matter is identified—in our case, the behavior of persons—what must it account for, and what manners of observing, formulating, theorizing, explaining, etc., are compatible with the subject or violate its integrity? And, crucially, are there concepts so fundamental to the subject that they must be maintained? Here's a first reminder: as a psychologist and a behavioral scientist, all of my professional work is the work only a person can do. This, of course, holds for all of us.

As a psychologist who practices psychotherapy my interests center on the behavior and characteristics of people, especially how we come to be the way we are and how we can change. This requires having the concept of a person in the first place. Fortunately, we already do, but it's mostly implicit. This book is about making it systematic and explicit. Being systematic and explicit provides clarity and facilitates negotiation about where we agree, disagree, or don't have a clue.

My introduction to the Person Concept came early fall 1972 when I read somewhere NASA had asked, "If green gas on the moon speaks to an astronaut, how do we know if it's a person?" God knows why it came up, but north of Nederland, high in the Rockies, warm around a campfire, a classmate said one of our professors had an answer.

I entered doctoral study having read Thomas Kuhn's *The Structure of Scientific Revolutions* and Stephen Pepper's *World Hypotheses*. Kuhn taught that when a scientific community encounters a sufficient number of empirical anomalies that do not fit the established paradigm, it is eventually replaced by a new paradigm. From Pepper, I learned the troubling idea that most contemporary personality theories stem from incompatible "root metaphors" grounded in ancient metaphysical assumptions that the world is a machine or an organism, and so on. Working my way through Wittgenstein's *Philosophical Investigations*, its end notes especially resonated, ".... For in psychology, there are experimental methods and conceptual confusion." From these texts I gathered that psychologists have significant knowledge and useful practices, but their theories aren't built on a coherent conceptual base. Fundamental concepts in one theory can mean something quite different in others. Nor, for that matter, do their theories start with a similar appreciation of what is real. One theory's thorny anomaly is another's starting point; an unquestioned given for one is treated as unreal by another.

It still seems that concepts of accountability, choice, reason, and intention—ideas at the cornerstone of civilization and *my* practice of psychotherapy—when taught along with a "scientific" requirement for reductionism and determinism, reside in contradictory intellectual universes. When I read physics, chemistry, and biology, the foundational concepts in one text resemble their use in the others, and when they don't, that problem is recognized as requiring a shared lexicon; and, if the data requires, an improved paradigm. Psychology is different. Psychology lacks a common lexicon *and* a comprehensive foundation. And psychology is different in other ways as well.

Psychology *is* special. It has, at least for me, a more interesting problem than sorting out the meat and potatoes of the natural sciences. Psychology must have a place within its domain for the creation and practice of science itself. The physicist, chemist, and geologist do not have to account for their personal interests as part of their subject matter, but the psychologist must. Inescapably, every scientific theory and experiment is someone's theory and experiment. Behavioral science has to account for scientific behavior—the sort of behavior *only* persons can do. Fundamentally, behavioral science has to provide an explicit and comprehensive account for the behavior of persons *as* persons—and not as if we are something else.

So, I entered graduate school ambivalent about the discipline, expecting contradictory and barely relevant theory, but with faith I would learn reasonable methods for establishing facts. Sticking close to the empirical seemed a smart way to go. But being no fan of theology, what was I supposed to do with all those theories? No surprise, I ended up in my chairman's office worried I'd made a bad choice. Not smiling, he responded, "I suspect you might like Pete's stuff," and with that I went off to meet the guy pondering the green gas problem. This book is mostly about what I learned from him and the people that formed a community around his work.

Peter Garcia Ossorio introduced me to the job of making explicit and systematic the knowledge and competence of living as a person in a world of people. He called this discipline Descriptive Psychology. By 1972 he was well into working on the Person Concept, the central concern of Descriptive Psychology. He told me to start with what I already know about people; to start with what is required to live as a person in the community of others. The work of Descriptive Psychology, he said, was to carefully and explicitly formulate concepts and rules that can systematically interconnect everything we know about people without leaving anything out. He also reminded me, "things that aren't intellectually satisfying tend to be unsatisfactory in other ways as well." Sharing this aesthetic, I began.

What I will present here is not the usual fare for the practice of behavioral science. Descriptive Psychology is not psychology in the conventional sense of a comprehensive personality theory. It is not a theory, but instead a preempirical conceptualization, a formulation of the essential attributes of persons and behavior that any adequate theory must encompass. The function of Descriptive Psychology's *Person Concept* is to provide an explicit, extensive, and systematic analysis and connection of all the "moving parts" of what we implicitly mean by persons and behavior. To accomplish this requires a shared lexicon and set of rules, clearly articulated and suitable for coordinating *all possible facts* regarding people and behavior. As such, one use of this project is a framework for comparing theories and judging their scope and adequacy. The goal is a map with a place for what is already known with room for what is yet to be found.

Why not call this a theory? Unlike a theory, a conceptualization of a subject matter attempts to establish its full possible range by identifying *what it is about* rather than the empirical or historically particular form it takes. *The focus is the range of possibility.* Finding out what really happens, on the other hand, is the empirical task. But before attempting systematic observation, it is usually wise to have some idea what you are looking for. Descriptive Psychology's mission is this sort of preempirical formulation. The job of theory is postempirical to explain why out of the possibilities only certain patterns occur. Good theory can then be vindicated by predicting new observations that are found and fit. We then face the dilemma of how to fit our theories together. Under current conditions, attempting integration can be a fool's errand.

The continued absence of a shared framework for investigation and practice has resulted in the fragmented state of current psychology and the neurosciences. As an aesthetic judgment, some find this more disturbing than others. Descriptive Psychology was invented in response to those who share this discomfort. To the extent the Person Concept is well-formed, its explicit conceptualization should sharpen observation and refine our ability to share and integrate what is found. I believe it has for me.

What follows is a work in progress. The essential nature of Descriptive Psychology requires room for significant distinctions yet to be recognized. Nonetheless, what is already built is nuanced, systematic, and entirely interconnected. The Person Concept has complex interdependent component concepts: Individual Persons, Behavior as Intentional Action, Language and Verbal Behavior, Community and Culture, and World and Reality. Tying these together are the transition rules of The State of Affairs System for unpacking and connecting everything.

Some words of caution. The foundational concepts are interdependent—resembling aspects of a map—so grasping them will be easier after they have all been filled in. The reward for effort will require patience. I have a promise for the practitioner. Descriptive Psychology is a pragmatic enterprise, its success rests on enhancing effective action. I earn most of my keep in the practice of psychotherapy. Any adequate understanding of persons and behavior necessarily involves an appreciation of how people change. If this is your interest, this book should hold some value for you. That's my intent.

A few more words before we begin. I am writing in first person. This book is my understanding, shaped by my interests. As a member of the community that developed these ideas, I believe they accurately represent Descriptive Psychology and the Person Concept. Still, this is my understanding, and the idiosyncrasies, examples, and digressions reflect my values, practices, and fascinations as an academic clinical psychologist.

1

What Is Descriptive Psychology and The Person Concept?

LET'S START WITH "PEOPLE MAKE SENSE"

"What makes an individual a person is, paradigmatically, to have mastered the concept of a Person." **(Peter Ossorio, 1998/2012, Place)**.

"The ability that people have that enables them to understand people is the ability to use, or act on, a certain concept. This concept is designated as 'the Person concept' or, interchangeably, 'the concept of the Person.'

Mastery and use of this concept are what is universal among persons. It is universal among persons because mastery of that concept and the routine spontaneous exercise of that mastery are what make a person a person." **(Peter Ossorio, 2006a, b, The Behavior of Persons)**.

When I first meet someone new to my practice, before I spend much time introducing myself, I ask them to orient me. I want to learn something about how they construct their concerns before I impose mine. Given my shopworn appearance, people sometimes suppose I've heard a story like theirs before. I am careful not to dismiss this recognition, but I point out I do not know them yet, and it will take time before I do.

Introducing the Person Concept creates a similar dilemma. Much will be familiar, because it is something every competent person already knows, but when the Person Concept is made explicit, when offered as the foundation of a unified behavioral science, it can be confused with *something else* already known. For example, it can be taken as some variety of philosophy or psychological theory. Wait before placing the Person Concept in any of those other already known categories. What follows is not conventional psychology in the form of a theory or a set of empirical findings. Rather, it is something prior to that, something preempirical, a foundation that provides a place for theory and data to coherently engage. Assembling this foundation will require patience; it will be akin to putting together a jigsaw puzzle. The picture we will construct is the conceptual structure of persons, a subject matter in which, one way or another, all the facts of behavioral science must have a place. This includes what people know about themselves and others; their theories and methods; and since every idea is someone's idea, what people take to be the case about their worlds. The goal here is *that* inclusive and *that* ambitious. As daunting and grandiose as it sounds, remember: *we are already prepared, because we already know how to act as persons.* And since concepts guide action, to the extent we act as "one of us persons," we practice the Person Concept, even if we have never put this understanding into words. My job here is to find the right words.

The Person Concept is not the same as a theory of persons nor is it an assemblage of empirical findings about us. Instead, it is a structure, scaffold-like, with places to hang whatever we know or come to find out. Like a jigsaw puzzle, the Person Concept is constructed from other interlocking pieces, but here the metaphor breaks down. A jigsaw cuts up the image in some meandering way to make it a puzzle and make it challenging. Any orienting shapes will come from the straight edges and right-angled corners that framed the precut image. This is not how we are going to construct the Person Concept.

Contrast a jigsaw puzzle with a scale model airplane, fresh out of the box, parts and instructions on the table. Even without the directions, many components can be recognized for their function: a propeller, a clear cockpit, wheels and struts, parts for wings and fuselage. Since we already know about airplanes, we can make sense of what is spread before us. The foundational concepts, the parts of the Person Concept, are more like the airplane to be: each concept is already meaningful and scaled to fit the others. The Person Concept's box holds the primary interdependent concepts: Individual Persons, Behavior as Intentional Action, Verbal Behavior and Language, Community and Culture, and Reality and World (Fig. 1.1). In turn, each of these concepts is formed from other concepts. Since these complex parts need to fit together properly, we will need guidance. As with the model airplane, there is a set of instructions: The Relationship Formula and The State of Affairs System provide the rules for transforming and interconnecting the concepts, at whatever level of abstraction we need.

A brief thought. Think of the box of the model that caught your eye in the hobby shop. Its cover had an image of the assembled whole. Consider the Person Concept in this light. We already understand people, akin to the way we understand the image on the box. Do the standard behavioral sciences have a box that shows what competent people already know about people?

Maps, puzzles, and model kits are a bit misleading. The primary components of the Person Concept are more like perspectives than parts. They are not simply parts that make up the whole. They are distinct ways of accessing the full logical domain of Persons. All of what we can attribute to an

The Person Concept

Individual Person	Behavior	Language	World	Culture
	Parameters	Parameters	Elements	Parameters
Paradigm Case Formulation	Identity	Concepts	Objects	World
	Wants	Locutions	Processes	Members
Engages in	Knowledge	Behavior	Events	Social Practices
Deliberate Action	Know How		State of Affairs	Statuses
in a	Performance		Concepts	Language
Dramaturgical	Achievement		Relationships	Choice Principles
Pattern	Significance			
	Personal Characteristics			

FIG. 1.1   The Person Concept.

individual can be represented by that individual's behavior. All behavior corresponds to something that can be represented verbally. And all the distinctions that can make a difference in behavior and language are distinctions in the world.

Peter Ossorio created what he called Descriptive Psychology as the domain for exploring and mapping the Person Concept. No one I know, including Ossorio, has ever been happy with the subject matter's name. (It is not even really a psychology; nor is it Franz Brentano's Descriptive Psychology, although both subject matters focus on intentionality.) The justification for "Descriptive" comes from the sense that if a description is clear enough, no further explanation is ordinarily required. This underscores the value of lucid, logically sound description. Descriptive Psychology is stocked with guidance and reminders for accomplishing this.

In orienting people to Descriptive Psychology, Ossorio offered these claims that capture the discipline's spirit. The devil, of course, is in the details.

1. The world makes sense, and so do people. They make sense to begin with.
2. It's one world. Everything fits together. Everything is related to everything else.
3. Things are what they are and not something else instead.
4. Don't count on the world being simpler than it has to be.

If everything fits together, any opening should connect to the entire world. Let's consider an ordinary encounter. On my way to meet a friend I see a young woman, a current student—I'm not sure—texting while walking in my direction. I can be ill at ease, awkward when bumping into students and acquaintances outside our usual context. As we pass, I hesitantly say hello—I fear she'll think I'm a stranger and not appreciate being greeted by an older man. Fortunately, just in time, she looks up and smiles in recognition. My discomfort ends. We chat a bit and go our separate ways.

These few details offer an example of mundane social engagement. The actors have common and differing statuses. They have some idea where they stand with each other and can appreciate what is afoot. Any competent member of the culture that includes the young woman and me, understands what's in play, including what would benefit from further inquiry. For example, what I just told you is not sufficient to definitively explain my awkwardness. What we have observed is easy to see, but further inquiry is required to understand the significance of what we observed.

This illustrates my first point: implicit understandings of this sort are expected. In ordinary interactions, each actor has a self-perspective and an observer's perspective on the circumstances. This includes what they take to be appropriate behavior, including recognition of the uncertainty of their understanding. These perspectives could be further elaborated, but usually aren't if things make enough sense for everyone to get along. Unless the interaction goes awry, there is usually little point explaining it further. Questions are mostly asked when something goes wrong or does not make sense.

Here is the second point: it is normal for things to make sense when people act together in a shared culture, not the exception. Generally, if we did not understand people, life would be chaotic. We could not cooperate. You could not understand this sentence. Understanding people *is* the central competence involved in being a person in a world of others.

Ordinary social interaction is predicated on most behavior going well enough, and this is my third point: that to recognize things not going well, a person must have the competence to recognize how it would appear going right, performed as expected, and achieving its desired goal. To recognize something as ineffective, there must be some concept of proper effect. *Behavior going wrong is a variation of it going right.* This goes for shared understandings too. Misunderstanding is the exception, not the rule. Before disagreement and misunderstanding can be identified, there must be some appreciation of what agreement and understanding looks like in a coherent world. We first need some sense of what it means to get along and communicate before we can identify its absence.

Some implications and reminders: people always act under some degree of uncertainty but always have enough information to attempt something. Normally behavior goes right. That is, unless it goes wrong in one of the ways it can go wrong.

This then follows: a person's actions can go wrong go in all sorts of ways, so explicitly identifying the conceptually distinct, changeable dimensions that constitute "doing something right" are relevant parameters for diagnosis and correction. Later, this will be formally reintroduced using a Parametric Analysis of Intentional Action, but for now, these few sentences should suffice. First, of primary social interest to people are intentional actions: behaviors that involve attempting to achieve some desired state of affairs. People are very interested in meaningful performances done on purpose. Second, a person's values, knowledge, and competencies are expressed in performances that try to achieve the person's goal. Intentional behavior involves recognizing an opportunity to get something wanted and having sufficient skill to try to get it. Doing this involves a performance, an implementation in real time.

The pragmatics of effectiveness is at the heart of this. *There are many ways to skin a cat*, an image not to be confused with *all roads lead to Rome*. Some ways work, some don't. (The infinite possibilities of doing something should not be confused with the random and arbitrary. A trillion chimps with typewriters might produce the works of Shakespeare, but don't hold your breath.) Here's the rub: there is no intellectually honest way to deny (1) that various performances can achieve or fail to achieve a goal and (2) that various personal characteristics can successfully or unsuccessfully be employed.

Despite complexity, uncertainty, and ambiguity, people within a community generally make sense to each other, their various understandings vindicated by effective engagement, including their means of correcting a course of action gone wrong.

A bit more orientation and another logical complexity: in a familiar circumstance, a person might repeat something done previously or try something different, even something that never occurred to them before. Sometimes we are surprised. But here is a troubling question. Are there systematic methods in our scientific psychologies to notice a spontaneous gesture as spontaneous? Do behavioral science traditions allow this? Is there a place for novelty and creativity as such? Similarly, does our scientific stance respect the foundations of contract and law built on the concepts of choice, responsibility, accountability, and negligence with the integrity of those meanings preserved?

Here's a problem. Articulation of what people do, expect, and require of each other is difficult, even impossible, when restricted or reshaped a priori by commitments to how behavior and the world must be. Historically, overreliance on deterministic, causal, and reductionist modes of explanation can set this trap (cf. Bergner, 2016). A way out can be found in something we already possess: our linguistic competence. But we need to be careful, very careful, when building science. We cannot afford to discard useful concepts and commitments where they work. Causal explanation and reductionist descriptions have places where they get the job done.

Here is my fourth point. For an adequate understanding of ourselves, our ordinary language with its extensive lexicon of nouns, adjectives, verbs, and adverbs already has most of the operations and distinctions needed. We have prepositions to open "unless clauses" pointing out the exceptions. We have plenty of actionable rules implicit in varieties of grammar and mathematics. When necessary, we invent technical vocabularies and procedures to cover new terrain. The elements and transformational operations required for identifying, describing, evoking, and explaining ourselves and our worlds are already implicit in our competence with language. Making this refined and explicit is part of the point of science. Good science is careful with language and attentive to its resources. Mathematics and logic are quintessential for this care. Descriptive Psychology is an example of this sort of attention applied to the scope and integrity of behavioral science.

Essence is expressed in grammar, says Wittgenstein (1953). "Think of the tools in a toolbox" … "there is a hammer, pliers, a saw, a screwdriver, a rule, a glue pot, glue, nails, and screws.—The functions of words are as diverse as the function of these objects. (And in both cases, there are similarities.)" The work of Descriptive Psychology involves carefully stocking the tool chest for constructing behavioral science. Its job involves curating the concepts and rules suited for systematic framing of observation, description, and explication. The rules are in the form of a behavioral logic, reminders Ossorio called status dynamic maxims. "…The work of the philosopher consists in marshalling reminders for a particular purpose" wrote Wittgenstein in a kindred spirit. (A listing of Ossorio's maxims can be found in Appendix 1.)

Descriptive Psychology is partly a response to Wittgenstein's observation of psychology's reductionisms and conceptual confusions; and to his challenge that whatever can be said can be said with complete clarity. As a clinician, I take kindred heart in another of his reminders, "There is not a single philosophical method, although there are indeed methods, different therapies, as it were" (Wittgenstein, 1953). Some of these methods will be illustrated shortly.

To anticipate a worry, Descriptive Psychology does not throw the baby out with the bathwater. Empirically, we know a great deal about actual babies and how they grow to become one of us. That which has been empirically vindicated remains intact. The goal is not to refute or argue against well-designed experiments, sound methodologies, and carefully gathered observations, nor against useful theory, but to establish a workable common ground where hard won knowledge can be honored and coherently shared. But it is also the mission of Descriptive Psychology to provide checks and guidance on the logical form of adequate description and explanation. An unavoidable consequence of increased clarity may be recognizing that certain methods and theories are more up to the task than others.

Building a framework where all the facts can be located requires considerable care and an openness that allows modification and expansion. What different frames will we need? Do they seamlessly interlock? Can we avoid napping in a Procrustean bed?

A FEW REMARKS ON SCIENCE AND WHAT A SCIENCE OF PERSONS SHOULD RESPECT

Descriptive Psychology's Person Concept provides a foundation for behavioral science so naturally the focus is the behavior of persons. But what about science itself? What commitments do we make calling something science? What is scientific behavior? Thinking a bit about the nature of science is not a bad way to start our thinking about the Person Concept.

Simply put, without the full set of the Person Concept's components, there is no science. Science is only produced by paradigmatic people. Nothing can be considered science that is absent of deliberate action, language, and a community of individuals that possess a certain set of values. In particular, science is created by a community that honors truth, rigor, objectivity, elegance, closure, fit, and kindred aesthetic values. Such folk find beautiful the well-formed formulas, the elegant experiments, and the clarity of parsimony. Of course, something similar could be said of music, art, and literature.

What sets science apart? This is answered all sorts of ways, but here's mine. Science strives for representation in exact and parsimonious language, is rigorously systematic, rule-following, teachable, and respectful of what actually happens in the empirical world. Science is constructed from shared, coherently connected concepts and theories that have been vindicated through methodical observation and recorded in a way that someone not present can understand and attempt to replicate. Standard lexicons and measures are vital for this. Where appropriate, quantification is a very good idea. Science is open to revision and reformation, not writ in stone.

Note I am saying scientific theories are vindicated rather than proven. Here's why. Unlike mathematics and logic where proofs are appropriate, to the extent science is an empirical enterprise that relies on data, its methods *only* vindicate or confirm that it continues to make sense to formulate and theorize in a particular way, and to do so until or unless a better formulation comes along. Scientific theories are judged by how well they fit the data, an aesthetic judgment. If the data fits, the theory remains vindicated, if not, it is disconfirmed.

Science is created and vindicated through systematic observation and description, and then situated within the currently accepted paradigm of what the scientific community counts as a "proper" explanation. Here preempirical assumptions, Stephen Pepper's (1942) world hypotheses and root metaphors, can cause problems. The explanatory and metaphysical assumptions of formism, mechanism, contextualism, and organicism offer some clarity, certainly more than animism and mysticism, but prove too restrictive or distorting when serving as the sole lens for viewing the lives of people.

Historical context shapes some of this. Prior to the 20th century, the Enlightenment offered faith in a "clock-work" universe organized by mechanical causes and their effects, constructed in a manner that allowed for composition and decomposition to basic units, such as atoms and the void. Reductionist practices and a faith in determinism served the scientific revolutions of the 17th century quite well. I doubt it got in the way of what chemists, physicists, astronomers, and physiologists were trying to figure out.

It would have been natural for the philosophers and physicians of the 19th century, as they morphed into psychologists, to look at the physics and chemistry of their time as the Yellow Brick Road to follow. Hard science's rigorous methodology, quantification, parsimony, and reproducibility are goals to emulate. But should we commit to them in a blood oath?

Sigmund Freud's motivational system is a good example of the conceptual dilemma of a priori commitments to what counts as authentic science. Everyone knows that Freud thought sexual pleasure, in one form or another, was a big motivator. Eventually, he settled on sex and competent mastery, but it took him 20 more years to get beyond the pleasure principle to his theory of competence.

In his attempt at a scientific topography of the mind, he transformed sexual desire into sensual pleasure. Pleasure, in turn, was to be understood as actually an energy called libido that followed the thermodynamic principles of Fechner's constancy principle. The libidinal system "sought" discharge to lower tension, pleasure being the phenomenology of tension reduction. I write "sought" to focus on the fact that this principle was also central to Freud's metaphysics of intentionality of goal direction. Why this convoluted reductionism? Well, he was an Austrian scientist committed to a preempirical decision of what constitutes legitimate science. Even when he acknowledged mastery was a primary motive, he attempted, very awkwardly, to reduce that to a repetition compulsion, a death wish, that followed the thermodynamic laws of entropy. Where did Freud's commitment come from? A blood oath signed by his mentor and laboratory director, Ernst Brücke.

In 1842, Emil Du Bois-Reymond, Ernst Brücke, Carl Ludwig, and Herman von Helmholtz signed this pact that dominated Germanic science in the century to follow.

> [We pledge] to put into power this truth: no other forces than the common physical chemical ones are active within the organism. In those cases which cannot at the time be explained by these forces one has either to find a specific way or form of their action by means of physical mathematical method, or to assume new forces equal in dignity to the chemical physical forces inherent in matter, reducible to the force of attraction and repulsion. (Ellenberger, 1970)

The extraordinary scope of Helmholtz's achievements in thermodynamics, optics, and physiology was persuasive testimony to the value of this pledge. It offered scientists useful guidance, up to a point, and that is where psychology got confused.

Think of the different ways we use force, cause and effect, and reasons for an action. I should not have to argue that the Newtonian force of mass multiplied by acceleration has little to do with forcing a person to act. To force an action suggests coercion. You might coerce me into a high-stakes game of eight-ball, but after I hit the cue ball, there is nothing coercive in the cause and effect chain of motion and impact. Causal language does that job well. But if you forcefully coerce me to play, I might resist, comply, or make a mockery of the game. How I choose to respond will follow from my reasons.

There is no place for choice in a world that only has room for causes and effects. I am using cause and effect when it is determined that whenever X occurs Y invariably follows. Scientists, engineers, and the rest of us make practical use of knowing when this is the case. I have no quarrel here. When playing eight-ball, I rely on this. But what about my decision where to hit the cue ball to break the rack apart?

For behavioral science, the shelf life for full reliance on reductionism and determinism has expired. Reductionist attempts to reduce or translate concepts of intention, choice, meaning, significance, and the like into language proper for physiology, physics, and chemistry have failed. There is very good reason to think such programs are misguided by category errors and confusions of logical types. A person's development is not suited to utter predictability nor are people's erotic motivations reducible to discharges of tension.

Psychology is splintered over fidelity to philosophies of reductionism and determinism. Some schools still pledge allegiance, but by the mid-20th century, the humanistic psychologies of Maslow (1943) and Rogers (1951) cashiered these concepts out of their programs. They argued that purpose, meaning, and self-actualization are robbed of meaning in a fully determined world, and moved toward person-centered psychologies of being. Likewise, the phenomenological and existential psychologies of Binswanger and Boss took concepts of freedom and liberation as a given (Hall et al., 1998).

In the mid-1970s, alert to critiques from analytic philosophy (MacIntyre, 1958; Peters, 1958; Wittgenstein, 1953), psychoanalytic theorists, such as Roy Schafer (1976) and George Klein (1976), began to disentangle their clinically relevant theories of maturation, intention, meaning, and conflict, from the physicist's language of energy and thermodynamics.

The tension between a therapy that attempted to free people from unexamined constraint and its underpinning in mechanistic metaphysics plagued psychoanalytic theory from the very start. "Free association" and libidinal determinism inhabit separate theoretical universes. Despite a lifetime of effort, Freud failed to reconcile the teaching of his two great philosophical masters, Hermann von Helmholtz and Franz Brentano.

Freud held tight Brentano's vision that intentionality is the hallmark of the mental and Helmholtz's dictum that scientific explanation requires the language of physics and chemistry. Freud offered libido, his sexual energy, as a force "equal in dignity" to Helmholtz's "chemical physical forces," attempting to bridge thermodynamics with intentionality. It didn't result in a coherent system. His fundamental attempt, the *Project for a Scientific Psychology* written in 1895, was only published posthumously.

In 1976, while reading Schafer's *New Language for Psychoanalysis* and George Klein's *Psychoanalytic Theory: An Exploration of Essentials,* I saw the beginning of a consensus that a paradigm shift was emerging in the grand narratives of psychoanalytic theory. The shift favored intentionality. More Brentano, less Helmholtz.

In 1985, Kenneth Gergen and Keith Davis edited *The Social Construction of the Person.* A hallmark of social constructionism is the description of persons, cultures, and worlds as an invention, a state of affairs built rather than discovered, inexorably woven from cultural practices. In the volume's introduction to its subject matter's domain was a chapter of Ossorio's providing *An Overview of Descriptive Psychology,* where he stated "the realist, subjectivist, and social constructionist, each make salient something the others do not …. they are only incompatible with each other when they are used imperialistically, … with the status assignment 'This is how it *really* is.' Although there is some overlap, the realist, subjectivist, and social constructionist are in general concerned with a different range of facts and possible facts, each one to the neglect of others." He contrasted the subject domain of social constructionism with Descriptive Psychology's goal to create "systematic formulations providing formal access to all of the facts and possible facts."

In 2015, writing in *The Journal for the Theory of Social Behavior,* Gergen declared "the 'science wars' of recent decades have largely subsided, giving way to what might be viewed as a condition of reflective pragmatism." In his abstract, Gergen writes, "Shifting from a view of knowledge as propositional, to one of knowledge as praxis—or practical 'knowing how'—I discuss research in a future forming direction, including critical inquiry, the creation of new practices, and collaborative action." This, I think is all well and good, but more is needed if the goal is a coherent science that provides a matrix for reflective practices.

Recognizing that science is a human creation, blind faith in determinism, reductionism, and an utter reliance on *time one, time two* causality is being replaced by a more inclusive requirement that science must be systematic, rule following, teachable, and vindicated by effective results. Science, unlike mathematics and logic, is not subject to proofs but is vindicated by results that show it makes sense to talk one way rather than another. Science is something people create where some ideas work much better than others. Some will get you three in a row and some won't.

Rather than build persons from the bottom up, from atoms and the void, Descriptive Psychology starts with a top-down approach in which persons are a given. This corresponds to acknowledging that the guiding principles of people's lives lose their integrity when treated as something else. To the extent there is an ongoing paradigm shift in psychology, it has been mostly a matter of fits and starts. Making explicit the Person Concept provides a coherent rule-following guide for this scientific revolution.

Moving from simple causality to pragmatics and rule following allows the actual persons present in ethics, aesthetics, politics, law, and religion to be found without distortion. If the science wars have "largely subsided," it would be good to have details of the treaty. Without an adequate foundational framework, it is very difficult for this treaty to achieve adequate interconnection and coherence; and accept modification as conditions on the ground require. The Person Concept provides the lexicon and rules, subject to expansion and revision, as discovery and invention proceed.

THE DESCRIPTIVE MAXIMS: BEHAVIORAL LOGIC AND SOME REMINDERS FOR WELL-FORMED DESCRIPTIONS

The status dynamic maxims constitute rules for a reasonable account of behavior. They are explicit reminders of how to make sense. The following nine are a fraction of the current collection, but they provide a good orientation. And, like well-formed formulas, most are tautological. As summary reminders, they are interspersed throughout this book in bold type, and are all tallied in Appendix 1, the 1998 list developed by Ossorio (1998/2012) in his volume, *Place*. Below are the nine that introduced me to the Descriptive maxims. They serve as an excellent sample of the rest.

Ossorio used the convention of "he" as a gender neutral third person pronoun and I will preserve that use when quoting him, as I do below. In my additions and paraphrases, I will employ the awkward "they" rather than he/she/it. I won't use "it." Even though a "possible person" might be a gender-free robot or what have you, as a personal value and a nod to Martin Buber (1958), among persons I prefer I to Thou.

THE ORIGINAL NINE MAXIMS

1. **A person takes it that things are as they seem unless he has reason to think otherwise.** Maxim One provides the reminder that people act on how it seems to them. It requires building a case if they are to be dissuaded.

2. **If a person recognizes an opportunity to get something he wants, he has a reason to try to get it.** Maxim Two is the reminder that behavior follows not just from motive but also from opportunity. The behavior occurs now because the opportunity, correctly or incorrectly identified, is occurring now.

3. **If a person has a reason to do something, he will do it unless he has a stronger reason not to.** Maxim Three is the reminder of the multiple perspectives that go into the appraisal of what a situation or circumstance calls for. There may be reasons not to pursue an otherwise desired course of action.

4. **If a person has two reasons for doing X, he has a stronger reason for doing X than if he had only one of these reasons.** Maxim Four holds for any number of additional reasons and is the reminder of the multiple reasons people often have for doing what they do.

5. **If a situation calls for a person to do something he can't do, he will do something he can do.** Maxim Five reminds us that behavior is an expression of a person's current values, knowledge, and competencies and not what an observer believes ought to be the case. People may not always do the best they can, but their action is always based on their appraisal of themselves and their circumstances. Not ours.

6. **A person acquires facts by observation (and thought).** How could it be otherwise?

7. **A person acquires concepts and skills by practice and experience in some of the social practices that involve the use of the concept or the exercise of the skill.** Maxim Seven reminds us that skill, competence, and know-how has a learning history and requires the opportunity to practice. In the absence of such practice a person may know what is called for but be unable to effectively act on that knowledge.

8. **If a person has a given person characteristic, he acquired it in one of the ways it can be acquired, i.e., by having the prior capacity and an appropriate intervening history.** Where Maxim Seven refers to the development of competence, Maxim Eight provides the logical structure for the development of personal characteristics and individual differences.

9. **Given the relevant competence, behavior goes right if it doesn't go wrong in one of the ways it can go wrong.** Maxim Nine simply restates what it means to be competent. Once competence has been acquired, successful behavior requires no explanation, but failures do.

These maxims are components of a preempirical structure for behavioral science and offer guidance for sound description. If a description is adequate, as Wittgenstein pointed out, there may be no need for further explanation. But there might. When more explanation is needed, theory might serve the purpose.

Let's turn to the Person Concept.

2

Individual Persons, Personhood, and the Problem of Definition

A person must be a being with his own point of view on things. The life-plan, the choices, the sense of self must be attributable to him as in some sense their point of origin. A person is a being who can be addressed and who can reply. **(Charles Taylor, 1985)**.

Persons and the status of personhood have an esteemed place in moral philosophy, law, politics, religion, and in the ordinary ways we are told to treat each other. At the heart of civilized engagement, we assert that persons are significantly different from other living things. But are we? And, if so, how? In contrast, some behavioral scientists treat these claims as convenient illusions, too soft-headed and fuzzy for serious scientific study. (Paradoxically, they could be questioning if any of us are really persons.). They ask how we can be both a product of biological evolution and hold ourselves categorically apart from other organisms? After all, our species, *Homo sapiens*, is just another mammal, one of the primates with a vertebrate anatomy that extensively mirrors the fishes and the frogs. Can we really be a special case, an exception to the laws of nature? And, if in some manner we are, what is different about us? Is it a matter of kind or degree? And how do we rigorously study that?

The systematic study of human nature in the humanities and natural sciences is a history conflicted over various commitments to what is meant by *human* and *nature* (e.g., Collingwood, 1945). As an undergraduate zoology student, I was wisely cautioned against anthropomorphism. Paradoxically, psychology and the behavioral sciences sometimes appear to urge the same. Not alone, I've come to wonder if the natural sciences' rigid avoidance of even a hint of anthropomorphism throws the baby out with the bathwater (see, e.g., Nagel, 2012; de Waal, 2016).

The philosophical naturalism "that reality is exhausted by nature, containing nothing 'supernatural,' and that the scientific method should be used to investigate all areas of reality, including the 'human spirit',"

(Papineau, 2016) is second nature to me. What is deemed supernatural on close inspection always seems to be something else. Still, the spirit in human spirit, not energy or matter, and clearly not weighing 21 g (MacDougall, 1907), is nonetheless a subject matter that requires reckoning. But how do we get at the essence, the essential nature and character of persons, human or otherwise? Scientific understanding demands methods appropriate for investigating whatever marks persons *alike and apart* from other things. This chapter will attempt that, respecting that people have bodies *and* conduct themselves in soulful ways.

What makes us think we are so special, other than we bother to ask? Usually this is answered by appeals to language, consciousness, and whatever is meant by free will. Human persons have a nature, are biological organisms, but apparently act in ways other animals can't or don't. (Unless, of course, some of them do.) Accounting for this setting apart is problematic if, in respectful imitation of our colleagues in the physical and natural sciences, behavioral scientists try to be scientists exactly like them. *Why not treat persons as simply another object entirely subject to the logics and methods that make physics and physiology successful?* (Sometimes, however, the physics that psychologists favor feels a bit Victorian, from a time when the math was easier.) And to complicate matters, although almost everyone agrees that human language is significantly different from the ways other animals communicate, there is no shortage of those arguing that free will is too muddled for science to take seriously. Many will not even get started trying to make sense of consciousness.

As a science of persons, Descriptive Psychology takes free will and consciousness seriously, while recognizing that these themes require considerable reformulation. In part, Descriptive Psychology employs methodologies that replace an a priori, faith-based determinism with rule-following systems. The Person Concept's point of providing a foundation for the behavioral sciences requires that whatever is actually special about persons cannot be ignored or treated as something it is not. Our task is to systematically give a detailed account of these themes. If successful, this ought to facilitate an authentic behavioral science that actually has a place for scientists, humanists, behaviorists, and all the other persons in the world. That psychology "has a place for the scientists" is a reminder that an adequate psychology must be reflexive. It must account for its own creation, that is, for the behavior of the scientists themselves. For this to work, the formulations of Persons and Behavior must be recursive and reflexive. The formulations must account for the behavior and the actor, must have a systematic place for representing ongoing and varying patterns of behavior, *and* a self-aware person who is creating and commenting on the action.

The Encyclopedia of Philosophy's (Edwards, 1967/2006) entry on Persons offers good examples of the special nature of persons that requires systematic accounting. Understandably, the normative moral philosophies are front and center. Interwoven, value-laden claims follow the implications of people being intentional, cognizant, and deliberate.

1. Persons and things. Kant et al.'s (1787/1998) position is instructive. Unlike mere things, he thought, respect is an attitude that has application specifically to persons. Kant's stance, his moral imperative, was that persons are of unconditional worth.

2. Persons are ends-in-themselves. Persons, Kant wrote, are "ends-in-themselves and sources of value in their own right." Hence, moral and ethical considerations apply to persons that do not apply elsewhere. Murder versus killing is this sort of distinction, in that only persons can murder or be murdered. Persons can also kill and be killed; but when a person kills another person deliberately or with premeditation, that killing is murder.

3. Accordingly, we have entry three: legal persons. Persons have responsibilities and are considered agents. This is a status that can be gained or lost. Consequently, some of us, sometimes, might not be legal persons.

Action, agency, and responsibility are big deals when considering relations among persons. There are at least two basic meanings of responsibility in psychological theory and ordinary life. One meaning is simply an indication of ownership: "that house with the vicious dog out back is mine," "I *do* feel that way," or "last night I dreamt." Similarly, people as responsible agents are expected to "own their actions" or to change them: "you need to get your act together, buddy."

A second foundational meaning concerns deliberate, premediated, chosen action. Psychological theories have a checkered past when approaching this. Early in my psychoanalytic training, I noticed this when I tried to sort out the contradiction between Freud's deterministic drive theory, his physicalism, and his hope for therapeutic liberation brought on by insight (Schwartz, 1984). On the one hand, Freud followed the party line of Germanic physical science, but on the other, he wanted to liberate and expand his patients' arena of choice, through the interpretative act of informing them of their hidden, unconscious options and motives. Later, as a cautionary tale, I'll return to Freud's problem of sorting out the dilemma of therapeutic liberation in a framework of reductive determinism.

Attributing responsibility is not cut and dried. We point to mitigating factors of competence and personal history. Emotional reactions and dreams also constitute a legitimate gray area. Sometimes we get away with, "I had no choice about what I felt and displayed," and sometimes we don't. So-called crimes of passion, feeling terrified and screaming in fear, being provoked and enraged, or having wanton transgressive dreams are excused, often enough, as being beyond self-control. Even so, people are held accountable by their neighbors for how they express their personal characteristics, a position Aristotle's *Nicomachean Ethics* made clear, long ago. Curiously, in an essay entitled "Moral Responsibility for the Content of Dreams" (1925), the sometimes determinist Freud wrote, "Obviously one must hold oneself responsible for the evil impulses of one's dreams. What else is one to do with them?" If a person claims he is not responsible for "his unconscious attributes," then, to quote Freud, "he will be taught better by the criticisms of fellow-men, by the disturbances in actions and the confusions of feelings" (p. 133).

Although people do not ordinarily choose what they dream, they might be held responsible for their ramifications. If rational and capable of insight, a person can be held legally responsible in the sense described in the various doctrines of negligence, criminality, and tort. "I can't help what I do when drunk" and "I can't control my desire" are countered with, "knowing that, why did you not avoid the circumstances that evoke your thirst?" This refers to the doctrine of "the reasonable man's," "know or ought to know standards," regarding negligence (Prosser, 1941). Because people are able to deliberate, they are expected to do so in certain circumstances. They prudently know what they should protect, avoid, or counter. We expect the person who owns the house with the vicious dog to keep it chained. They may be legally negligent if they fail to do so. For that matter, we implore some people to get a grip on their emotions.

In contrast to the ambiguity of owning one's personal characteristics, the acts that attend deliberation and choice are the grounds on which ethical and legal attribution and accountability always arise. Legal persons are those who knowingly can choose or refrain from a list of sanctioned behaviors. They are agents able to exercise adequate self-control. From these concerns follow *The Encyclopedia of Philosophy*'s next subheading.

4. Self-consciousness. Persons are morally responsible agents because they are at least sometimes self-consciously aware of their actions, options, and choices.

P.F. Strawson (1959) takes a different tack than the moral and legal philosophers. Strawson's conceptualization of persons, with his "M" and "P" predicates, opens the door to other possible persons besides those of our species. The M-predicates concern the embodiment, the material body, or object that happens to be the person in question. The P-predicates are those special attributes that apply only to persons. For an object to be a person there must be at least one P-predicate as part of its description. Strawson's definitional liberty of "at least one P-predicate," will be useful to remember when later in this chapter we build a Paradigm Case Formulation. Paradigm cases allow for deletions up to the point that only one P-predicate is left standing. We can argue then, if that is enough.

Since all the Person Concept's foundational ingredients are interdependent, it's dealer's choice where to begin the unpacking. Ossorio generally opened with intentional action because he wanted his students to become familiar with Parametric Analysis, one of Descriptive Psychology's principle methods. (This chapter's Paradigm Case Formulation is a variety of parametric analysis.) I favor starting with Individual Person before moving to Intentional Action, a step I'll make next because a variation of Intentional Action, that is, Deliberate Action, is a cardinal feature of what persons do. People, at times, are cognizant and deliberate actors who knowingly make choices. After addressing individual persons and intentional action, sufficient concepts should be in the mix to tackle language, community and culture, and world and reality.

The crucial first step is deciding and then agreeing on the orienting *preempirical* parameters. Compare this to drawing a map. Without using compass points it is difficult to show locations and relations. But after the north, south, east, and west coordinates are drawn, and a scale for distance has been decided, it is easy to show how to get to Duluth from Winnipeg, and the time it might take for the journey (with the additional empirical considerations of weather, traffic, and pesky border guards). Notice what is important to decide, preempirically, before coloring in the map's details: the orthogonal distinctions relevant to what we mean by "the lay of the land." And consider the value of a common lexicon. How long exactly is a mile or kilometer, and which unit are we going to use? The parameters of longitude, latitude, north, south, east, and west, along with scaling in miles or kilometers are not distinctions discovered in nature, but concepts we invent, and words we share.

Another key point. I will separate the Person Concept's individual person from the fact we are human beings, *Homo sapiens*, even though we are the only empirical example most of us take for granted. The value of this separation should be clear when I introduce Paradigm Case Formulations, in a manner that modifies and expands Strawson's M- and P-predicates. I don't know if there are actual persons out there other than us. There might be, but to *look* for them we will need an appropriate "east, west, north, south" equivalent for locating persons. Explication of the concept of Persons while honoring the historically established meanings is vital to the preempirical nature of Descriptive Psychology.

In the preface, I wondered if talking green gas encountered on the moon might be a person. Let's return briefly to the campfire above Nederland. Someone had to control the sparks and blaze. Asserting my Eagle Scout status, I took over the job. A man *and* his fire. Gas is too unstructured to do what we expect of people, I thought. Accordingly, I argued that green gas encountered on the moon, even appearing to speak, is a poor candidate. I'd consider little green men, but not gas. Pay attention to the man behind the curtain. Some other entity is giving the gas a voice.

As afternoon approached sunset, and we got to know each other better, my classmates agreed that people talk, are more or less self-aware, use tools, and build things. When all that is present, we felt on firm ground that at some point a person was there; a fairly conventional solution that still left questions about the status of the talking gas. Developing tools and manufacturing stuff did not seem easy for a formless gas. In our test case, no artifacts were visible except those brought by the human astronauts. Still, there was this gassy speech.

By early evening, we had reached no consensus about whether the talking gas was a person. It got very cold, started to snow, and we made our various ways down the mountain. Let's keep the group's uncertainty in mind, since it will be part of the reason employing a Paradigm Case Formulation is useful. Keep in mind that we took actions such as speech and the presence of objects that appeared to have been deliberately constructed, to be the observable, empirical evidence required for building a strong case that a person is or was present. Notice how these observables are different from what we can't directly observe: someone's first-hand experiences, their unvoiced deliberations, and their contents of self-awareness. None of us, as far as I can tell, have direct access to other's motives or awareness. We observe performances, including what we say we are up to.

That afternoon's campfire opens a number of themes to explore. Everyone in the group was already an expert in *being* a person. Implicitly, we already knew most of what is at stake in questioning personhood status. Our conversation veered all sorts of ways. Given the group's diversity in terms of gender, race, ethnicity, and cultural belief, different compelling ethical and moral dilemmas surfaced. Some of us were particularly sensitive to how in the real world one's personhood status is a very big deal. Historically, members of our species have not granted the full status of persons to others who share the same human embodiment, and have been able to enforce that social degradation. And beyond its place in mythology and science fiction, some of us wondered if human beings are, in fact, the only persons around.

Why is this important? As Kant reminded us, personhood confers rights and obligations not relevant to nonpersons. Here I am necessarily wandering into the polemical weeds of values and politics; but doing so will demonstrate an application of a body-neutral person concept. By way of example, here's a simple question. Is it proper to kill, eat, or keep as property a member of our species? Now ask the same about a nonhuman that also happens to be a person. With regard to humans, we use concepts and locutions that imply responsibility and consequence that we do not usually or appropriately apply to nonhumans. If one's culture allows, cattle may be deliberately slaughtered for food, but when a person is deliberately killed, that constitutes murder. (I am sidestepping state sanctioned killings legally identified as exceptions to murder as in warfare, capital punishment, and euthanasia. And, as legal constructions, therefore not writ in stone, they can be deconstructed and changed.)

Following a legal reasoning successfully employed to liberate African American slaves, *writs of habeas corpus* have been argued, so far unsuccessfully, for captive chimpanzees and elephants (Wise, 2000). Prior to the American Civil War, Native Americans and African Americans were frequently denied this basic person protection. For that matter, are humans at whatever state of development granted the rights and protections of persons? Consider the passionate disputes regarding abortion. Even theology aside, abortion debates boil down, in part, to the personhood status of the not yet born. A fetus granted personhood has different legal, ethical, and moral standing than mere developing tissue. As a nascent person, a human fetus has a moral and ethical value that comes with its future, hence the painful legitimacy of positioning a pregnant woman's rights against the purported rights of her fetus. Similarly, we treat human corpses with a different respect than other cases of dead flesh. I point this out to foreshadow the apparently inescapable moral and ethical conflict that comes with being capable of deliberate action, the dilemmas of conflicting perspective and choice. How does or should a person, a deliberate actor, regard another deliberate or potentially deliberate actor? Shoulds, oughts, and the whole normative gamut of ethical and moral value has an intrinsic place in the lives of deliberate actors since they provide considerations and priorities that are part of a person's potential for making a choice.

For some time now, nonhuman personhood has been suggested and argued for a variety of vertebrates, mostly but not exclusively mammalian. In some quarters, the person status of the nonhuman Great Apes, the Cetacea, the Elephants, and some birds is fiercely advocated. How can we rationally sort this out? Partisanship aside, any reasonable negotiation of who's in and what's out comes down to the preempirical question of what we mean by a person in the first place? We need some handle on this to intelligibly wonder if anything other than us might fit. While at it, we might identify, I think *should* identify, close cases, actual ambiguity, and reasoned disagreement. False positives, I feel, are less harmful, *are less immoral,* than the reverse. You might disagree. Back at the campfire, my classmates hoped that if the gas even appeared to talk, the astronaut would exercise the respect and caution due when encountering a stranger of uncertain status and intent. We all agreed that it was problematic, ethically and prudently, to treat something as a nonperson and get it wrong. People tend to become hostile when their status as persons is degraded. And some held with persons it should always be I to Thou.

PARADIGM CASE FORMULATIONS

A few years back I attended a conference at Yale, *Personhood Beyond the Human*, and presented a paper entitled "What is a person? How can we be sure?" (Schwartz, 2014). My focus was the thorny question of what we take to be a person, what counts as relevant data, and on what grounds can we sensibly negotiate agreement and disagreement on specific cases. Center stage was the question of granting civil rights to captive chimps and the future status of sentient robots. I did not argue for a revised definition of person; the discussions made apparent that the varied meanings of personhood were too complex for that. Instead, I employed the Descriptive method of constructing Paradigm Case Formulations (PCFs for short). Along with Parametric Analyses, PCFs were developed by Peter Ossorio (1981) as conceptual-notational devices employed when traditional definitions fail to capture the full possible range of a concept, and to show how any appropriate example is alike or different from any other. At Yale, competent critics had reasonable and compelling grounds for agreement and disagreement. I tried to offer a systematic way to negotiate.

Finding a fully inclusive definition presents a common conceptual dilemma. Consider how difficult it is to exactly define what is meant by the word "family" or the word "chair" if we wish to achieve agreement on all possible examples of families and chairs. Must all families have two parents of different genders plus their children? Must all chairs have four legs and a backrest? For example, most would agree that a group of people living together consisting of a married father and mother and their biological son and daughter is a family. But what if there is only a husband, his husband, and their dog? Or three best friends who live under one roof and make their significant decisions together? What elements must be present and what can we change, add, or leave out and still honor what different reasonable people call a family?

The status of persons clearly presents us with a definitional problem. When definitional boundaries are fuzzy, and disagreement easy, establishing some sort of PCF helps. Paradigm Case Formulations are used to achieve a common understanding of a subject matter where ordinary definitions prove too limiting, various, ambiguous, or impossible. These formulations are helpful when it is reasonable to assume there are legitimate grounds for disagreement about specific examples. When is it reasonable? The answer is usually when competent, reliable judges who represent legitimate stakeholders disagree. But all of us have skin in the game.

PCFs take note of ordinary usage and start by providing competent users an example that begins with their full agreement. The trick is to find an example with enough detail and nuance that it can be transformed in ways that get at all other relevant cases. A PCF should start with a complex case, an indubitable one, or a primary or archetypal example. It should be sort of "By God, if there were ever a case of X, then that's it."

At this point you have probably noticed my use of the phrases "competent users," "informed quarters," "reasonable judges," and other kindred expressions. My justification for this language, a pragmatic matter, should be clearer after the entire Person Concept is presented, although it will be elaborated some in the next section on Intentional Action. But let's get back to PCFs.

Let's try this out. I expect everyone will agree the example below looks like a family. If not, I assume you live in a culture that doesn't significantly share any ordinary meaning of family, or you're from another planet, but, in that case, you are not likely reading this. Here's how to proceed. First, do you agree that the following paradigm case is an example of a family? If so, then look at the transformations. Do any of them violate what you consider a family? Can you see how someone might draw the line differently? Can you accept marginal and ambiguous cases as grounds for reasonable disagreement?

By starting with a paradigm case that everyone readily identifies as within their understanding, it should be possible to delete or change features of the paradigm with the consequence that with each change some people might no longer agree that we are still talking about the same thing. But because of the shared paradigm, it should be possible to show where agreement and disagreement lie and where various reasonable judges draw the line.

Building a PCF often works this way: Stage 1, introduce a paradigm case specification for the domain in question; Stage 2, introduce one or more transformations of the paradigm case.

In the example that follows, notice the parameters of gender, number of participants, presence or absence of marriage, presence or absence of children, presence or absence of living together, and so on. Each of these parameters is subject to deletion or substitution, with the result that with each alteration a judge may no longer accept the new variation as within the domain of what they take to be an appropriate instance of the concept of family. Here follows the example.

PCF OF FAMILY

A married couple, husband and wife, living together under the same roof with their biological children, a 14-year-old daughter and a 5-year-old son, and their dog, cat, and turtle.

Transformations

T1. Eliminate the parents being married.
T2. Eliminate one parent but not both.

T3. Change the gender of either parent.

T4. Eliminate both parents.

T5. Change the number of children to N, $N > 0$.

T6. Change the gender distribution of children.

T7. Change the ages of the children to any values compatible with the ages of the parents.

T8. Change or eliminate the pets.

T9. To any combination from T1, T2, T3, T4, T5, T6, T7, and T8 add any number of additional parents.

T10. Add adopted and other legally defined children.

T11. Keep the pets but change the number of children to zero if parent or parents are living together.

T12. Eliminate the pets and children if the parents are living together.

T13. Eliminate the requirement of living together.

How did you do? Do you see how some people might reasonably differ with you?

I want to build something similar for the concept of an individual person.

THREE DEFINITIONS AND A PARADIGM CASE FORMULATION OF PERSONS

Descriptive Psychology's definition of an individual person has undergone a history of refinements. In the volume *Persons* (1966, 1995), Ossorio defined a person as "an individual whose history is represented by a collection of a series … of intentional actions, successful, unsuccessful, and abortive …." (p. 82). In 1972, when I first encountered this definition, I remember we argued it would let in the lions, tigers, and triffids as well. By 1976, Ossorio said in a seminar "That's why I'm considering changing it to 'deliberate'. Keep in mind that deliberate action is a special case of intentional action. It's not wrong; it's just misleading. The change is to a more restricted definition. The other one would still be true. It just may not be restrictive enough." (1977, p. 80). When the dust settled the Descriptive community finally accepted "a person is an individual whose history is, paradigmatically, a history of deliberate action."

This last definition was elaborated in the final years of Ossorio's life to "a person is an individual whose history is, paradigmatically, a history of Deliberate Action in a dramaturgical pattern."

Furthermore:

1. A Human Being is an individual who is both a Person and a specimen of *Homo sapiens*.
2. An Alien Being is an individual who is a Person and has a biological embodiment other than that of *Homo sapiens*.

3. A Robot is an individual who is a Person and has a nonbiological embodiment. (Ossorio, 2006a, b, 2013, p. 9).

At the *Beyond the Human* conference I expanded upon this with a PCF of the individual person as follows.

A PARADIGM CASE FORMULATION OF A PERSON

1. A person is an individual who paradigmatically engages in Deliberate Action (an intentional or goal directed action in which the actor is cognizant of what they are doing and chooses to do it) and is:
2. Linguistically competent (employs deliberate symbolic verbal behavior and engages in linguistic self-regulation).
3. The significance of the deliberate actions reflects the person's perspectives and concerns with:
   a) Hedonics (pleasure, pain, disgust, noxiousness, etc.).
   b) Prudence (self-interest, what is to my advantage or disadvantage, etc.).
   c) Aesthetics (fittingness in the artistic, intellectual, and social domain).
   d) Morality/ethics (right or wrong, fair or unfair, just or unjust, and carrying duty or obligation).
4. Resulting in a dramaturgical pattern with significance patterns called *through-lines.*

Transformations
Change

   T1. The embodiment of the individual (human, nonhuman, robot, etc.).
   T2. The form or degree of cognizance/consciousness that limits Deliberate Action (asleep, dreaming, dissociated, unconscious, etc.).
   T3. The degree and/or development of linguistic competence.
   T4. The specific language employed.
   T5. The presence or absence of hedonic, prudent, aesthetic, and moral/ethical perspectives informing deliberate action.
   T6. Add additional motivational perspectives.
   T7. The presence or absence of coherent through-lines.

Let me clarify. "A person is an individual," but not in the sense of hives, colonies, collectives, or corporations; nothing akin to the Borg in *Star Trek*. Those are something else, perhaps composed of persons or whatever. Although a community is required to become a person, each individual is more or less autonomous. In Chapter 6 I will point out, formally, that language can only develop in a community.

The phrase "who paradigmatically engages in …" is a locution indicating something that fulfills a full paradigm case or something with the essential qualities or attributes that identify the subject matter. Deliberate Action is goal-directed behavior, a variation of intentional action, and involves an awareness or cognizance of a choice. Deliberate actions are a demonstration of personal autonomy insofar as autonomy is linked to the ability to make choices. A person's values, knowledge, and competence inform their choices and characterize the actions selected. I will say much more about this in Chapter 3 when examining the person as an Actor, Observer, and Critic.

An individual person's status can involve different states of cognizance, consciousness, or awareness. (State, a Personal Characteristic, is a concept we will get to soon.) Cognizance can be limited, altered, or, at times, absent in actual empirical persons. Sometimes humans are asleep, dreaming, dissociated, intoxicated, enraged, comatose, and so on. Nonpathological persons, however, are cognizant enough to engage in the social practices of their Communities. Asleep in bed is usually fine, but asleep at the wheel is problematic.

Paradigmatic persons hold each other more or less responsible for the choices they make. This is an implicit premise of civilization: awake and aware people have a degree of choice and can weigh their reasons for a course of action. To the extent people choose what they want to do, they are accordingly accountable for their behavior. This accountability is made explicit in the law and in negotiations, sworn contracts, and the like. A fundamental premise is that people act in a social world whose civil fabric of contracts and laws are senseless without personal and accountable choice.

DELIBERATE ACTIONS AND INTRINSIC MOTIVATION

Deliberate actors have a multiplicity of perspectives that provide their reasons for acting one way or another. I am going to have more to say about this when examining intentional action but here is a preview. As deliberate actors, paradigmatic persons have Hedonic, Prudent, Aesthetic, and Moral/Ethical reasons they might weigh when selecting a course of action. Why only these? These are the ones we know. There may be more; if another is invented or recognized it would be included, in the way cooks now agree there is a fifth taste, umami, in addition to sweet, sour, bitter, and salty. A hallmark of Descriptive Psychology is a required openness to inclusion of new distinctions. When fundamental behavioral concepts are recognized that are not in the Descriptive canon, the canon is enlarged or modified accordingly.

These four classifications are *family resemblance groups*. Hedonics referring to the value of pleasure, pain, disgust, and so on; prudence to self-interest; aesthetics to the artistic, social, and intellectual values of truth, rigor, objectivity, beauty, elegance, closure, and fit; and morality and ethics with right and wrong, fairness and justice, the level playing field, the Golden Rule, and kindred notions. For purposes of brevity, I'm going to condense morality and ethics into simply ethics even though there are distinctions to be drawn between the two concepts.

Hedonics, prudence, aesthetics, and ethical concerns provide people with intrinsic, fundamental motivations. By intrinsic, I am saying they offer reason enough on their own merit to do something. They need no further justification. Seeking and responding to pleasure or pain, acting in one's self-interest, producing something elegant, beautiful, or well-formed; attempting to get closure; renouncing privilege; and not taking undue advantage because it would be unfair, are all fundamental motivational stances and reason enough for a person's behavior to make sense. These reasons can stand on their own in justifying a course of action. And naturally and unavoidably, they conflict, operate in a complementary or independent fashion, and so on. Tautologically, if you have two or more of these reasons to do something, you have more reasons than if you had only one of them. That last sentence is a maxim.

People's hedonic, prudential, aesthetic, and ethical perspectives inform their appraisal of what they want to do. This is the dynamics of motivation. *It provides a person's perspective on what matters.* Individual differences in character correspond to how people actually weigh these—not as lip service—but as actual guidance of their behavior. Later, when we examine the concept of judgment and appraisal, we will look at the distinction between a person claiming a set of values versus actually acting on them.

There are some interesting differences among these groupings regarding choice and deliberation. Hedonic and prudent motivations inform both deliberate and nondeliberate intentional action. As a fundamental motive, they are probably features of all sentient animal life, whether human or not. They provide a basis for cross species empathy and shared understanding. I do not think I am being overly anthropomorphic when I think my dog's hunger and pain resembles mine. For that matter, I believe my dogs are somewhat sensitive to mine, but not appreciatively sensitive, given how often they grab my snacks.

I am paving the way for formulations I will offer later about verbal behavior, empathy, and shared understanding among persons and nonpersons.

Among the intrinsic motivations there are, I think, some logical differences in what is required for them to make sense. Aesthetic and ethical motivations are formally different from hedonic and prudent concerns. Aesthetics and ethics, as formal categories, require deliberate action to be possible. I waver between a strong position that ethically and aesthetically based actions always involve an awareness of choice versus a weaker claim that choice facilitates and justifies these categories after an action, even in the absence of recognizing other options when the action occurs. Both strong and weak assertions still take it that aesthetic and ethically grounded actions require the ability to choose or refrain, to potentially think over possible or desirable courses one could follow. Choice is essential. If I am coerced to do the right thing, even though the act yields a fair or just outcome, my action did not follow my sense of justice, but likely represents prudent compliance. The law agrees. Attributions of crime and tort rest on the assumption that a choice was involved, or should have been.

At some point, cognizance or self-awareness is important for behavior to follow from an aesthetic and ethical perspective. Some awareness of options: this phrase or that, which shade of color, a tux or business casual, the high road or the low path, is required for deliberate action. But I'd like to return for a moment to my weaker assertion that the recognition of choice is required for deliberate behavior but might not be a necessity for a specific action to be grounded in ethics and aesthetics. I can imagine that a person's ethical and aesthetic perspective can be so dominant it becomes the stance always taken in certain circumstances. No questions asked, no decisions made. Some people, I suspect, simply *see* what is ethical or fitting and act accordingly without deliberation and without a moment's cognizance of choice, akin to the immediacy of emotion. They live the aesthetic or ethical way of life. I'll return to similar themes when considering through-lines. Similarly, when we look at emotional behavior in Chapter 5 we will explicate other learned tendencies to act without deliberation.

In summary, it is reasonable to claim I can't help that it hurts or feels good, and for a host of dilemmas, that I recognize my self-interest. The pains and pleasures of the flesh come with the territory. When the lion enters the room, lacking whip and chair, I try to escape. Under those circumstances, saying I had no time nor reason enough to consider the ethics and aesthetics of my dilemma would pass muster. Nonetheless, as a paradigmatic person, even if I directly experience visceral pleasure, disgust, advantage, and disadvantage, I can deliberately attempt to refrain from seeking pleasure or self-interest on aesthetic and/or ethical grounds. And, perhaps unsurprisingly, I might set my ethics and aesthetics aside for the sake of pleasure and self-interest. The actual weights I give to my opportunities and dilemmas depend on my character.

As a measure of community standing, character, and integrity, people judge each other on the choices they make. This reflects how they weigh their hedonic, prudent, ethical, and aesthetic reasons. To maintain good standing in the community, we expect some of these perspectives to be given similar values. Any adult who does not have these interests, or does not know how to appropriately weigh them, will likely seem primitive, ignorant, pathological, or criminal.

We expect that the normal mature human can employ all of these motivational perspectives. Accordingly, any general theory of human behavior that does not adequately address these motivations will be defective.

A last point for now. Insofar as behaviors motivated by ethical or aesthetic perspectives are deliberate actions, ethics and aesthetics are quintessential person qualities. Any action that appears motivated by an ethical or aesthetic concern is evidence of the involvement of a person. Not proof, mind you, but evidence. Hedonics and prudence are less compelling.

WHAT ABOUT LANGUAGE AND VERBAL BEHAVIOR?

> In short, the natural history of man is the history of a convention-forming, rule-following, concept-exercising, language-using animal—a cultural animal. *(P.M.S. Hacker, 2015).*

Paradigmatic of persons is linguistic competence, an ability to share symbolic representations that correspond to the concepts used in social engagement. People talk about what is happening, not happening, what they want to have happen, and what has not happened yet. And anything else that suits their fancy. This requires symbols suited to the flexible improvisations and negotiations of life.

Much of the debate concerning the person status of nonhumans focuses on language. Do chimps and porpoises talk to each other? Can we teach them to talk to us? And what should we make of Wittgenstein's (1953, 2009) assertion that we wouldn't be able to understand talking lions? And, not being a lion tamer, what do you advise, if the lion that enters the room, licking its chops, tells me not to be afraid?

I'm going to take the conventional position that the detection of language is vital but problematic in assigning the status of persons to a nonhuman entity. Why so? It's a matter of sharing. We know a great deal about how human folk generally behave and are usually able to recognize some behaviors as involving language, ours or foreign, even if we don't know how to translate their locutions into our native tongue. Some things easily look or sound like speech, song, writing, signing, and so on, even if they aren't. This is the case since we humans share "forms of life" that follow from our embodiment and common social practices that occur cross-culturally. All of us are members of cultures where we eat and drink, take care of each other, compete, attempt to negotiate conflict, mate, rear kids, sing songs, and play sports. Shylock asks, "Hath not a Jew eyes? Hath not a Jew hands, organs, dimensions, senses, affections, passions; fed with the same food, hurt with the same weapons, subject to the same diseases, healed by the same means, warmed and cooled by the same winter and summer as a Christian is? If you prick us, do we not bleed?" Or as Harry Stack Sullivan (1953) wrote, "All of us are much more human than otherwise."

When it comes to nonhumans, to the extent it is difficult to identify social practices, an identification that rests on behaviors resembling *in some way* what humans do, language detection and translation is difficult. Never mind the thorny question of whether an utterance or representation means what it says (Cavell, 1969/2002). Some have a policy never to give a sucker an even break, practice deception, and maintain two sets of books. Consider the fate of the poor frog that let the scorpion talk him into a ride across the stream. Translation works best when we know we share similar perspectives and are expected on average to mean what we say.

Shared social practice based on shared forms of life, as Wittgenstein (1953, 2009) put it, creates a dilemma. Embodiment, environment, and life's needs and concerns are relevant to what can or will be shared. In the absence of shared perspectives, it is difficult to determine what, if anything, is being talked over, let alone agreed.

The problem of detecting language does not alter the essential place language has in the paradigmatic concept of persons. Verbal behavior is a deliberate action. Evidence of language is compelling for determining that a behavior was deliberate since language can symbolically represent choice; what was chosen and what was not. You see me take the low road but unless there is some way of representing that I was aware I could have taken a higher path, you'd be hard pressed to successfully argue I chose my lowdown ways. (Unless you get away with arguing that it is simply my character. Recall the scorpion.) Despite actions speaking louder than words, what people say is a powerful way to know why they are doing what they do. We don't see choice through their mind's eye. We see their performance, including what they tell us, whether we believe them or not. And they may truly believe their own claims, even if the available evidence speaks against it. We will return to this when we examine the interpretation of self-deception, disclaimed, and unconscious action.

(When my colleague Clarke Stone saw this last paragraph he remarked, "Have you ever read an entire first chapter, where the protagonist says to herself, 'I'm not going to the party,' literally, over and over—as she showers, picks out a dress, puts it on, fixes her hair, calls a cab, and arranges for a baby sitter. She hands the baby over and says, 'I'm going to the party.' I hated her so bad, I stopped reading the book.")

A last key point for now. Language facilitates a person's ability to reorder priorities, a vital ability to manage complicated social life. Since language can represent actions and consequences not yet undertaken, it is ready made for negotiation, self-regulation, and justification. I talk things over with myself and I talk them over with you. I weigh the consequences of my potential acts and you tell me your thoughts about them. This also allows the behavior of persons to be less stereotyped and predictable than the behavior of nonpersons. People can develop, invent, and reconsider. They can think about their thinking. They can change their mind (or at least try). They can change course in the middle. In Chapter 3 we will examine another Descriptive formulation of the person as a self-correcting Actor, Observer, and Critic and the facilitating role of linguistic self-regulation. We will also return to language, social practices, and forms of life in the Chapter 6.

INDIVIDUAL DIFFERENCES AND PERSON CHARACTERISTICS

In some ways, we are all the same, and clearly, we have our differences. Persons have personalities. No matter how similar we are, identical twins included, we are all separate individuals finding and creating our own historically unique path. Let's start with some behavioral logic, a maxim: **A person acquires their personal characteristics by having a prior capacity and a suitable intervening history**. This begins with an initial capacity, a state of affairs that comes with the initial developing body and its immediate context. From there on, a person's characteristics develop.

Each person's behavioral history results in what Ossorio (2006a, b) well named, a **dramaturgical** pattern. Patterns, actually, since people have a multiplicity of personally significant concerns, entertained in their varied ways. These patterns reflect the multifaceted engagement of an individual with particular personal characteristics living in a specific time and place. This wash of overlapping events creates a person's world in its wake, a world that is discovered, invented, and created. No surprise, the word "world" comes from the Old English and Anglo-Saxon "woruld" that meant, roughly, the age of man or the course of a person's life (Ziff, 1960).

The concept of dramaturgy, first developed by Lessing (1967/1962) for analyzing the stage composition and representation of actors and props, offers guidance for our Descriptive account of persons and their worlds. Why drama rather than narrative? Almost, but not quite, six of one and half a dozen of the other. Dramaturgical shares key features but is more inclusive than the compatible idea of narrative. As a form of verbal behavior, we voice and write narratives, that when nuanced enough, capture the dramas we live. The concept of narrative respects that every verbal act is someone's that reflects that person's perspective. This book is my narrative, but was produced and exists in the broader context, the drama, of my life. Unwritten here is the wider dramatic context of this writing's opportunities, dilemmas, and significance to me.

To digress a bit, I sometimes show my clinical students how canonical playwrights and novelists construct characters and worlds, and how critics have categorized the resulting patterns. I am especially fond of Northup Frye's (1957/1967) taxonomy of the comic, romantic, tragic, and ironic visions. Another writer I admire, the psychoanalytic action theorist Roy Schafer (1976), employed Frye's categories to describe what his patients believed their life ought to be like, and noted how this vision changed as they became more insightful. As a clinician and pragmatist, I share Frye's and Schafer's perspective that life is more realistically portrayed through the nuance of tragedy and irony than comedy and romance. (This seems an entrenched belief among psychoanalysts and their ilk. I recall Freud's pessimism that the result of a successful psychoanalysis was to transform neurotic misery into ordinary human unhappiness.) Tragedy's uncertainty about the outcome of choice, and the inevitability that choices are made under constraint, fit a dramaturgically constructed **Real World** of actual persons.

Individual differences and personal characteristics can be divvied up all sorts of ways, but should follow the logic of a few questions: What is *possible* for a specific person to do? And, what is *likely* an individual will do? In addition, in what fashion will they accomplish it? The first question is answered by reference to a person's **Powers** and the second and third by their **Dispositions**. This roughly corresponds to what a person is able to do and how frequently they do it in their particular way.

Just to keep the jargon straight, the technical term "powers" refers to an aspect of the logical structure of the concept of Individual Person and not to some mystical occult or supernatural process or force. Powers are not forces but logical categories. If it turns out someone actually has the power of X-ray vision and can leap tall buildings in a single bound, these potentials will be classified under **Abilities**, one subtype of the three Powers. (If so, let's hope they are disposed to exercise these abilities in through-lines characterized by Superman's commitment to "Truth, Justice, and the American Way." But with some serious reflection on the various "American Ways.")

Another class of individual differences providing for or derivative of a person's powers and dispositions are their **psychological states, capacities**, and **embodiment**. Psychological states differ over time and correspond to available and active powers and dispositions. And, whatever powers and dispositions a person demonstrates, they are an expression of a set of prior capacities. The capacities in question, at whatever state of development, are provided by the embodied form of the person, whether animal, vegetable, mineral, robot, or what have you. The individual's worlds, communities, and culture provide the context for this development.

Once in place, firmly established as part of a person's repertoire, in-character behavior does not call for an explanation. It becomes unsurprising when they do similar things in comparable situations. This does not mean they always act this way, but it is understandable when they do. What calls for an explanation is out-of-character behavior. Here "unless clauses" provide the logical reminders. During ordinary circumstances we expect people to act as they usually do *unless* the circumstances are not what we thought, or they don't recognize the usual circumstance as they usually do, are perhaps not in their usual state, have acquired or lost ability, had a change in embodiment, and so on. And, it may turn out, we do not know them as well as we thought. Last but not least, they might do something wholly unexpected, even to them. Novelty happens. People have their limits, but one of these limits is not knowing what those limits are.

POWERS

Whereas **Dispositions** are person characteristics based on frequencies and styles of action, **Powers** are standing conditions that must already be in place for there to be any behavior at all. Dispositions concern what we can expect; powers limit the possibilities. The Powers concepts are **Abilities, Knowledge**, and **Values**. In Chapter 3 these concepts will correspond to the parameters of behavior that identify what a person specifically knows about their circumstances germane to what they want to achieve given what they know how to do.

If Pedro did not have the **ability** to throw a ball, he could not have mastered the changeup fastball and curve. If I **knew** nothing of the location of Fenway Park, unless I got really lucky, I could not expect to walk directly there from my apartment. And, if I didn't **value** the roar of the crowd more than traffic noise, I might not have followed the cheers and beheld the awesome Green Monster.

Abilities, Competence, and Skill

A person's abilities, competencies, and skills, corresponds to their potential to achieve something under ordinary circumstances without it being a matter of luck or accident. Abilities range from a mere capability to an exceptional talent. I'm going to lump competences and skills under abilities, despite subtle differences in use.

With every ability we have the disability that corresponds to a person being significantly less able to accomplish what is normally expected under ordinary circumstances, or when it becomes less possible for an individual who ordinarily could rise to the occasion. Maintaining good standing in social life and community usually involves an expected degree of ability, competence, and skill required to do the various done things. Chefs are expected to skillfully slice and dice. Significant deficits in a person's powers and dispositions to manage the expected social practices can result in pathology descriptions, diagnosed or described clinically, morally, ethically, educationally, and so on. For now, let's define pathology as a significant restriction in a person's ability to engage in deliberate action or, equivalently, to participate in the social practices of the community (Bergner, 1997).

A significant subcategory of Ability is **Sensitivity**. Sensitivities refer to a person's refinement in discerning or detecting, through observation and thought, the nuance and content that constitutes **Knowledge**. Sensitivities range from sharp and perspicacious to insensitive and impervious. Another subcategory is **Judgment**, the ability to make appropriate appraisals and decisions given the circumstances. Judgment will necessarily overlap with **Values** and range from wise to foolish.

Along with ability concepts, **Know How** is used as a technical term in the Intentional Action Formulation in Chapter 3. The Descriptive concept of Know How corresponds to Gilbert Ryle's (1949/2002) use in *The Concept of Mind*, where he distinguishes knowing something in contrast to knowing how to do something. Know How is a parameter in the Intentional Action Formulation that identifies what a person specifically knows how to do in the performance of a particular action, such that *that* performance was not a matter of luck, chance, accident, or coincidence.

Some relevant Ossorian maxims are provided here:

> **A historical individual acquires a given individual characteristic by virtue of having the prior capacity and the relevant intervening history.**
> **A person acquires a given person characteristic by virtue of having the prior capacity and the relevant intervening history.**
> **A historical individual having a finite history has some nonacquired characteristics during some part of that history.**
> **If a person acquires a given person characteristic, they acquired it in one of the ways in which it can be acquired.**
> **If a person acquires a given relationship to something, they acquired it in one of the ways in which it can be acquired.**
> **A person acquires concepts and skills by practice and experience.**

Knowledge

Knowledge is the set of facts, concepts, and distinctions that a person has some competence to employ in their behavior. Akin to the pragmatic reminder that meaning follows use, a person's knowledge informs their behavior. Knowledge is informative, as Gregory Bateson (1972) put it, "a difference that makes a difference." A person's knowledge is the cognitive repertory that supports their behavior potential. If they lack the appropriate facts, concepts, and distinctions they can't be expected to appropriately or successfully act when such knowledge is required. Lacking appropriate or necessary knowledge results in the dilemmas and pathologies of ignorance and negligence.

Here are two relevant maxims: **people acquire their knowledge of the world by observation and thought**. And there are stopping points in justifying knowing something: **people take it that things are as they seem unless they find reason enough to think otherwise**. This last point was Descriptive Psychology's original Maxim One. It serves as a foundation for the possibility of there being any sort of knowledge: personal, scientific, whatever. Without some stopping point ending with how it seems (at least now), we invite an infinite regress. Maxim One echoes Wittgenstein's (1972) opening reminders in his final work, *On Certainty*:

1. If you do know that here is one hand, we'll grant you all the rest. When one says that such and such a proposition can't be proved, of course that does not mean that it can't be derived from other propositions; any proposition can be derived from other ones. But they may be no more certain than it is itself ….
2. From its seeming to me—or to everyone—to be so, it doesn't follow that it is so. What we can ask is whether it can make sense to doubt it.
3. If, e.g., someone says "I don't know if there's a hand here" he might be told "Look closer."—This possibility of satisfying oneself is part of the language game. It is one of its essential features.

You have to rest at how things seem; unless you have sufficient reason not to. Further maxims include:

**What a person takes to be real is what they are prepared to act on.
A person acquires knowledge of the world by observation and thought.
For a given person, the real world is the one they have to find out about by observation.
A person takes it that things are as they seem unless they have reason enough to think otherwise.
A person takes the world to be as they have found it to be.**

Values

A person's behavior follows from their particular set of **Values**, Knowledge, and Abilities. Values are more or less stable standing conditions that establish a hierarchy of priorities of what a person wants to happen or accomplish in their changing circumstances. Notice "values" is plural and my frequent use of "more or less." In psychology, as in life, much is precisely more or less. Ordinarily, moving through our day, we have a multiplicity of values in play, some being dearer than others. This weighing of significance is the hierarchy of preferences that enable a person to make choices. Values provide the weights we balance in judgment—immediate or thought out—when choosing to do one thing rather than another. Having values is fundamental to paradigmatic persons, since in the absence of values, nothing would qualify as a deliberate action. I'll illustrate this concept in Chapters 3 and 4 using variations of the **Judgment Diagram** and in considering the **Actor-Observer-Critic** model of self-regulation.

Cultures and communities have a stake in what ought to be valued, have characteristic **choice principles**, which typify a culture and community's normative ways of acting. If a person ignores or lacks the values that guide their culture and community's choice principles, their social participation will likely appear quirky, inappropriate, misguided, criminal, or pathological. Upholding and maintaining moral and ethical values are especially significant for people to remain in good community standing. Deficits in honoring a community's core moral and ethical values set the stage for moral indignation and the restrictions that can result in a degraded status. We'll return to this **status dynamic** by unpacking the implications of Harold Garfinkel's (1956) degradation ceremonies and the related practice of accreditation ceremonies in Chapter 7. Descriptive Psychologists have made extensive use of these concepts in understanding and treating psychopathology (Bergner, 2015; Bergner, 2010; Holmes, 2013; Ossorio, 2006a, b; Schwartz, 1979).

An inevitable consequence of the complexity of what we value is conflict. Our diverse personal and social roles, our memberships in different communities, create conflict. With conflict comes successful and unsuccessful compromise; along with feeling at odds with others and ourselves. The foundational values required of good standing members in our different communities don't always work well together. This can create defensive conditions of bad faith and self-deception, resulting in bungled actions, denial, and symptom formation. Or simply being stuck, not knowing what to do. Worse, some actual values, usually in the form of transgressive desire, can be self-intolerable to the extent a person refuses or is unable to acknowledge having them. Some of what is valued might also be "unthinkable," yet influence action, as some theories suggest. We will return to these themes in Chapter 4 when examining the logic and dynamics of unconscious action.

Further maxims include:

> **A person values some states of affairs over others and acts accordingly.**
> **If a person's relationship to something is such that they are in a bad situation or circumstance, they have a reason to try to improve it.**

If a person's relationship to something is such that they are in a good situation or circumstance, they have a reason to act to maintain it.

If a person is in a good situation and has an opportunity to improve it, they have a reason to try to do so.

If a person is in any situation and it may be expected to become worse, they have a reason to act to prevent that.

A person will not choose less behavior potential over more.

If a person values a specific something, e.g., an object, a circumstance, a behavior, or more generally, a state of affairs, they will thereby also value other specific things of the same kind to the extent that they are relevantly similar to the original.

If a person values a general something, they will thereby also value a specific something to the extent that it is a paradigmatic instance or realization of the more general value.

If a person values something general, they will be sensitive to (will tend to evaluate) the relevance of their circumstances to that something and act accordingly.

DISPOSITIONS

Where Powers define what a person is potentially able to do, **Dispositions** describe what they are likely to do and the fashion in which they do it. Based on the frequency of what a person does, the concepts of **trait, attitude, interest**, and **style** describe a person's **Dispositions**. Since these features of personality are identified by an observer's account of their occurrence, a natural question is what counts as enough? The boundaries here are inherently fuzzy. The answer will be some version of "more or less than what's generally expected." Or, they act this way in a manner that seems worth noting. As with most stable features of personality, dispositions develop slowly and change gradually. Ordinarily, we are unsurprised by how the people we know well, behave. Still, from our perspective, given what we know of those we know best, they can appear to behave out-of-character. Our judgment, of course, can be based on our knowledge being wrong or incomplete. Bear in mind, our knowledge is always incomplete. And, given we are dealing with persons and not machines, one of the hallmarks of deliberate action is invention, creation, and novelty.

Traits are general, consistent, persistent, and stable patterns of behavior. To have a given trait is to be disposed to engage in a certain kind of behavior in a certain way, independent of the significance or the goal of the action. Both low-frequency and high-frequency patterns will generate trait descriptions. For example, some people are customarily more generous or stingy, irritable or calm, worried or carefree, modest or boastful, honest or deceitful, and so on, than others.

An **Attitude** is an attitude toward something or someone in particular. Attitudes are context specific and focused on a particular set of objects or states of affairs. An attitude is like a trait except more specifically targeted. An attitude may surprise an observer when it appears as an exception to a more general trait. For example, John is generally a hostile guy, except when it comes to his mother where he exercises an attitude of kindness, deference, and compassion.

An **Interest** is an interest in something. Interests are seen as a general and intrinsic valuing of something demonstrated by various actions that concern the object of interest. For example, an interest in fishing can be shown by practicing casting, attending to the tides, and subscribing to fishing magazines. Interests can range from the causal and occasional to the passionate and obsessive.

Style refers to the manner a behavior is implemented. The style of a performance is often given as an aesthetic appraisal. With sophistication, elegantly, boorishly, ineptly, awkwardly, boldly, sneakily, directly, and so on, are ways all sorts of behavior could be performed. He trips the light fantastic across the ballroom floor. She precisely bites her words in the mid-Atlantic lockjaw style.

Since dispositions are summary formulations of prevalence and frequency, observers not only collect different impressions about what counts, but can appraise the significance of what they observe differently. Consider the following example: most of Humbert's acquaintances think him cheap. He's a lousy tipper who balks at suggestions to evenly split the tab. In contrast to this parsimony (a trait), he loves travel (an attitude) and is fascinated by the late Victorian explorers who searched for blues, coppers, and hairstreaks (an interest). Few know about his expensive cross-country reenactments to mountain parks, where he draws butterflies (an interest), impeccably dressed (a style) in the fashion of a late-19th-century naturalist, slyly concealing his companion, Dolores, a youth of uncertain status (an obsessive pathological interest), or so Quilty said before he was dispatched.

Given the inherent lack of exactness in determining and labeling dispositions, different judges can come to different conclusions. Modifiers, quantifying adjectives, and unless clauses provide useful wiggle room. "Unless clauses" work well when a trait and attitude appear in contradiction. Humbert squeezes a nickel until the buffalo groans, except when bidding on eBay like a drunken sailor. Is Humbert simply a penny pincher? Or is the considerable money he spends on travel and gay-90's lepidopterist garb and kit more descriptive of his character? All these attributions fit, but in context, some descriptions are more germane than others. Humbert has a naturalist's knowledge. He can tell a beetle from a bug. Still, from my perspective, Humbert is not so much stingy as paranoid he'll be cheated; a suspicion consistent with his other fears that he will be found out. He is careful about money but spends lavishly on costumes, road trips, and attempts to impress his illicit other. And he has good reason to think he's being followed. The **Through-Line** concept's focus on the significance of the path the actor followed, implemented in various ways, will help sort some of this out. *Humbert resentfully and suspiciously guards his resources to support a never ending and unconsciously compulsive attempt to undo his loss of Annabel.*

ADDITIONAL INDIVIDUAL DIFFERENCE AND PERSONAL CHARACTERISTIC CATEGORIES

Here are three more categories of individual difference: **States, Capacities**, and **Embodiments**. Capacities and Embodiments provide the possibility to acquire particular powers and dispositions. States refer to specific, transiently active configurations of powers and dispositions.

States

We expect a person's powers and dispositions to be acquired slowly and to remain fairly stable. We don't expect to wake up in the morning a changed person, nor is it wise to accept at face value anyone announcing they are no longer *that person*, they've seen the light, can now be trusted, relied upon, have given up the bottle, what have you, without evidence they have undergone a sufficiently transforming history. Even the stories of sudden spiritual enlightenment generally follow the preparation of, "I once was lost but now am found. Was blind but now I see."

Personality change requires relevant and sufficient experience for a power or disposition to be altered or acquired. Given the sorts of persons we are, including all the other mammalian candidates, relevant practice is necessary to acquire a stable competence or skill. It might be different for robots or other person embodiments. But for now, here's a reasonable rule of thumb for humans: it takes considerable time and practice to acquire and expand a person's powers and dispositions although they can be degraded or damaged in a heartbeat. Humans can be traumatized fast, can change immediately, with reactive and restrictive characteristics a result. Damage can be quick, but personality maturation, at least for human persons, is slow.

Within the overall stability we expect of normal, undamaged, and nonpathological persons, there are more or less sudden, temporarily, and reversible presentations that we refer to as **States**. A state involves a systematic difference in a person's powers and/or dispositions. As such, the state concept is employed both to compare one person to another and to compare how an individual may differ from their usual or normal way of being, a temporary intrapsychic change. Since the state concept refers to systematic changes in a person's typically available powers and dispositions, a change in state does not imply any particular behavior will follow but rather whatever set of behaviors that then occur will be chosen and/or executed in a manner that reflects the change in power and disposition. We behave differently in whatever we do. These changes can be profound, perhaps easy to observe, or hard to notice at all. Since a person's ordinary powers and dispositions establish their expected in-character presentation, it should come as no surprise if out-of-character actions, brought on by an unusual state change, look like they come from an entirely different person. In-character and out-of-character are observer's judgments subject to the scope and accuracy of the observer's knowledge. Sometimes Joe is not willing or able to exercise his basic caution and good judgment. Rarely, but occasionally, Suzy drops the wise constraint she normally shows when suffering fools.

In the course of a human's day and life, there are regularly expected changes in state. Humans sleep and dream, are sometimes famished, intoxicated, enthralled, overjoyed, disgusted, enraged, horny, and so on. For many of us this is normal. We also speak of exceptional and altered states of consciousness (ASCs), such as trance states, dissociated states, psychedelic states, and states of rapture. States can be pathological when a person is panicked, dissociated, psychotic, manic, or morbidly depressed.

Capacities

A **Capacity** is a potential to acquire a **Personal Characteristic**. This starts with some set of original capacities provided by the individual's initial **Embodiment** that, with history, develop into specific **Powers and Dispositions**. Capacities are different than Abilities. A capacity only provides the possibility to acquire a particular characteristic or behavior potential. An ability, on the other hand, provides the reasonable expectation that in the relevant circumstances something wanted that requires that ability will be accomplished. Given an initial normal embodiment, and an average expected developmental history, we aren't surprised when the resulting person ends up a version of "one of us." Still, given the deliberate actor's potential for creative improvisation, some of us turn out quite different and thrive. The idiosyncratic happens. Vive la difference!

Some histories are more fortuitous than others. The resulting competences can range from absent to barely able, to skills that looks like magic (Putman, 2010). Here the interplay between capacity and history corresponds to the potential of the capacity and the relevance of the history. A history similar to the one that brings out Jack's gifts may fail to develop Jill's. This is the case even if Jack starts out with lesser gifts than Jill. It can turn out that Jill's extraordinary ability is never seen unless she finds the right teacher. The average expected learning environment has uneven results. Life, for humans, doesn't start on a level playing field. Capacity and experience matter; that and luck.

Moving from the conceptual to the empirical and theoretical, we can ask what variety of capacities and histories are relevant in becoming, developing, and/or creating paradigmatic or near paradigmatic persons? What capacities and developmental histories foster linguistic competence, deliberate action, and dramaturgical patterns? I'll play with this in the next section on embodiment and later, in Chapter 5, when examining emotional competence.

Embodiment

Embodiment concerns the object status or body of the person whether animal, vegetable, or mineral; whether human, Martian, or robot. This being the case, we can describe relevant identifying features of a particular body. Given the different requirements for developing and sustaining a particular embodiment, expect corresponding differences in initial capacities, with attendant powers and dispositions along with corresponding vulnerabilities and pathologies. *Do Androids Dream of Electric Sheep?*

Aspects of a person's embodiment provide the object basis of their capacities. Accordingly, embodiment and capacity have a relationship of particular interest to the physician, the neuroscientist, and the robotics engineer. For example, our human anatomy and physiology provides for the capacity to speak and move about in human style. Absent legs or larynx would mean we move about and speak differently, if at all. Given sufficient neocortical absence or damage, we don't expect a human to produce or comprehend any language. An authentic humanoid robot would require "parts" of equivalent capacity. I understand that Anakin Skywalker got C-3PO's photoreceptors on Tatooin in a chase through Mos Espa. I got mine, somehow, from my mom and dad. God knows about the Martian.

SOME EMBODIMENT THEORY

Evidently, our bodies provide the stuff persons can grow from. But what about our human embodiment lends itself to this? Bear with me as I stray from the preempirical Person Concept to the empirical and theoretical question of why the human body works well for producing persons. Since we have decided on the attributes of the paradigmatic person, we can more clearly ask about the relationship of embodiment to the conceptual requirements of personhood: a body suited to engage in deliberate action in a dramaturgical pattern.

Before encountering Descriptive Psychology, I spent my college years with a teacher who took this question to heart. A formative period of my education was spent sitting with the anthropologist Weston La Barre, whose teachings were centered on the question of why our primate biology produced humans with ethical and religious concerns. La Barre thought of our species as, "half reprobate ape and half apprentice angel" (1954, 1968) and had me read a lot of Freud. He pointed out that Freud's German *die Steele* was scientized and improperly translated by James Strachey into "the mind" (e.g., Bettelheim, 1983), when it should be translated as "soul." Souls, I gather, are a better fit with angels. Be that as it may, La Barre thought one of Freud's central interests was how our mammalian embodiment provides the nature in human nature. He told me to worry less about the historical context that shaped Freud's arguments and focus more on what Freud was trying to figure out.

La Barre held the essence of Freud's (1912a, b) work was to make sense of a cultured beast whose "anatomy is destiny." La Barre was trying to teach me to identify the intent of the theorist, to find the crucial parameters of the subject that organize the theorist's writing. With this in mind, Freud's theories took on a different light. Apart from how interesting and problematic I found his historically situated claims, I learned to attend to the themes that Freud considered necessary to understand human development, motivation, and individual differences. My assignment was to drop the historical details, but to keep an eye on the organizing concerns: the socially dependent human body with its specific needs felt as "urges"; how our awareness of these urges inform, direct, and compromise intentional action and self-regulation; and with that, shape the aims and rules of culture. This tutoring was good preparation for revisiting persons and embodiment through the lens of Ossorio's Descriptive Psychology. To my delight, it was consistent with the way Ossorio taught Freud in the first seminar I took from him entitled Personality and Personality Theories (Ossorio, 1977/2015).

Although the Person Concept is open to any embodiment that provides the capacities for the behavior of persons, I have a mammalian bias. Here is my take away from La Barre. Green gas is a lousy candidate. Some embodiments, no doubt, are better contenders than others. La Barre's conclusion that primate mammalian features give us good footing, offers a reasonable start for what to look for in nonhuman persons. Here is a list of the features La Barre considered prototypically mammalian; characteristics more exaggerated in us than the other primates. He considered humans the most "generalized mammal." By that, I think he meant we have greater flexibility in our employment of our embodiment than our other mammalian kin.

1. Long infantile dependency is a really helpful start for growing people in the natural world. That, and a body that develops slowly, lives a

long time, and is forever interdependent on others for survival. A body that lives long enough to produce, protect, and hand down culture.

2. A body with varied and sensitive modes of perceiving and manipulating the objects found in the environment. Our eyes, ears, hands, and feet do the trick for us. It is useful to have a body with multiple means to build and transmit technology.

3. Fundamental characteristics, biological and social, liable to produce competition, conflict, and vulnerability manageable through cooperation, negotiation, and established rules that serve survival and safety. Humans have needs, urges, and social complexity that are best managed through deliberation, order, and when necessary, renunciation. Our nonseasonal sexual desire, our infants that require intense and constant nurturing and protection, and our states of vulnerability such as sleep, are part of our human set up. La Barre noted that our sexual desires, arousals not confined to reproduction and free from an estrus cycle, opens the door to all sorts of mischief that needs sorting out. And, since this free-for-all desire often produces infants, growing them into adults takes a village with rules.

4. A capacity for complex and novel communication in the form of broad and varied organs capable of vocalization, signing, or what have you, that can store and transmit the knowledge of how things work and the rules of conduct.

So, with all that in place, what's a body to do?

THROUGH-LINES AND THE DRAMATURGICAL PATTERN

Over the years that I have taught Descriptive Psychology, I have noticed that students with a background in theater come already equipped with a serviceable account of the Person Concept. They tend to nod at the right times when I lecture about intentional action and the dramaturgical patterns. They seem to appreciate how a person's life is akin to the drama of an improvisational play. And, especially if they have studied directing or method acting, they have explicit ways of getting at the complex moving parts of character, action, and setting.

Dramaturgical concepts and the idea of through-lines hold an honored place in the arts and humanities where the traditional meanings bear a strong resemblance to their use in Descriptive Psychology. Let start with Shakespeare:

> All the world's a stage,
> And all the men and women merely players;
> They have their exits and their entrances;
> And one man in his time plays many parts ... (*As You Like It*).

Kierkegaard and Journalen (1843) notes that what I call a through-line must be a retrospective construction: "Life can only be understood backwards; but it must be lived forwards." Goffman (1956/1990) brought the dramaturgical model to sociology, "I spoke of performers and audiences; of routines and parts; of performances coming off or falling flat; of cues, stage settings and backstage; of dramaturgical needs, dramaturgical skills, and dramaturgical strategies. Now it should be admitted that this attempt to press a mere analogy so far was in part a rhetoric and a maneuver." And here is Ossorio's (2006a, b) formulation: "In the Dramaturgical Model, behavior is intrinsically and fundamentally a matter of creating and realizing personal and social dramas. Human lives are intrinsically and fundamentally dramatic in form …. A drama is a structured behavioral episode or series of episodes that makes sense to Us."

Some years ago, Bryan Harnsberger, working on his dissertation (Harnsberger, 2015), discussed method acting and Constantin Stanislavski's (1936/1989) *An Actor Prepares*, "You do not know that your intentions will be carried out, but you can suppose that they will be. Then you must have an idea about the rest of your day. Don't you feel that solid line as it stretches out into the future, fraught with cares, responsibilities, joys, and griefs? In looking ahead there is a certain movement, and where there is movement a line begins." The notion of a through-line seemed a good structure to fit the problem Ossorio (2006a, b) acknowledged when he wrote that, "dealing with heterogeneous behavior patterns as a single type of behavior does nothing toward elucidating the pattern. And yet the understanding of such full-scale patterns in real life is essential for understanding the behavior of persons."

If you have the right concepts, and you follow a person long enough, their life will come to make sense, not because their specific performances are predictable, but because they fit in some way that person's perspective on what matters and the flexibility to choose how to go about honoring that. Life is an improvisation and only when looking back do we see if the results fit the aim. The characters and stage change and the audience wait to see how it turns out. If a script is eventually written, it's in retrospect, after the action has occurred. But once you know a character really well, you are rarely surprised by what they do. When you finally understand what significantly matters to them, what earlier might have seemed out-of-character, now appears an implementation true to pattern.

Accidents and the unintended happen; but for the most part, people have *their* reasons for doing what they do. Over time, from these personally motivated attempts, patterns emerge. These patterns, more or less stable, implemented in different ways, occur intermittently through the course of our lives. If we need to justify what we are up to, it will finally boil down to what we actually hold intrinsically significant. Implicitly or explicitly, we employ our recognition of these through-lines when describing behavior as in and out of character. It can be hard to tell, since we implement what matters in all sorts of ways. Some performances require careful thinking to understand if they share a common thread. And, like every other accounting of motivation, absent a pipeline to the truth, we can get it wrong.

Life is complicated. Our lives have unfurling, overlapping episodes of action that reflect the complexity of our agendas. People simultaneously and sequentially live on many fronts. Some through-lines may appear consistent, while others may not. Some may appear for a time, disappear, later to reemerge. Some may end in satisfaction or be abandoned in frustrated disappointment. They can be given up with insight or because of an absence of opportunity for expression. Some may seem to go on forever.

In summary, through-lines are an observer's conceptualization of what someone frequently does because of its personal significance. What a person finds significant organizes their selection of specific behavioral implementations that follow from recognized opportunities and the actor's competence. Since what a person actually finds personally significant should reflect their motivational hierarchy of intrinsic core values, through-line descriptions should reveal these values. The values revealed may not be the values a person claims they hold most dear. Actions speak loudest.

EXAMPLES OF THROUGH-LINES

Any personal characteristic and behavior can be an aspect of a **Through-Line Pattern Description**. What keeps the line together is the shared significance of the behaviors, not whether they express any particular trait, attitude, interest, style, or state, although some of these personal characteristics may frequently attend the pattern. The through-line description should be a summary or abstract of themes of ongoing significance that also captures what is ordinarily achieved by the efforts and implementations.

Here are some examples of how they look. All examples should start with: *when there is opportunity and perhaps while doing other things as well.*

She heedlessly and perhaps unconsciously goes through life attempting to score competitive victories with women who resemble her mother, and does so with an eye toward currying favor with unobtainable men.

While fearfully avoiding degradation, he manages his affairs in such a way as to offend no one while never stepping outside of what he thinks are his competencies.

He consciously and unconsciously strives to put people in a helpless position in a manner that keeps him, in his view, on the moral high ground.

Terrified of being alone and doubting her worth to others, she seeks satisfaction by tolerating the abusive needs of others or in actions that undo and distract her from being aware of her loneliness.

Requiring a sense of specialness, he looks for opportunities to demonstrate his worth by achievement in competitive arenas while making sure not to out-step the values and achievements of those he considers the conventional esteemed judges.

You might notice how the insistent, noncognizant, and pathological weaves these examples together. Some through-lines end in satisfaction, some are eventually outgrown or no longer relevant; some are extended compulsively without satisfaction, others are extended because the satisfactions are and remain valued. But why are these unhappy examples the ones I offer first? Hint, I'm a clinical psychologist with a psychodynamic bent. No doubt, one through-line of mine is a concern with identifying pathology. So please allow me a short digression into the dynamics of human embodiment and self-deception.

Through-lines organize a descriptive narrative in a manner that highlights a status dynamic similar to what Roy Schafer (1976) called psychoanalytic action language. Analysts employ this sort of locution while interpreting the significance of an action, especially those seen as defensive or unconsciously motivated. Here's why: a through-line that has significant unconscious aspects is prone to unsatisfying repetition since the actor is not in a good position to critically modify their behavior or reorder priorities *or even recognize the significance pattern.* Human compulsive repetition frequently involves our body-based urges and social desires. Sex, trauma, and unmet dependency needs can become compulsive when the desire for satisfaction and release, restoration, and support remains without a self-aware practicing of alternative and serviceable implementations. Without adequate self-critical awareness, a person may repeat a tragic pattern, unable to learn from misfortune. (We'll return to these themes in Chapters 4 and 5 when we look at psychopathology and emotional competence).

Still, I am troubled by the negative, restrictive, and pathological tone of my examples. On logical grounds, I think, to the extent that a person's behavior is rigid, insistent, and notably restricted, it is easier to identify patterns. Pathology restricts performances in a way that produces stereotyped behaviors. This lets diagnostic categories work. Pathology is simpler than health. It is easier to classify when the boundaries of motive, toleration, and knowledge narrow. A happy and healthy life is less predictable than one restricted by fixation and compulsion. The significances that organize the through-lines of the healthy are satisfied through varied and flexible implementations, free of insistent repetition. So, how's this:

Aware of the rights and plights of others, mindful of her failing, careful not to overly compromise herself, she deliberately seeks novelty, pleasure, and beauty ironically embracing that what's good for the goose might not be good for the gander.

NONHUMAN THROUGH-LINES

Ossorio once joked, but seriously, that a zilch particle is a person with almost everything left out. This boundary condition on embodiment is hardly a candidate for a person and their through-lines. There is simply not enough there. That's why we start with a paradigm case to examine the close calls, near misses, and the no way in hell would that count.

I can always derail a seminar by asking the class their thoughts about dog psychology. I remember an exchange that started, "dogs are like children with impulse control problems," and the wag who responded, "cats are sort of on the autism spectrum." I have already indicated that I don't discourage heuristic anthropomorphism. Dogs *are* impulsive. Maybe not all of them, but the dogs I live with could do a better job at restraint. And the cats I love seem a bit indifferent.

Be any of that as it may, some person attributes are easy to see in dogs: individual embodiments, what looks to me to be intentional action, even deliberation; evidence of cognizance, and so on. Accordingly, I was game, when my colleague Clarke Stone asked about through-lines in dogs. Here's my response. It can serve as illustration of the top-down approach where we look at nonperson actors—for us, the other nonhuman animals—as only more or less filling out the full paradigm.

THROUGH-LINES AND DOGS—THE SIGNIFICANCE IN DOG PSYCHOLOGY

You can trust a dog with your life … but not your lunch.
(Stephen Huneck).

A through-line description is, paradigmatically, the description of a non-contiguous sequence of a person's courses of action as having a shared significance. For me, that's sufficient formulation.
(Greg Colvin).

Happy and grateful, I spend a lot of time in the company of dogs, each with their personable ways. Of course, a lot of what they do is pretty doggy.

With dogs, I employ person qualities where they seem appropriate. We can argue about this, but I think no one in their right mind doubts dogs have personalities, with individually different abilities and dispositions. If you know a dog, you recognize a character. And while never knowing exactly what a dog will do, we come to know what they find important. They sometimes surprise us, but *mostly* they act in-character in their dogged ways.

That dogs have personal characteristics and engage in intentional action, paradigmatic intentional action, carries the logical requirement that their behavior involves courses of action with significance. In retrospect, their lives have *through-lines* organized by what they found important. I think this is the case for many animals. The through-lines descriptive of humans may seem more complex than those of dogs but that claim might be an artifact of our failure to recognize the nuanced sensitivities and forms of life that matter to our canine companions. Obviously, they hear and smell beyond my competence to judge what they appreciate. These sensitivities inform their natural needs and provide information beyond my ken. Why do they roll in dead worms with such obvious delight? Here, "try it, you'll like it," is not going to happen.

All personal characteristics develop from an individual's prior capacities, their in-born and developed sensitivities and body-based needs, and their intervening experiences. Dogs and humans alike find themselves in environments with restricted possibilities where they find, create, and practice their individual ways. Pet dogs are usually more restricted than humans. We keep them this way, as we do with human children.

I think it's appropriate to think of a dog as a sort of person with certain paradigmatic attributes absent. Let's start with the question of whether an individual dog has a history of Deliberate Action in a Dramaturgical Pattern. A person's actions follow from their individual characteristics and their circumstances, reflecting what they try to achieve given their values. Having values means being able to want some state of affairs over others. This in turn produces patterns. Dogs have patterns.

Earlier, we established that a human being is an individual who is both a person and a specimen of *Homo sapiens*. This last sentence carries the reminder that nonhuman individuals could also be persons. But could a dog be a paradigmatic person? Paradigmatic, you recall, refers to a full or undoubted case, a case where all competent judges likely agree. Along with the ability to engage in deliberate acts, paradigmatic persons have language. Dogs don't talk. Ask them to speak, and if willing, they bark. Dogs, to me, are deficit case persons.

A problem in understanding dogs is we can't expect an answer if we ask, "what are you doing?" let alone, "why did you choose that" or "how does it matter?" We can't get dogs to tell us if they choose and renounce, or anything about what they are up to. This does not mean their behavior was not deliberate, it just means it is hard to gather the evidence that comes with a verbal description of choice. Choices are easiest to see when the speaker can tell us the option not selected. We will return to this since some behaviors, especially those that involve ethical or aesthetic values, may require the ability to engage in deliberate action. Choice involves renunciation, at least in the moment. Did my dog not chew my tasty boot today because he'll get yelled at? Because it's not the right thing to do? Or because the boot looks best without bite marks?

Hard to tell, but I suspect it's not a concern with ethics or aesthetics but the prudent recollection of the scolding that followed last time. And, the time before that.

I have no trouble arguing dogs have hedonic and prudent concerns. Clearly, they're pleasure seeking, pain avoiding, and self-interested. I don't doubt they are cognizant and deliberate, but I'd have trouble making a strong case that dogs have ethical and aesthetic values, even though I think some might. I treat my dogs as *deficit case persons*, worthy of respect, but they're dogs so I don't trust them with my lunch (but then again, I might not trust you either).

Do dogs have an ethical sense? A study in *Proceedings of the National Academy of Sciences of the United States of America* (Range et al., 2009) suggested dogs respond to unfair treatment, cooperating less when they witness a partner dog getting a bigger share of food. Since I don't know of a case where a dog has acted to make sure another dog gets a fair share, this seems to me more a matter of self-interest than an ethical concern with fair distribution. Perhaps they only really care when they are at the short end of the stick. But I can't speak for what the dog is actually considering.

Here's a thought of Clarke Stone's on this topic. "They essentially have one social arrangement—top dog to bottom—so any dog getting more resources is getting elevated. No dog would reasonably allow that without some kind of conflict. Noting that combat is *only one kind* of conflict, I observe our older dog becomes a little more insistent about getting attention when our younger dog gets more, even if the attention is negative. She doesn't want to lose her place. This is why you can't trust your dog with your lunch: more lunch = higher rank. Stealing your sandwich is stealing a move on you. But since your dog takes it you and your dog are in the same pack, you can trust your dog with your life. It will always defend *one of us* against an interloper."

Dogs are clearly less competent than humans in language use, although I don't write them off completely. I think the strong case is that their communications, as effective as they are, do not have the improvisational flexibility to qualify as language. (Another point to argue.) Their limited verbal repertory along with the importance they give hedonics and prudence, and an apparent lack of ethical and aesthetic perspective, keeps them as deficit case persons in my book. Here are all sorts of reasons to argue. I argue with myself about this.

SOME LIMITATIONS TO A DOG'S THROUGH-LINES

Dependency, rapid maturation, and an extraordinary awareness of smell and sound, inform and shape a dog's all too short life. In the span of my children growing from infancy to adolescence, most dogs live their entire lives. By the time some human folk have just begun to understand what they find fundamentally significant, a dog has come and gone. This makes for shorter through-lines. As a human with a limited ability to appreciate the nuanced world my dog senses, the through-line descriptions I can construct are less complex and differentiated than those I construct for the people I know well. My limited appreciation limits my competence to adequately describe what they find significant. This, I suspect, is also partly why dogs are sometimes described in the ways we talk about children. A dog's life and a human's youth span a similar number of days. And dogs, like human children, are domesticated, bred, and socially shaped to fit the worlds, the cultures, of our human adult ways.

Since very young children and domestic dogs are dependent on the support of a more mature human community, their through-lines, informed by their idiosyncratic abilities, experiences, and discoveries concern their standings with each other, and with their keepers and providers. As they begin to do their own thing, privately, or with others, we watch them sort out whether to lead or follow, whether they've been individually recognized, and whether they're in good standing. That and food seem front and center. When human kids thrive, they are like pups, but up to much more as they discover and practice new roles; find, create, and spontaneously practice their strengths while becoming mindful of their vulnerabilities. Dogs probably do too, but with different restrictions. When human children play, status assignments are central, and humans have an extremely extensive set of statuses. How many statuses do dogs have? Certainly, not so many.

The through-lines I construct for my dogs are mostly descriptions of how they manage their dependency and the imposed restrictions on their lives. That and the stuff they just seem to like doing.

Since through-lines are an observer's production, the descriptions I develop center on how I see them interact with me, each other, our family, neighbors, strangers, other dogs, and other animals encountered on walks. And all that stuff they look to gobble down. The trick with describing their through-lines is finding a nuance that captures the pattern. So, here's some for the dogs I live with.

Hart, a dachshund rat terrier mix:

Tirelessly keeping his eye on the "ball," he seeks potential allies, incessantly imploring them to play his games so he can show off his varied moves and respond to acknowledgment.
Sweetly obstinate, heedless of the other's power and direction, he makes a show of a resistance to follow. Knowing he will eventually come along, he digs in his heels and delays any attempt that distracts him from a mission to sniff and mark where he's been.

And two for Banjo, a dachshund–lab mix:

Following from behind the pack, insistently eager to connect and please, he seeks acknowledgment and a secure place where he'll not be bothered.

Disregarding the consequences, if it smells palatable, it's to be grabbed and eaten. (Actually, this describes both Banjo and Hart.)

Not that competent with language, but very communicative, both dogs mix and string sounds, phatic and evocative, along with body gestures that convey meaning. My understanding of their intended meanings, varied and sometimes complex, is vindicated by their response. If I respond with what they want, they stop imploring. The signal-to-noise ratio seems largely signal. If there is grammar to what they convey, it is simple and conforms to the forms of life, the social practices, which matter to them. It seems to me that if I keep my vocalizations short and relevant to their concerns, they mostly respond accordingly, unless they don't want to. But that's the case with everyone I deal with.

When I play with Banjo and Hart, sometimes I find reason to think they might have a limited ethical and aesthetic perspective. At some point nightly, Hart will stand in front of me, catch my eye, and bark. Then he'll stare. Banjo will run in from the bedroom, check out the scene, and for reasons hard to fathom, remain or return to the bedroom where he has likely rearranged the pillows and snuck in some item of my wife's clothing, never mine. I might try to ignore Hart. I have my own agenda. But if he can hold my eye, he'll bark again, make a puppy whine and then turn his head to the mantle where his toys are almost hidden. He'll try to catch my eye and when he does, he points to the balls. He moves his eyes from mine to the mantle and waits, eagerly. I know he wants to play.

If he's caught me in the right mood, I take one of the squishy balls and toss it. Grounders, popups, and fakes to the right or left. Gleeful mid-air catches and in-air toss backs. This goes on and on and on and on. When Hart makes a particularly artful catch he wiggles the way he does when excited. He catches better than he throws, I'm lazy, so if he hasn't tossed the ball right to me I'll say, "not close enough." He'll look at me again and if he wants to continue will nudge the ball closer. Sometimes he doesn't want to give it back, especially if Banjo intrudes. Banjo, awkward with the game, mostly runs interference. If he can, instead of bringing it back to me, he'll steal it and return to the bedroom inviting chase.

This is a game. It has shared rules of fair and foul, and, I think, a mutual appreciation of the beauty of a well-executed play. Seeing it this way and acting accordingly, makes it work for all of us.

Here are some additional maxims for this chapter:

If a person has a given person characteristic, they continue to have it until and unless it changes.

If a person's personal characteristics change, that calls for an explanation.

If a person has a given person characteristic and their behavior is an expression of it, then that calls for no explanation, whereas if their behavior violates that person characteristic, that does call for an explanation.

Some Implications

The PCF of Individual Persons allows for nonhuman persons, potential persons, nascent persons, manufactured persons, former persons, deficit case persons, primitive persons, and fictional persons. Us individual humans are persons who happen to be *Homo sapiens*. Akin to my ruling out *Star Trek*'s Borg, I am not going to include the legal claim that corporations are persons. That construct involves a political and legal claim that makes whatever sense it does owing to corporate liabilities, contracts, and similar rights and obligations. Resistance to this employment of language, I hope, is not futile.

A PCF allows different judges to draw lines differently. At this point, the only examples I know that fill out the full PCF of persons are us. Even so, not all humans match the entire paradigm; not at all stages of life nor in all states of consciousness. Maturation and the cycle of the day present different configurations of available powers and dispositions. Maturational and developmental stage, and the presence of pathology, matters in the social world regarding the extent of deliberate action expected or possible. Language ability is especially crucial. Although deliberate action is not dependent on the availability of language, verbal behavior is a form of deliberate action essential for the full paradigm. A person without language would be a deficit case if adult, or a nascent case if an infant or toddler still in the process of developing linguistic competence.

Must a person have hedonic, prudent, ethical, and aesthetic perspectives to count as a person? Or is the ability to engage in any sort of deliberate action enough? Even though our conversations are pretty one sided, I have little doubt Banjo is a deliberate actor. He has, I feel sure, hedonic and prudential perspectives. About his ethical and aesthetic perspective, I'm not so sure. I would have a hard time building a case that he has these values. I think he appreciates affection and gentleness in some ways similar to me, but I would not expect him to share a favorite treat with Hart. I do not doubt that he is an intentional actor, but I am uncertain about the range and nature of his deliberate actions and what he thinks over. Regardless,

Banjo has some person qualities, certainly enough to be a beloved member of my family. I am sure it works both ways. From Banjo's perspective, I bet he thinks I'm more than a bit doggy and that's OK with him.

And what of humans who appear lacking or deficient in the paradigmatic values? The ability to weigh hedonic, prudent, ethical, and aesthetic interests are personal characteristics often required to participate successfully in complex cosmopolitan culture. We make judgments about anyone who clearly lacks or overplays *any* of these motives. Significant imbalances result in problematic self-regulation and social engagement that can get labeled as psychopathology or moral failing.

The dramaturgical pattern of a particular life is significantly dependent on a person's values. Given its physical form, a robot person might not respond to the visceral sensations of pain or pleasure. If it has a hedonic perspective, it might be significantly different from mine or yours. A chimpanzee person, if we have sufficient reason to assign that status, if lacking language, probably has limited or absent ethical and aesthetic concerns. This suggests a sort of primitive person status, adequate for the forest but not Manhattan.

Underdeveloped or limited is different from absent. Our descendants, if we don't blow ourselves to extinction, may look back and find our perspective underdeveloped. We're a work in progress.

Treating something as engaged in deliberate action, using language, or exhibiting a dramaturgical pattern is not without ambiguity. At times, the line is drawn arbitrarily or with self-conscious uncertainty. Here PCFs are useful to negotiate resulting confusions, uncertainty, and disagreements. Even what differentiates language from nonlinguistic communication is blurred. Do any of the other primates have linguistic competencies? There is some evidence that chimpanzees and other great apes use a flexible system of nonvocal gestures to communicate in "sign language" (Hobaiter and Byrne, 2014). But is it flexible enough? Does it allow or invite novel constructions? Can a story to be told and passed on?

Full personhood status is finally a matter of political and legal decision; a changeable decision we make about each other. The PCF I offer provides a way to classify different sorts of persons based on language and the motives they are competent to use in recognizing their options and choosing a course of action. The ability, competence, and disposition to speak and deliberately employ hedonic, prudent, aesthetic, and ethical values are relevant to a consideration of appropriate rights, expectations, and responsibilities. Implicitly or explicitly we employ these distinctions in our interactions with others, whether adult or child, human or otherwise.

Other species and entities aside, we don't even treat all humans as full persons. The classification of a human as an alien or a savage has historically carried a degraded status in the service of depriving those labeled of the rights, expectations, and obligations accorded to paradigmatic persons. Stripped of full person status, they are more readily treated as chattel or disposable. For that matter, human children have a nascent person status and are treated differently than full legal persons. They, too, are sometimes treated more as parental property than as limited but autonomous persons (Godwin, 2015). The distinction between childhood and adulthood is clearly arbitrary. Is adulthood reached at 21, 18, 16, 12, or 35?

WHAT ABOUT OTHER ANIMALS?

Years back, I was pursuing a pod of bottlenose dolphin when a small one smacked the stern of my kayak, hard. As the calf reapproached, a large female nudged it away. I was astonished, grateful, and relieved. Not wanting to push my luck, I paddled back to shore.

Are the Cetacea good candidates for personhood? Do they engage in deliberate action in a dramaturgical pattern? Do bottlenose dolphins speak to each other? Did a dolphin protect me from mischief? I do not know. I do not have sufficient evidence that dolphins fill the paradigm case, even though some people have their considered reasons to think they might. Using a PCF, I can point to where the evidence is robust and where it is lacking. Language seems to be a sticking point. They left their hands behind and moved into the sea, perhaps 50 million years ago. So, without good ability to make tools but with the possibility of speech, what are the chances we have of understanding whatever it is they might be saying?

What about the other Cetacea, and the elephants, the nonhuman primates, and crows and parrots? I suspect they fill out some of the paradigm case. Other judges reasonably believe they fill out more (Wise, 2000).

Do animals in the wild talk with each other? Could they talk with us? We may not have sufficient shared social practices to make interspecies communication, speech, and translation feasible, so it is very hard to tell. This is a difficult empirical issue. Rather than simply communicate, some observers believe they speak to each other in a linguistic fashion. There is no consensus, but the evidence is mounting that some do (see, e.g., Savage-Rumbaugh et al., 2009). And then there is Wittgenstein's, "if the lion could speak, we could not understand him." Nonhuman animal communication, including the possibility of language use, is difficult to study when there is an absence of "shared forms of life." But, if the lion could speak, given our common mammalian form, could it not demand I scratch him harder and more to the right? We will return to this in Chapter 6.

Another ethical judgment. Since language requires shared social practice, an animal's ecologically bounded options limit its expected communicative range, concerns, and actions. Humans are adept at disrupting natural environments and are skilled at coercing or killing animals to further our goals. If they wanted to talk to us, I am not sure we would welcome what they have to say.

If someone actually taught nonhuman animals to competently use language, would that be teaching them to be a person? This is an implication of the paradigm offered here. By this same reasoning, we teach our human children to be persons, too.

SOME ETHICS ABOUT THE UNCERTAINTY OF PERSONHOOD—ANOTHER VALUE JUDGMENT WILL FOLLOW

What should we do with our uncertainty? Logically, we are never in a position to prove that something is a person, but we can adopt a policy that if we have any strong grounds for seeing the other as one of us, we should treat that entity as a person until we have reason enough to feel we are misguided. Here, I am promoting the value that with persons, it should be I to Thou. There are people whose cultures and social practices leave me mystified, but it is prudent and ethical to proceed from the belief that I simply do not understand what they are about. Perhaps the same should hold for other animals. I am not particularly concerned with initial false positives. In my scientific training, I was told to avoid anthropomorphism. I have become skeptical about the morality of this stance, whether it involves an animal's possible slavery or how I treat them as food.

A significant ethical question remains: after the line on personhood is drawn, what considerations apply to the treatment of animals that do not fall into the full person category, near miss or not? Sentient animals are intentional actors and have an interest in the avoidance of suffering (Singer, 2009). Is it ever ethical to inflict harm if there is a way not to? What perspectives and priorities can and perhaps should be weighed?

Person status defines a domain where social and legal rights reside, hence a proper abhorrence of slavery and murder. Judges in good faith might differ as to what animals are included as persons, but it is morally and ethically problematic to limit concerns about the quality of a life to whether that life is also a person. Part of being a person is a potential to appreciate this. Since a paradigmatic person can weigh hedonic, prudent, aesthetic, and ethical concerns, all these perspectives have a place in judging the consequence of an action that involves harm, damage, and suffering. It ought to. Since humans can deliberate, we have the inherent potential to reorder values and change our mind.

3

Behavior as Intentional Action

Chapter 2 used a Paradigm Case Formulation for negotiating reason-able agreement and disagreement about what constitutes a person. Our next core constituent of the Person Concept is Behavior as Intentional Action. This chapter will take a close look at Intentional Action and its Cognizant and Deliberate variations. Our principal method will be Parametric Analysis, an alternative to Paradigm Case Formulations. With these tools, we'll think about self-regulation, appraisals, and reality test-ing; and examine hypnosis.

Let's return to the distinctive mission of Ossorio's odd psychology: Descriptive Psychology is a *preempirical discipline* structured by the logical requirements of the Person Concept and designed to systematically orga-nize this subject matter's full range of possibilities. This is odd because psychology is usually anchored in theory. Descriptive Psychology is some-thing else entirely, *something formally prior to theory*. Those of us doing this work do not start with a theory saying what might be the case, but with a set of concepts open to all possibility, including concepts we might have missed. As Ossorio put it, "All the facts—*and all the possible facts*—about persons and what they do." This is independent of what we historically, empirically discover to be the case. This sort of preempirical conceptu-alization should provide a modifiable, theory-neutral framework for the systematic study of everything that fits the subject matter. This distinction between a subject matter's possibilities and what, empirically, turns out to actually happen is codified by our convention of restricting the term *reality* to the full range of logical possibility, and limit *real world* to the empirically, historically vindicated data. Reality is the limiting structure of the possible, the real world what is found to be the case, our walkabout world where we know how to act and can imagine ourselves doing do. Our formulation of intentional action is preempirical. It covers (and can expand to cover) all intentional action, those actions already done and those possible.

55

SOME QUIBBLING ABOUT CONCEPTUALIZATION AND THEORY

This distinction between theory and preempirical conceptualization is a hallmark of Descriptive Psychology. Still, after I exhaustively explain that the Person Concept is a conceptualization of the possible rather than a theory of the actual, students and colleagues continue to ask about Ossorio's "Theory of Persons." Some say our distinction is too picky, and they call "a theory" any complicated network of ideas, so this becomes theory to them. Whatever you want to call this, please keep the distinction between identifying a subject matter and the empirical job of going out and observing the actual actions of individuals. Then, if you ask, "Why this specific pattern and not some other possibility?" you'll be concerned with what we mean by "theory." A conceptual network is more akin to definition; theory to explanation; thus the following is not a theory of intentional action but what we commit to when we describe something as intentional.

SOME ACTION VOCABULARY

Just as the Descriptive lexicon distinguishes *reality* from *real world*, we have conventions for the family of intentional concepts. These distinctions are consistent with ordinary use but, unless further clarified, invite ambiguity. Too often, the behavioral sciences have a tradition of employing the same terms in vastly different ways without regard to their ordinary meaning, or very different terms to mean the same thing. We will avoid this messy confusion by clarifying our technical meaning.

Here is how we will use *intentional, cognizant, deliberate* (the adjective), and *deliberate-with-a-long-a* (the verb). For our purposes, intentional indicates personal agency, and refers to any goal-directed, purposeful, or meaningful behavior. We will focus on two forms of intentional action: cognizant and deliberate. **Cognizant Action** involves a knowing awareness or recognition that one is acting (to know X is to be able to act on the concept X. In this case, X is the action I know I am performing). **Deliberate Action** is cognizant action that involves an awareness of choice, that is, out of the possibilities to achieve a goal, version X was chosen instead of Y, Z, etc. Deliberate-with-a long-a (i.e., to deliberate) is simply the ordinary meaning of mulling something over, of considering the possibilities. To deliberate is to engage in a cognitive act that has duration, a beginning, and an end; and like any behavior, it can be interrupted. We will abbreviate the intentional action as **IA**, the cognizant action as **CA**, and the deliberate action as **DA**.

The IA formulation is reflexive. Cognizant actions involve the possibility of representing self-observation and self-knowledge. I can think about what I am doing while doing it. "Here I am, up at bat." The IA formulation is recursive. A linked chain of related intentional actions makes up a social practice, but an individual IA, itself, can be a social practice. For example, the IA "taking a swing at the ball" is a meaningful social practice, and a series of linked IAs, such as "hitting the ball over the fence," "running the bases," and "jaunting to the dugout," can be another. (The concept of an IA as a social practice also provides the pragmatic foundation for language and verbal behavior as something necessarily sharable.)

In summary, the distinction between intentional and deliberate follows their use in ordinary language. The adjective, *deliberate*, and the verb form, *to deliberate*, catch the notion that people do things consciously and on purpose and can consciously consider, reconsider, and think things through. They don't have to, they don't always, but they can. Intentional only commits us to "done on purpose" or "done for a reason." Deliberate Action requires the possibility of choice, of recognized alternatives to do what is done. Any deliberate action could be done differently or refrained from entirely.

When we say we observe a deliberate action, we are claiming what happened was not utterly coerced, fated, or destined; was not luck or accident. (Not that there can't be a degree of coercion. When I assign this book as a required text and threaten pop tests, my students have a choice and a threat for noncompliance. On the other hand, the social practice of "taking a course" includes testing, so maybe I'm overstating the case when I say "threaten.") Without this commitment to what deliberate means, the concepts of responsibility, criminality, tort, negligence, contract, and the like have no substance. Ethics, morality, and all the normative "oughts" ride on this. Civilization's contracts, laws, promises, rewards, penalties, and the like are built from the shared understanding that people are accountable for the behaviors they choose *because* they can choose them. None of this makes sense without a place for choice in our conceptual formulation.

This is not to claim choice involves some absolute "anything goes" freedom. Here, pragmatics intrude. Is there an actual alternative? Choice is constrained by our previous choices, our bodies, our other attributes, and our circumstances, including the world we inhabit. (Try making a silk purse out of a sow's ear.) By making choice the core of deliberate action, I am trying to avoid the rabbit hole of "free will," whatever that has come to mean. Free from what? Choice is always constrained by the actionable options. Within a locked cell, I can sit down or stand up, but I can't walk through the bars. Writing this, I remember a Facebook discussion on free will, determinism, and causation where the philosopher Owen Flanagan responded, "I have said in print that if I were the benevolent dictator of philosophy, I would issue an edict banning the use of the word 'free will' for 100 years. We would do fine." In the exchange that followed, similar points were made about the muddled use of "causation." The pragmatics of "choice" and "option" avoids this mess because choices are constrained by circumstance, by what is known and valued, by the ability or competence to act on the option chosen. You will soon recognize these constraints as some of the parametric distinctions in our formulation of intentional action.

INTENTIONALITY, BACK WHERE IT BELONGS

For many in the behavioral sciences, the study of intention has found its way back to center stage. There is considerable talk and argument about intentionality, but it is hindered by a lack of shared meaning. Without common ground, it is hard to negotiate overlap and disagreement. A coordinating map, some sort of Venn diagram would help. The Person Concept's formulation of Intentional Action addresses this.

The paradigms of science's logical forms are expanding. None are more significant than reexamining the place of cause-effect reductionist determinism as the necessary given for scientific progress. The unavoidable problem is us. The ordinary meanings of intentional and deliberate action have no reasonable place in a deterministic scientific theology. If persons perform deliberate acts, they cannot be reduced to something wound up like God's clock. If science requires this, a science of persons *as persons* is ruled out. If we want to understand persons, the faith that science requires reductionist causality founded on determinism has outlived its value. I say faith with purpose. Determinism is not something discovered in nature, but an idea, at times very helpful, that guided and legitimized the use of cause and effect accounts of nature. Cause and effect work just fine for some explanations, but determinism is a hammer that treats everything as a nail. Our toolbox needs something more than hammers. A tool box of rules and reasons has space for causes and effects. That's what we need.

Can you imagine a fully functioning person who never behaved intentionally? Or a world where people never do anything on purpose? We take it people have *their* reasons for what they do. Not everything is done on purpose, but without acknowledging intention as central to personal behavior, none of us are one of us. The ordinary meaning of intention must be preserved for behavioral science to treat persons as persons and not as something less. An adequate portrayal of persons requires concepts that acknowledge the intrinsic meaning of intention-related concepts: purpose, wants, reasons, responsibilities, accountability, and the like. If these ideas are violated or ruled out, the subject matter portrays something different than a person.

This concern with intrinsic meanings illustrates Descriptive Psychology's top-down approach. We start with a subject matter's necessary commitments and make sure the necessary attributes of that complexity are not violated in its analysis. Accordingly, we employ Paradigm Case Formulations that start with the full complexity intact.

Starting on top acknowledges that competent humans hold each other accountable. It would be negligent not to. The meaning of negligence requires this. People make choices given their understanding of their circumstances and personal characteristics. Would you trust anyone who behaved otherwise? For that matter, would "trust" mean anything? Why then, put faith in a behavioral science "beyond freedom and dignity" (Skinner, 1971)?

Evidence that the science wars over reductionism and determinism have subsided is seen in the reemergence of intentional action as a central concept. Here's Jerome Bruner's forward to *Intentions and Intentionality: Foundations of Social Cognition* (Malle, 2001): "… there was little room for a concept like intention in the self-professed 'tough' psychological theorizing of the twentieth century." But he then concludes, "The nature of intention and the means whereby we recognize one another's intentions has become a central issue not only in philosophy but also in psychological theory and research—and not just in psychology in general, but in enriching our understanding of how the growing child comes to know his or her social world and, indeed, how *Homo sapiens* managed to take the crucial step of developing human culture." A tough minded but coherent appreciation of culture is hard without intention.

Since I've advocated top-down formulations, let's dismantle reductionism. Consider the dilemmas that come with an atomistic approach. Try building a paradigmatic person from the bottom up, constructed entirely from some elementary atomic unit—some zilch particle. If, as Democritus claimed, there are only atoms and the void (Schofield, 2002), when and how do we introduce intention, choice, consciousness, and self-knowledge into our scientific narrative? If you respond that consciousness, intention, and the capacity to deliberate are emergent properties, fine, better than smoke and mirrors. Emergence is consistent with these attributes being easily observed in highly differentiated animals, and nowhere else, at least as far as I know. I've no doubt some form of organic evolution produced us. Alternatively, you might go the route of panpsychism and argue that zilch particles already have a bit of the psyche about them or that consciousness is an inherent quality of the universe (Nagel, 2012). Theorize the origins of consciousness to your heart's delight if the integrity of intentional action is respected. I have my theories, you have yours, but theory is not the primary Descriptive game. The "hard problem of consciousness" is a different kettle of fish (Chalmers, 1995).

(In critiquing a draft of this chapter, my colleague Clarke Stone suggested, "You might make the Descriptive case here: "… cause-and-effect, reductive, deterministic science *is something we do.* We who? We persons. So, persons are prior to science. Or, as we have noted, pre-empirical; thus, our generalized formulation of 'what we do' precedes the formulation of a more specific 'something we do,' such as science.")

Top down, we start with Deliberate Action. We are not going to sort out here how to build a person from the bottom up. If some variety of reduction has the provisions for ending up with a Person, fine. I'm more concerned with the problematic reductionism that makes intentional action a "billiard ball" causality and a simple T_1, T_2 change. That is not enough to manage the complexity and significance of intentional behavior. Total puppets, performances *fully* forced or coerced, things moving accidently or by reflex are not intentional actions. Such objects, processes, and events are something conceptually different. They have their place *within* another fundamental component of the Person Concept, the concepts of World, Reality, and the State of Affairs system. People are incidentally objects in the world but paradigmatically agents. People attempt to achieve something when appraising the opportunities and dilemmas they encounter in the circumstances of their worlds. Deliberate actors have a degree of autonomy, with their own reasons for doing what they do.

WHAT ABOUT ROBOTS?

The autonomy of persons presents opportunity and dilemma. A student once asked me if the purpose of Descriptive Psychology was to better humanity and I said no, it could be used that way, but it could be used other ways as well. If there are intrinsic values that attend Descriptive, they are an intellectual-scientific aesthetic of coherence, elegance, and fit. The analysis of Deliberate Action might be of use in constructing an artificial intelligence able to act deliberately. But how would it be disposed? Remember when Skynet became self-aware?

Deliberate agents can invent and create, but also damage, harm, and destroy. The history of humanity holds cautionary tales that should apply to nonhuman persons, too. Consider the hypothetical "singularity" moment in which a machine becomes a super-person. On formal-logical grounds, if you grow or build a person, the result will have its own intentions and its own choices. No wonder Isaac Asimov (1950) wanted these three laws built into his robots: (1) a robot may not injure a human being or, through inaction, allow a human being to come to harm; (2) a robot must obey orders given it by human beings except where such orders would conflict with the First Law; and (3) a robot must protect its own existence if such protection does not conflict with the First or Second Law. Let's hope they don't stumble upon or figure out the override. Asimov's "laws" are designed to be built in, programmed constraints on the range of Deliberate Actions, not weighed perspectives such as hedonics, prudence, aesthetics, and ethics. Without inherent (hard-wired or programmed) boundaries, who knows what mischief an authentic robot might find satisfying. Remember HAL 9000, "I'm sorry Dave, I'm afraid I can't do that" (Kubrick and Clarke, 1968).

OBSERVATION, PERFORMANCE, MEANING, AND SIGNIFICANCE AND SOME PRELIMINARY CONNECTIONS TO VERBAL BEHAVIOR

Intentional actions understood as social practices provide the pragmatic basis of our ability to understand each other. Not being a mind reader, I have no direct knowledge of your experience. I am not you. What I have are my thoughts and understandings of what I observe you do. This is informed by your deliberate verbal behaviors including what you tell me when I ask what's on your mind. (I take it on empirical grounds that none of us are mind readers who know how to perform a Vulcan mind meld (Wincelberg, 1966). If I am wrong and some of us do, it will only add to the list of skills, sensitivities, and perceptions that can inform observation and thought.)

Verbal behavior is meaningful because it reflects, accompanies, and is part of our shared social practices. Our communities' practices have corresponding locutions. Their meanings, as Wittgenstein (1953) pointed out, follow their use. We speak of things that make a difference to us, a difference we can act on. I cannot know directly how you experience things, but I can recognize what you are doing. Your private experience is beyond my ken, but your actions show and tell.

A simple example. I watch you walk to the intersection, stop at the red light, wait, and cross when it turns green. Your stopping and going make sense to me. I usually do the same. We both live in a community where red and green lights on street corners have specific purposes. We take for granted the usual human condition that our eyes are sensitive to the light's color. People with color blindness are expected to know which color is where. Most of us learn red means stop and green means go—we fudge a bit on yellow. We take it that most folk beyond a certain age have sufficient competence to know how to walk and stand still, even when chewing gum. Thus even without direct access to your experience of red and green, since you appear to treat these distinctions as I do, I do not suspect your experience differs much from mine.

Another point. My sensitivity to red and green, the physiological responses of my retina's cone cells, are not of the same logical type as what red and green *mean* to me. The meaning of red and green, stop and go, is nowhere in the description of a photoreceptor protein response to absorbing photons. This holds for any explanation limited to physiology.

Don't roll your eyes at this profundity: this confusion of formal categories is frequently ignored or lost in textbook definitions of behavior. The Descriptive remedy is a full parametric analysis of behavior, a formulation that has a place for both physiological processes and the meaning of the behavior.

Here is something else to keep in mind. Implicit in intentional behavior is the distinction between a performance as a process or movement and the behavioral significance of that process or movement. A favorite example comes from Elizabeth Anscombe's (1957/1966) classic, *Intention*. To paraphrase and quote her: It is sometime in the dark 1930s, when we notice from a distance a "man's arm is going up and down, up and down." On further inspection, we see this movement, provided by "certain muscles, with Latin names which doctors know, are contracting and relaxing" and that he is "pumping water into a cistern which supplies the drinking water of a house." Anscombe then asks, "What is this man doing? What is *the* description of his action?" She points out that a multiplicity of descriptions fit, from his sweating to his muscular pumping. But Anscombe's target is his intention. She is interested in *the significance of all this pumping and sweating*: what he is doing with all this motion and sweat? She answers: The man is a hero attempting to save the town's Jews and prevent a world war. How? He has put a deadly poison into the cistern that supplies the water to the house that is "inhabited by party chiefs ... who are in control of a great state; they are engaged in exterminating the Jews and perhaps plan a world war."

Before I detail the Parametric Analysis of Intentional Action, bear with this stage-setting a bit longer. I want to address some confusions that attend "behavior."

WE NEED A COMMON LEXICON

Finding common ground for the practice of behavioral science requires a sufficiently shared lexicon of basic concepts to communicate within and across disciplines. Is there any doubt the behavioral sciences have a lexicon problem when something as basic as what we mean by "behavior" is such a mess? Let's look at some of what the Descriptive Psychologists, C.J. Peek and Raymond Bergner have done and written about this.

Anyone who has spent much time in a large institution that provides services to diverse communities; houses multiple professions; and necessarily interacts with political, legal, and funding bodies has had, I'll bet, the difficult task of getting the diverse interests on the same page. Consider navigating the paperwork and conversations across departments in any metropolitan hospital. With this problem in hand, C.J. Peek developed methods for creating common lexicons in complicated health care organizations that house different disciplines, missions, and stakeholders. Peek pointed out the wider problem that:

> it takes a generally understood system of concepts and distinctions to do good science. Here is one example of lexicon development from nineteenth century science: At the time of the first International Electrical Congress in Paris in 1881, complete confusion had reigned in this field; each country had its own units. Multiple different units were in use across researchers and countries for electromotive force, electric current, and resistance. At this first Congress, agreements were reached on the ohm and the volt—with ampere, coulomb, and farad also defined, all done as one conceptual system. Governments saw that it had become necessary for commercial transactions to create an international system of definitions and to provide a forum of scientists, manufacturers, and learned societies to establish terminology for the whole field of scientific and technical concepts (*du Couëdic, 1981*).
>
> Without this system of electrical concepts becoming community property with standing across all electrical researchers, the field could not have developed into the mature form of empirical science that we now witness. (*Peek, 2013*)

My colleague Raymond Bergner's essay, *What is behavior? And so, what?* (Bergner, 2010), underscores this mess in psychology and the behavioral sciences. He begins by quoting the *New York Times* science writer, Natalie Angier, "Certain things should never be taken for granted, among them the precise meaning of words that are at the heart of your discipline" (Angier, 2009). Paraphrasing Bergner: psychology, although describing itself as the science of behavior, has not arrived at any consensus about the meaning of behavior, a concept "at the heart of its discipline." In reviewing 26 psychology dictionaries and glossaries, he found only 7 provided a definition of behavior. When they did, "the most prevalent formulation is typified by the following: behavior is 'observable overt movement of the organism generally taken to include verbal behavior as well as physical movements.' According to this definition, behavior is essentially observable physical activity: a pigeon pecks a disk, a woman says hello, a student raises his hand, and so forth."

The closest consensus Bergner found was that behavior is either some verbal utterance, or some other observable time-one, time-two movement. Absent is anything about motivation, meaning, competence, or significance. The only consensus is that behavior involves change, and that change is some sort of performance over time. Obviously, the behaviors that most interest us are more than *just* that. From holding hands while waiting for the red light to turn green, to pumping poison to kill Nazis, distinctions beyond mere movement are required if the meaningful behavior of persons is within behavioral science's scope. Knowing how a clock works is not the same as understanding the behavior of the person who built it, or the point of knowing the time of day.

AT LAST! THE PARAMETRIC ANALYSIS

Some preempirical conceptualizations are simple, some are not. Keep in mind that while parsimony is desirable, things are what they are and not something else. And, don't count on things to be simpler than they are. In our analysis, we need to maintain the meaning and complexity of intentional behavior. Since a plane *is defined* as two-dimensional, we can plot all planes, all flat surfaces, on two dimensions without worrying if more will be needed. Behavior is not so limited, simple, or of such a low-dimension. Further, there is no formal reason the list of parameters I present is complete or can't be refined. Behavior is complex and nuanced.

In Chapter 2, we looked at Paradigm Case Formulations as a method to systematically negotiate consensus and disagreement about what constitutes the essential nature of a subject matter. Another distinctive Descriptive tool, **Parametric Analysis**, is a method designed to identify how any example within a common paradigm is the same or different from any other. This method has similarities and overlaps with Paradigm Case Formulations but is a better fit for certain problems.

A Paradigm Case Formulation (PCF) is a useful method when the unity of a complex case needs to be maintained to preserve a subject's conceptual integrity. A Parametric Analysis (PA) is a systematic way to unpack a subject matter's range of logical possibilities and to show how any example can be the same or different from all the other examples (Ossorio, 2006b).

Let's look at the parts of a PA, starting with what we mean by "parameter." A parameter identifies a necessary and independent dimension of the subject matter. Consider plane geometry. Back in middle school, most of us learned everything in Flatland falls on the X and Y axes. These parameters provide for and limit every two-dimensional surface. Every figure in plane geometry is the same or different, depending on its location on the orthogonal parameters of the X and the Y axes.

Similarly, when we consider color as a subject matter, we can see all colors are the same or different depending on the parameters of hue, saturation, and brightness—the HSB color wheel. Color differences are subtler than what defines the logical space of a plane. Some color systems add additional or different distinctions as nuance, complexity, and use dictate. We have a red, green, and blue model (RGB) for computer screens, a cyan, yellow, magenta, and black (CYMK) for printers, and the LAB format, of luminance and A and B (the chromatic components), designed to be serviceable across devices.

Behavior is more varied than plane geometry or color wheels because it has more necessary, independent dimensions. Not only do we need to decide on those dimensions, those parametric distinctions, we need to figure out how to fill them in because their content varies in its essential form. Ossorio put it this way:

> Because a parametric analysis as such is a purely formal conceptual device, there is no general restriction on, or prescription for, the kind of values that a parameter can have. For example, some parameters have numbers as their values (in some color schemes, Brightness, Hue, and Saturation have numerical values). Some have letters as their values; others have facts; some have concepts; and so on. The only restriction is that all the values of a given parameter are of the same kind. (If it appeared that we had more than one kind of value for a given parameter, we would conclude that we were really dealing with more than one parameter or else that we needed to make the choice of which set of values we wanted.) Different parameters in the same parametric analysis may have different kinds of values.
>
> For example, a sow's ear is unlikely to change into a silk purse, but since they are both material objects, it could happen. (In this case, we would say that the material object had changed from having the characteristics of a sow's ear to having the characteristics of a silk purse.) In contrast, a mechanism could not become a motive, nor could an internalized parent become a conscience or become the ability to do arithmetic (neither could a history of reinforcement become either one), and a flowerpot could not become the number seventeen. The general principle is that if X is in one logical category, it cannot change into something of a different logical category. The flowerpot example brings this out most clearly. You can't get there from there. *(Ossorio, 2006a, b)*

THE FORMULATION OF INTENTIONAL ACTION

An adequate Intentional Action (IA) conceptualization needs to work across the behavioral sciences. It should be useful not only to show how one behavior is similar or different from any other. For example, it should provide a format to compare and coordinate different theories. Further, it needs to be expandable and revisable. The current version works, but even well-formed formulas can be refined. Although I see no formal way to improve $1 + 1 = 2$, I'll not make the same claim for the intentional action formula:

Intentional Action = <Identity, Want, Knowledge, Know How, Performance, Achievement, Significance, Personal Characteristic>

If the formulation is adequate, it can keep the promise to fit all intentional behaviors; and it can establish common ground for behavioral science to negotiate and connect its isolated, siloed theories and practices. After applying the IA formulation, some conflicting or competing theories may be less in disagreement than focused on different parameters. Similarly, what counts in practice as methodologically or clinically relevant may involve some parameters but not others. For example, stimulus response and operant conditioning descriptions can be completed without reference to the Significance parameter. Stimulus response interventions focus on coupling a stimulus with a targeted recognition (Knowledge) to alter a response frequency (Achievement), while the operant conditioner tries to manipulate the Performance by attempting to control the Achievement. In contrast, psychoanalytic transference and resistance interpretation's key parameters would be the Wants, Knowledge, and Significances of an action. Cognitive behavior therapy emphasizes the Knowledge and the Know How parameters.

The IA formulation should provide common ground and span all of behavioral science, but if found inadequate or incomplete, it can be refined, expanded, or modified. This flexibility is required for an open-to-possibility, theory-neutral subject domain.

To summarize: since actions occur simultaneously and sequentially in real time, and a person can be cognizant of this, the IA formulation must be amenable to recursive and reflexive representations. It must allow linkage to other actions performed individually and socially that are being done sequentially and in parallel. And it must have a place—the knowledge parameter—within itself, to represent itself.

An intentional action requires something wanted and an opportunity to try to get it. The actor might rely on competence and not reflect on any of this. Also, finding an opportunity to do something wanted is independent of the accuracy or clarity of what an actor takes to be the case. What a person knows can be ill-formed, inaccurate, or delusional; but except in pathological cases, this is the exception rather than the rule. And, this is separate from what people might be willing to acknowledge to themselves and others. People can be intentionally deceptive and intentionally self-deceptive.

THE PARAMETRIC ANALYSIS OF INTENTIONAL ACTION

What distinct parameters, what conceptually separate factors, can apply to describe what a person is doing? I am asking "can apply" rather than "must apply." At times, we might only be interested in describing how a behavior is performed, or what was achieved, or the behavior's significance, and so on. From the necessary parameters, we can choose the ones most useful for the task at hand.

A reminder. The parameters are preempirical. They refer to distinctions that locate the empirical data but are not a discovery in nature. Akin to the X and Y axes of plane geometry or the geographer's longitude and latitude, these distinctions are conceptual inventions that guide and organize discovery. They tell us what to look for and tell us what kind of observation would qualify as a valid observation under each parameter. Here's the formula and its application to a ball player whose identity is disguised to protect mostly me. We observe his high, inside fastball close to the face of a batter he had previously hit with a wild pitch.

Behavior = Intentional Action = <I, W, K, KH, P, A, S, PC>

The *Identity* of the actor. An index or name, such as "Bob Jones" or "Moon Unit."

W. What the actor *Wants* to accomplish in the circumstance. The circumstances the behavior is designed to *Achieve*. (Wants to throw a strike, high, and inside. Wants to scare the batter)

K. What the actor *Knows*, distinguishes, or recognizes in the circumstance that is relevant to what the actor Wants. (In Deliberate Action the actor recognizes different options, in Cognizant Action the actor is aware of the ongoing behavior) (Knows the strike zone. Knows the batter is afraid of getting his face hit.)

KH. What the actor *Knows How* to do given what is wanted and distinguished. (Knows How to throw accurate fast balls)

P. The implementation or *Performance* of the action in real time. (The windup and the pitch)

A. The *Achievement* or outcome of the behavior. The difference of whatever sort or magnitude it makes in the world. (Strike three. An angry destabilized batter)

S. The *Significance* of the action for the actor. What the actor is doing by doing the act in question. (Ends the inning, wins the game. Satisfies without acknowledging his sadistic longings for revenge)

PC. The *Personal Characteristics* expressed by the action. (Professionally focused; self-deceptively hostile)

Let's look more closely at the parameters and at some examples to see how we can use these distinctions. In later chapters, I will show how emotional behavior fits this scheme, its use in understanding pathology and implementing behavior change; in understanding and restoring empathy, and other clinically relevant issues.

The IA parameters should provide coordinates that map all behavior, not just those in my examples. Check their adequacy by asking if they address the subtleties that interest you. If they do not, what refinements and additions do you need? They should already be in the IA parameters, but do your worst. If you're stumped, ask me. You might have found a reason for an additional parameter.

When considering the content of the parameters, hold in mind the preempirical/empirical distinction. The parameters are preempirical concepts. For example, the Wants parameter simply indicates that intentional action is motivated, not what those motivations are. Filling in those details (i.e., identifying what someone wants), requires observation and thought. The observations should be thought out and presented as an empirical assertion, stated as fact. As such, further observations or considerations might make the statement false, unclear, or mistaken. As deliberate actors, we are free to revise.

I frequently use the IA Formulation when I am trying to figure out what a person is up to or what they understand about a third party not present. Questions relevant to each of the parameters help me focus when my understanding needs to be tested or made explicit. This is especially the case when the question, "what's wrong with this picture?" draws a blank. What someone cannot say points to a place to look closer.

IDENTITY (I)

Every action is someone's action. That someone has a name or title or some other individual marker. Ordinarily, this only needs a name indicating whose behavior it is. Jack or Moon Unit. The identity parameter specifies that. In its simple form, the identity parameter underscores the fact that one of the ways a behavior can be the same or different from any other is whose behavior it is.

The identity parameter simply indicates a name for the individual acting and does not carry the implications of a further status assignment. Status refers to a person's place in some community, ranging from a specific, limited domain (such as a chess club), through their entire world or culture, to their place "in the scheme of things." Descriptive Psychology's concept of status is not limited to social hierarchy. Rather, it resembles the ecological idea of a niche, plus the idea of the world that includes all niches.

Still, keep in mind that identifications in the broader sense are used as a status assignment. Names or titles used out loud or silently frame how people appraise each other. Labeling, addressing, or responding to someone by their nickname has different implications than Sharon, Ms. Smith, Professor, Doctor, Miss, boy, or "hey you." Whether an encounter is deemed appropriate, degrading, affirming, empathic, etc., can correspond to the means of address. The identity parameter, per se, is not a means of address nor, as will be clarified later, an appraisal that carries motivational significance, but the IA of addressing someone by a name is.

WANTS (W)

The most general answer to the question of why someone does something is answered by something the person has a reason to bring about. Wants, desires, and purposes are ordinary terms of intention that contrast to something random, arbitrary, out of reflex, and the like. Want is the motivational parameter. What a person wants depends on their current circumstances, reflecting the weights a person gives their reasons then. Actions require motives, and something distinguished in the current circumstance that provides opportunity to act on the motivation. The Wants parameter expresses the state of affairs you have a reason to achieve when there is opportunity.

Wants are to be distinguished from values. Values are part of the Personal Characteristics parameter. To be observed, personal characteristics must be expressed, to be exhibited in action; thus we watch a person try to achieve something to determine the rank they give what they want. Values correspond to the observable rank of wants, the person's "motivational hierarchy." Within the Wants parameter, singular or multiple motives can be described. In the case of Cognizant and Deliberate Actions, the Wants parameter has as one of its values the specific IAs that also appear in the Know parameter. This lets us formulate a self-representation of the ongoing action and how I regard it compared to other ways of going about. Sometimes, I know what I am doing. Sometimes, I know I want to perform a particular intentional action among other possibilities; and I know I am doing just that.

SOME THOUGHTS ON EMPIRICALLY IDENTIFYING OR INTERPRETING WANTS AND MOTIVATIONS

Accurately identifying motives can be tricky. The paradigm case of human behavior is a deliberate individual who is able to choose what they want, but people can act on reasons they do not consciously or accurately recognize. Reasons can be simple, clear, easy to say; or they can be complicated, conflicted, murky, ambiguous, unspeakable (because they cause offense). This latter is unsurprising if a person expects to be misunderstood or blamed. Even when clearly known, people can resist spelling out their reasons. As deliberate actors we can avoid, deny, divert, misdirect, and lie.

For that matter, telling someone the reasons *we think* they act is frequently met with, "… but it's more than that," since usually it is. And some take offense when told, accurately or not, what they are feeling. When pegged and labeled, humans can be a touchy lot.

Consider Sharon. When she flips her hair, bats her eyes, and blushes while speaking to John, we might take it that the flipping, batting, and blushing are a show of romantic interest—she's acting out the relationship *possible-girlfriend*. Sharon can't help the blushing. It's an unintended aspect of her Performance, but still a feature of it. But the batting and flipping?

Regardless of what Sharon knows, and depending on what she is trying to accomplish (what she wants), these gestures and responses have a Significance that would correspond to different intentional actions—different behaviors. If we ask Sharon if she is flirting, what should we make of her response if she laughs and says, "no"? What was *she doing by doing that* with John (the Significance parameter)? If we think she exaggerates her gestures, we might wonder if she is mocking John. The significance of her action could be "flirtatiously mocking."

In Chapter 2 I described four family-resemblance classes of values, i.e., hedonic, prudent, aesthetic, and moral/ethical. They intrinsically provide reason enough to do something, i.e., when a person in good faith justifies their reasons for doing something on these values, they have provided "reason enough." An intrinsic value is one that requires no further justification.

These classes of reasons for acting can conflict, operate in a complementary or independent fashion, and so on. If you have two or more of these reasons to do something, you have more reason to do it than if you only had one of them. How many are in play with Sharon? And what sort of dynamic results? Judgments about reasons can be tricky, but over time, we may come to believe we know Sharon's "true colors" and decide what we observe is something in-character or not: "Yes, under those circumstances, that is something Sharon would do." But if not: "No, Sharon wouldn't do that under those circumstances. Something is missing. We need more observations."

Here are a set of Ossorian maxims relevant for logically sound descriptions of Wants:

> **A person values some states of affairs over others and acts accordingly.**
> **If a person wants to do something, they have a reason to do it.**
> **If a person recognizes an opportunity to do something they want to do, they have a reason to do it.**
> **If a person wants to do something, they have a reason to create or look for an opportunity to do it.**
> **If a person has a reason to do something, they will do it unless they have a stronger reason not to.**
> **If a person has two reasons for doing X, they have a stronger reason for doing X than if they had only one of those reasons.**
> **If a person wants to engage in any given behavior, they would thereby also want to engage in other behaviors to the extent that they are relevantly like the behavior in question.**
> **If the situation calls for a person to enact a behavior for which they lack the requisite motivational priorities, they will enact some other behavior for which they have the requisite motivational priorities.**

KNOWS (K)

Know is the cognitive aspect of an intentional action. To know something is to be able to distinguish it, to tell X from not X. (Note that X/not X is a spectrum of difference, not a binary difference.) Knowing something is demonstrated by being able to act on that X/not-X distinction. The Know parameter is where we specify the concepts being acted on in the given behavior.

The Know parameter contains the range of concepts, facts, and distinctions a person can use in their ongoing situation; the differences that make a difference, then. Knowledge, part of the Personal Characteristics parameter, is the full set of distinctions a person can act on, *all* the things they Know.

When we ask the basic question of motivation (why a person does something), we also ask why they are doing it *now*. The answer is always some version of their recognizing, correctly or not, that the current circumstances provide an opportunity to achieve something they want.

Intentional action requires both wanting something and knowing there is something in the current circumstances that might provide what is wanted. Because not everything known is wanted, the relation between Know and Want is asymmetrical. Know has priority over Want. We don't want everything we recognize. What a person wants and recognizes is weighed against other states of affairs that are also recognized in a current circumstance. We will illustrate this with the Judgment Diagrams in Chapter 4.

People tend to notice what they value, including what they want to avoid. Individuals are continually scanning their environment for items of motivational significance. People can also act on distinctions without knowing they are making those distinctions: competence allows some kinds of knowledge to be employed unconsciously.

Knowledge is judged on how effectively the known distinctions can be used. A person might be ready to act on an incorrect distinction; or be ready to act incorrectly on a distinction; or both. These mistakes will have consequences, especially if they take it they are competent or eligible in ways they are not. This is the unfortunate Dunning-Kruger effect (1999).

The Know parameter can include the distinctions "my own actions" and "my potential choices"; thus the Know parameter is the place for the reflexive representation of an IA. This is represented in the K parameter by single or multiple IAs, depending on whether the action was simply cognizant (CA) or also deliberate (DA).

As with Wants, finding out what a person Knows has its problems. Like Values, Knowledge has a learning history. What people know is influenced by their communities, their culture, and their idiosyncratic life course. Even when community membership involves an expectation of knowing the community's choice principles, we should be careful what we presume. An individual might have an exceptional capacity—either beyond or short of—the expected. People make use of learning opportunities in ways that reflect what was available. The observer's knowledge of the other's knowledge should take this into account.

Maxim: **If a situation ordinarily calls for a person to do something, if they lack the relevant knowledge (or values or competence), they will do something else instead**. A person can only act on the values, concepts, and skills they have available.

Here are some other relevant Descriptive maxims:

A person acquires knowledge of the world by observation and thought.
For a given person, the real world is the one they find out about by observation.
A person takes it that things are as they seem unless they have reason enough to think otherwise.
If a person knows something, they continue to know it until and unless they forget it or change their mind.
If the situation calls for a person to enact a behavior for which they lack the requisite knowledge, they will enact some other behavior for which they have the requisite knowledge.
People know about themselves.
People know about their relation to the world and their place in it.
A person always acts under conditions of uncertainty.
A person always has enough information to act on.

KNOW HOW (KH)

Know How is the competence aspect of behavior. An action is an expression of know how, competence, or a skill if it is something a person can expect to perform non accidently. Competence is acquired through having a prior capacity and the appropriate practice and experience. At whatever degree of competence, knowing how to do something is different from simply knowing something. The umpire knows a ball from a strike. The pitcher knows this, too, but knows how to strike out enough batters to keep his job. We don't expect to find the umpire on the mound; he doesn't know how to throw like a pitcher.

Having the relevant know how means a person can perform an action with the expected outcome that the action **Achieves** what is intended, whether driving a car, dancing with a friend, or throwing a fastball, high and inside.

Under ordinary circumstances, once we want to do something we know how to do and have an opportunity, we expect to achieve it. Once adequate competence has been achieved, only behavior gone wrong calls for an explanation; behavior going right requires none. Tommy, an able-bodied teenager, walking to the couch and sitting down requires no explanation, but his repeated stumbling does.

Specific collections of social, intellectual, and emotional competencies are part and parcel of the roles we take on, willingly or not. There are things a person is expected to want, know, and know how to do to engage in the practices of our communities. We may expect members of a community to have certain core values, knowledge, and competences—the things the community expects from *one of us*, acquired as we mature from infant to adult. This gets complicated by our idiosyncratic attributes, circumstances, and experiences.

SOME ISSUES ATTENDING KNOW HOW DEFICITS

Akin to what some call procedural memory, once competence is acquired, a person ordinarily takes their skill for granted and does not deliberate about each move necessary in the **Performance**. We tend to be self-conscious as we develop our know how, but not so much after that competence has been acquired. We also tend to be self-conscious when we believe, correctly or not, that we lack the competence to act as a situation demands.

Prior capacities are not established on a level playing field. Fairness is not something that comes with our embodiment but is imposed through social negotiation. Not everyone has the needed prior capacity, practice, and experience to develop the competences a community might require (or take for granted). Some people are more sensitive, talented, or lucky than others. When a specific KH is required but deficient, the outcome is often awkward or blundered—if performed at all. Faced with a self-recognized absence of requisite competence, people try to do something else instead; something they believe they know how to do. This holds for what people want, know, and find significant. As a rule of thumb, a person will try to maintain or improve their place in their world. The class clown, expecting academic failure, while garnering the teacher's ire, may still think it is in his best interest to boorishly entertain his bros—from his perspective.

Knowing how to do something valued can lead to the expectation of a satisfying outcome. In contrast, worry, anxiety, and panic can be evoked when a person believes they lack the relevant competence to handle a problematic or desired goal. The absence of self-recognized competence can turn what otherwise might be opportunity into threat, a manageable hazard into feared danger. The expected failure can elicit anxiety and shame. Inhibiting and crippling performance anxieties understandably follow a self-conscious expectation of incompetence, making it all the worse. Similarly, a person's competence is relevant to what they can tolerate (Schwartz, 2002). We tend to tolerate what we know how to handle.

Here are some relevant maxims:

If the situation calls for a person to do something they can't do, they will do something they can do.
A person acquires concepts and skills by practice and experience.
If a person has a given set of skills, they continue to have it until and unless it changes.

PERFORMANCE (P) AND ACHIEVEMENT (A)

The **Performance** is the procedural or process feature of an action. A performance is an episode of behavior that occurs at a specific time and place with duration in real time. It has a beginning, an end, and can be interrupted. The outcome of the performance is the **Achievement**.

We do not directly observe what a person wants, knows, and knows how to do. Those parameters are part of the conceptual requirements for there to be any action. In the absence of something wanted, known, or known how to do, there is no behavior. Instead, what we observe is someone's performance and achievement at a specific time and place. Performances achieve some difference in the world, whether trivial or profound. The difference can be as slight as typing this sentence. Or, as profound as getting my point across.

Performances are implementations of something that has **Significance**, our next parameter.

Here are some relevant maxims:

Behavior goes right, if it doesn't go wrong in one of the ways it can go wrong.
A process is a sequential change from one state of affairs to another.
A process is a state of affairs that has other, related processes as immediate constituents. (A process divides into related, smaller processes.)

SIGNIFICANCE (S)

Significance is the meaning of the behavior which may include the action's ulterior, hidden, and nondisclosed meanings. The Significance parameter provides a place to specify what a person is up by doing the act in question—it's point. In contrast, the **Want** parameter only specifies what is recognized as specifically wanted in the current circumstances. This will be directed toward a particular implementation. For example, Roger pitches a fast ball, high inside, and over the plate because he knows the strike zone, knows how to throw a fast ball, and wants to throw a strike, and, as it turns out, wants to disturb the batter by throwing as close to his face as possible while remaining in the strike zone. Why he wants to throw a strike this way is its **Significance** to him. What is Roger doing by doing that? "Brushing back the batter."

A behavior is sought or chosen for its significance and implemented through the specific practices and **Performances** engaged in. And, just as multiple motivations can be in play in any behavior, a behavior can have multiple significances. At times, people kill two birds with one stone.

If a person has two reasons for doing X, they have a stronger reason for doing X than if they had only one of those reasons.

Significance has a multilevel aspect, a ladder of significance that begins with a performance that implements something the actor holds significant and finally culminates in an intrinsic practice that requires no further justification. Consider this series of questions and responses: In the act of pitching a curve, Roger is attempting to get a strike. But doing that is doing other things as well. "Why are you throwing a curve ball?" "What? To strike out the batter." "Why do you want to strike out the batter?" "To end the inning so we can bat and score." "Why does that matter?" "What's the matter with you? That's how you win a game." "So, why do you want to win games?" Shaking his head, "Jeez, that's how the game's played." And the ladder ends with an intrinsic social practice: winning a baseball game. "Listen, dummy, do you have any idea how much I get paid to throw little white balls?" (A prudential reason.) "And how cool it is to be me, with the stuff I get to do?" (A hedonic and aesthetic justification.) But the questioner continues, "You know, Rog, you keep hitting that high inside corner, that brushback spot, close enough to make batters flinch. And you do it even after beaning that guy last week. What's with that?" And with that, Roger smirks, gives his interviewer the stink eye, shrugs, and walks away.

SIGNIFICANCE, IMPLEMENTATION OF SIGNIFICANCE (PERFORMANCE), AND SOME THOUGHTS ABOUT PSYCHOTHERAPY

Here's a story I tell psychotherapy trainees that illustrates significance and implementation. Near the start of my training analysis I realized my mostly silent analyst, seated behind me, wrote with a scratchy pencil. Evidently, not everything I said warranted noting; but trusting he wasn't doing crosswords, he did note some of what I said. "Operant conditioning," I commented. Just the sort of remark to irritate a classical psychoanalyst. I figured I could tell what held his attention. The sound of that scratch was all the reward I needed to produce more of the same. But more *of the same what*? No surprise, he soon switched to a silent pen.

The premise of operant conditioning or instrumental learning is that following a behavior with reward or punishment will increase or decrease the behavior's frequency. Operant conditioners focus on changing the **Performance** by manipulating the frequency of a valued **Achievement**. Thorndike and Skinner taught this. Using this sort of reinforcement, we can teach pigeons and dogs tricks. In animals with a limited behavior repertory, this sort of training tends to increase or decrease a specific performance. Rumor has it, it might work with infants and young children, but not that well. To be honest, operant procedures work with one of my dogs, but not with the other who seems more interested in training me.

Here's what interests me. When operant conditioning is applied to socially complex animals that exhibit few routinized or stereotypical behaviors, what often follows is not an exact reproduction of the conditioned behavior but variations on a theme, kindred behaviors with shared significance. I think this was first observed in porpoises, who, when rewarded for doing something they'd not previously done, eventually responded with novelty (Pryor et al., 1969).

What did I produce in response to my analyst's sounds? No dummy, I didn't simply reproduce my previous comments, nor did I try to figure out another way to say the same thing; instead I began to understand the concerns and meanings he thought were significant.

I'm a psychotherapist, not so interested in training cats and dogs. My job involves helping people with what they identify as problematic and unsatisfying. Accordingly, I spend time wondering about the effectiveness of their actions and the significance of what they are trying to accomplish. They pay me because they want something to change. Attending to significances and implementations serve this goal.

When a person describes or illustrates a problematic behavior, I might ask questions that target implementation, "How's doing it that way working for you?" Or, I might ask about the action's significance, "What difference does it really make? What's really at stake?" Asking about how something is working leads to questions about alternatives, more useful implementations. Asking how something matters brings up questions of what might matter more, or might conflict with other important aims and values, now or later. *Does insisting on doing it* really matter when you consider the other things that do?

Psychotherapy, as I see it, should enhance a person's potential for flexible, improvisational responses to challenging circumstances. My work involves helping people increase their ease in changing behavior patterns performed with inadequate knowledge or skill, or performed inappropriately, often without adequate appreciation of the action's significance. My intent is to invite reflection and discussion of alternatives and significances. The conversation itself can provide practice for doing something different and new.

Every intentional action, conscious or unconscious, involves a person trying to achieve something that carries significance. Asking people if it might be better to do something differently, wondering if the significance of what they are attempting best serves their overall interests are questions good to pose. Like with our dolphin and porpoise cousins, something new and better might follow.

There is always the matter of perspective. The significance and implications of an action are only sometimes shared and similarly appreciated.

What's good for the goose might be bad for the gander. What something means to me may be more idiosyncratic than common. What a person's behavior signifies to me may be different to what it means to them. I try to keep in mind, regardless of how compelling the evidence, that another party might not appreciate what I see as the significance of what they are doing. Not having a pipeline to the truth, I try to respect this uncertainty while keeping in mind the compelling evidence. What I have learned to do is to not insist my perspective is superior. (Whether, I think it is or not.) Insistence is often one of the problems, so my job is to model flexibility with my perspectives.In interpreting the significance of an action, especially problematic ones, all the dilemmas of attempting to get someone in touch with what they are reluctant to see come into play. Therapeutically, confrontation requires tact. I also believe that being seen and described in ways a person might be reluctant to acknowledge is akin to the vulnerability of intimacy. Tact requires empathy; it requires an empathic appreciation that a person can tolerate only so much. One's lovers, close friends, and therapists *only might* have permission to test the boundaries of self-understanding, and even if insight comes from one's beloved confidants, it can be intolerable. I'll return to these themes in Chapter 9.

SOME EXAMPLES AND DILEMMAS OF SIGNIFICANCE TO THE ACTOR AND THE OBSERVER

Let's return to Roger, the consummate pro who can consistently throw a fastball precisely at the high inside edge of the strike zone. He mixes this up with a nasty curve and an additional plague to batters: the occasional wild pitch. He's hit more than a few on the helmet. This fits what I've been told about his behavior outside the game. More than once, he's been seen teasing his wife and children in ways that have made his audience very uncomfortable. His teasing clearly upsets his kids, but Roger doesn't respond or even appear to recognize their unhappiness. With wife and children, he acts like he believes he is just a playful tease, and he gets away with it. Never would he describe his actions as mean-spirited taunts, even though they look that way and have that effect. I've come to think he's a cruel, sadistic guy who gets his kicks making people helplessly uncomfortable. This is consistent with his preferred first pitch to a batter he's previously hit. With a gleam in his eye, that pitch is fast and very close to the batter's face.

To me, Roger is an all-star celebrity athlete, who experiences satisfaction in his skilled performance, and in his place in public life. I also take it he is more than a bit of a sadist, deriving pleasure and satisfactions in putting people in helpless, vulnerable positions of fear and embarrassment.

I don't think Roger would agree with my interpretation and the case I'm building. Nor do I suspect anyone can successfully present him the evidence. Notice my use of "building a case" and "successfully presenting the evidence." Later, I will show how interpreting the significance of problematic behavior resembles a lawyer pleading a case, with all the attendant dilemmas of truth and persuasion.

Recall that a personal characteristic is acquired by having a prior capacity and a suitable intervening history. Roger didn't become a star athlete overnight. He started life with a set of capacities and potential sensitivities that he practiced and fine-tuned over decades of disciplined work facilitated by expert coaching. Like most professional athletes, his body had an extraordinary performance potential. I bet his vision, coordination, and muscle characteristics are different than most humans. His coached and practiced arm and eye accounts for his fast balls.

But what accounts for that gleam in Roger's eye? Here's a possibility. Roger had a loving but rigid, punishing, and moralistic father; a dad he admires and emulates. He points to this upbringing as the foundation of his discipline and success. But what if someone confronted him about his alleged sadism? Can he see himself in that light? I doubt it. Given Roger's success and acclaim, his pride in what he takes as his moral strengths, he looks at himself as a man of superior virtue. He is insistent about this. Owning cruelty doesn't fit the place he's given himself in the scheme of things.

He views himself as hypercompetitive but fair, only aiming to throw the pitches hardest to hit. The third time he hit a batter, he was fined for a near lethal beanball. He claimed he was just trying to strike the guy out, nothing more. He will not consider if making the batter wince is a pleasure too much to resist. Does he notice his wife and children's distress? Is he unaware his satisfactions signify more than simply a well-executed pitch, or an affectionate tease? Is he hurtful in ways he could better control? I doubt he is interested in wondering if the helplessness and punishments of his childhood inform his actions; or whether his sadistic motives bungle what could otherwise be strikes.

Given Roger's world and self-assigned status, he does not acknowledge or confront his alleged sadism. It simply has no place within his self-concept. Or more properly, sadism cannot be self-attributed, given his current perspective. I am not employing theory-laden concepts such as repression, isolation, reaction formation, splitting, or projection. I am merely saying he lacks the power or disposition to see himself the way some of his observers do. And it shows up in problematic social behavior and bungled actions. His observers, when not cheering as fans, may have ethical and prudential concerns. He doesn't. So far, no one has dared speak their truth to his power.

Some foreshadowing. I am building a case, familiar to those of a psychodynamic ilk, that a person can have noncognizant motivations. Or motives they are reluctant to consider. I am keeping in mind the many problems that attend interpreting motivations, especially problematic ones. Who is right or in position to effectively interpret and confront? Confront, because what warrants interpretation is something someone thinks should change.

PERSONAL CHARACTERISTICS (PC)

People's behaviors are an expression of their personal characteristics. People vary in their Powers and Dispositions, and their actions reflect this. The Descriptive concepts of Personal Characteristics was detailed in the last chapter. The PC parameter carries the reminder that the values of the W, K, and KH parameters require the knowledge, motivation, and skill the person possesses. If not, behaviors that require the presence of those powers and dispositions will not be in the person's current behavior potential.

A BRIEF SUMMARY AND SOME PRACTICAL QUESTIONS FOR STRUCTURED INTERVIEWS

Competent action in the world of people means having the concept of a person and knowing how people behave. Much of this is implicit. Hence one reason for this book. But what understanding is required to manage social life? This understanding, compatible with ordinary meanings of action and responsibility, is made explicit through systematically unpacking the Person Concept's formulation of behavior as Intentional Action.

To review, our parametric analysis of intentional action consists of (1) an Actor; (2) what the actor Wants to accomplish; (3) what the actor Knows or distinguishes in the circumstance relevant to what the actor Wants; (4) what the actor Knows How to do; (5) the real time Performance of the action; (6) the action's Achievement; (7) the Personal Characteristics expressed by the action; and (8) the action's Significance.

The IA analysis provides a checklist. Here's a corresponding set of questions, easily modified, for all sorts of structured interviewing. I frequently use them in psychotherapy and supervision. In my misunderstandings and failed empathy, they've helped me get back on the same page. As I will explain later, I am treating empathy as empathic action. When a person is empathic they accurately recognize (K) and know how (KH) to tolerably perform (P) their appreciation of the significance (S) of another person's ongoing circumstances and intentional actions (IA). This is toleration as I have discussed earlier. A tolerable presentation of our understanding of another requires an accurate Knowledge (K) of what the other person knows how (KH) to handle.

Here's my checklist.

1. Given their understanding of the overall circumstance, what does this person want and value? (And do we share an understanding of what the overall circumstance calls for?) (The W parameter)
2. What exactly do they recognize in their circumstance that is relevant to what they want and value? (And do we share a common appreciation of the situation?) (The K parameter)
3. What do they know how to do, given what they see as their current opportunity or dilemma? (And do they have the skill or competence that is needed to successfully manage the circumstance?) (The KH parameter)
4. What is the significance to them of how they behave in these circumstances? (The S parameter)
5. What personal characteristics are they employing and what is the significance of these characteristics to them? (The PC and S parameters)

SOME NOTATIONAL DEVICES: THE INTENTIONAL ACTION DIAMOND, AGENCY DESCRIPTIONS, AND SELF-REGULATION

I don't know if a picture is worth a thousand words, but students pay more attention to PowerPoints than my lecturing. Grasping a visualization of something already understood can be instantaneous. My problem is their initial understanding. I need a thousand words for that.

Ossorio used a Diamond to represent a unit of intentional action, something he called the Agency Description (Fig. 3.1). Let's start there.

The Agency Diamond is a shorthand way to represent single Intentional Actions (IA). When presented as a series, one following another, a social practice or a course of action is represented. (The IA formula is recursive.) Social practices are usually linked intentional actions, actions done in parallel or in some sequence; done alone, or with others. A social practice can be merely a single socially intelligible IA, or the more usual case where an action, *move one*, is played out alone or with others, and invites or requires *move two*, etc. A hop, skip, and jump played with just me and my shadow; bouncing a ball off a wall; inviting my pup to fetch; or playing catch with you.

In Fig. 3.2, when the small diamond is in the Knows position, on top of a larger agency diamond, the person is cognizant of the ongoing

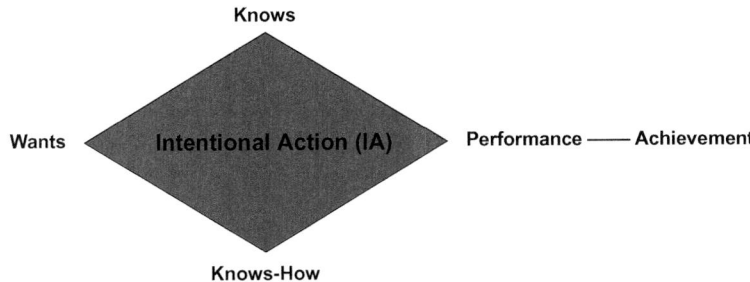

FIG. 3.1   The Agency Diamond.

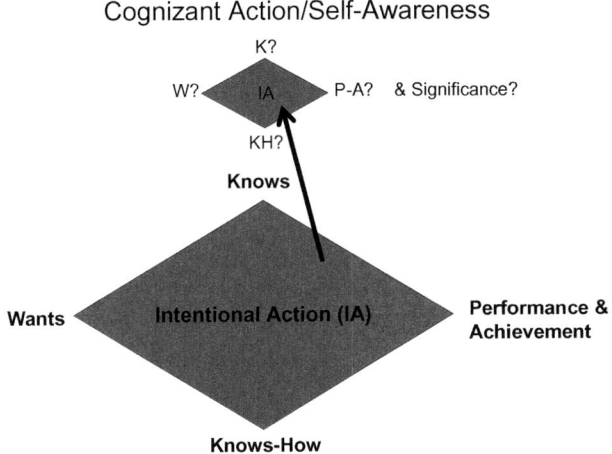

FIG. 3.2   Cognizant Action/self-awareness.

action. (Remember, the IA formula is reflexive.) People can reflect on their action as it occurs, not merely an actor but an actor-observer of their ongoing behavior. This potential for self-monitoring is also a feature of Deliberate Action. The question marks next to the parameters mean persons may be cognizant of their being in action, but they may be uncertain, inattentive, unaware, or mistaken, etc., about those aspects of what they are doing.

In Fig. 3.3, when the small diamonds are stacked one on top of another in the Wants position, and side by side in the Knows, it shows the available options for implementing a Deliberate Action. The small diamonds indicate available implementations of the intended Significance. Acting deliberately, the actor plays not only the role of observer, but also an observer-critic on their ongoing performance. This self-monitoring and

Behavior as intentional action

Intentional Action

IA = < I, **W**, **K**, KH, P, A, PC, S >

Deliberate Action

DA = < I, (**IA** | IA, IA, IA, ETC.), (**IA** | IA, IA, IA, ETC.),
P, A, PC, S >

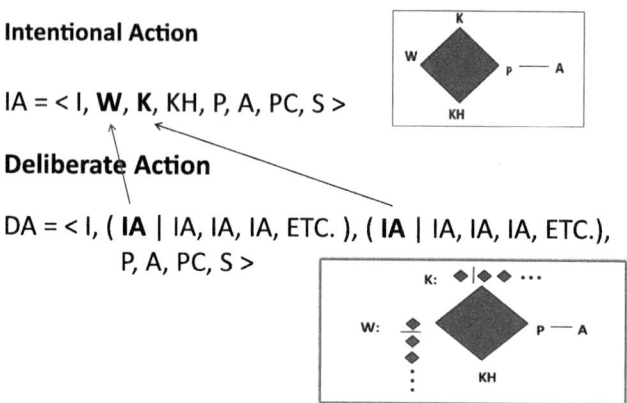

FIG. 3.3   Behavior as Intentional Action.

self-correcting can be personal or an ordinary feature of social observation, negotiation, and correction.

THE ACTOR-OBSERVER-CRITIC MODEL OF SELF-REGULATION AND THE DRAMATURGICAL PATTERN

What Truth is to the Observer and Describer, Authenticity is to the Actor. There is no appeal beyond that. In any given case there is no possible guarantee, in either procedure or principal or theory, that we have truth or authenticity. We are not missing anything here, either, and the absence of such guarantee has never kept us from legitimately distinguishing truth from falsity, authenticity from inauthenticity, and reality from unreality .... (*Peter Ossorio, The Behavior of Persons*).

Deliberate Action involves intentional self-regulation, a feedback loop involving cognizance and choice (Fig. 3.4). Although this feedback can be a process of deliberation, of thinking through possibilities, ordinarily it isn't. For the most part, we simply recognize what we take as our best option and act. Deliberation occurs if the result feels off course, when correction seems needed. Sometimes deliberation is more trouble than solution. Improvisational spontaneity can be bungled by second guessing. Deliberation can distract, inhibit, and confuse; can choke a flow of action better performed without overthinking. Ask any athlete or lover.

Persons as Deliberate Actors self-regulate or adjust their behavior to fit their changing circumstances in response to their appraisal of how effective they see themselves at achieving their goal (Fig. 3.5). In becoming a paradigmatic person, people learn the three fundamental jobs of Actor,

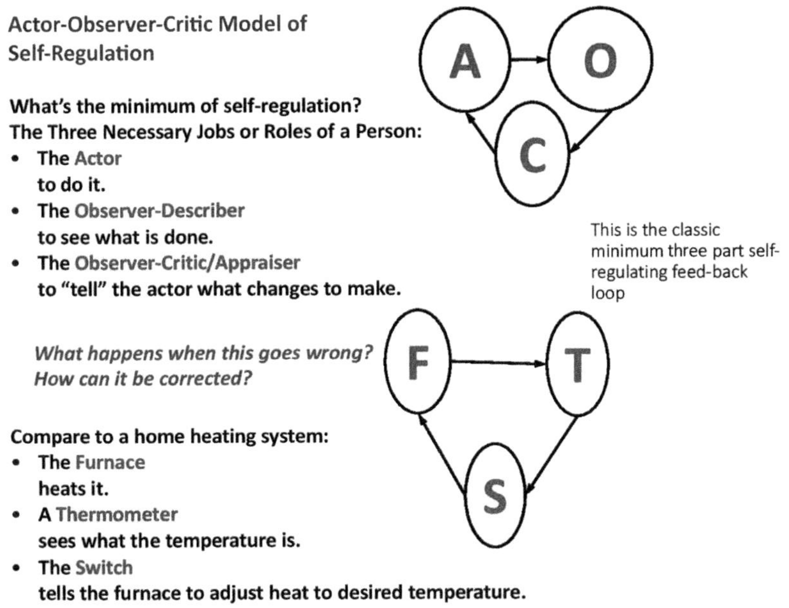

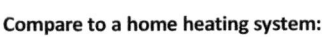

Actor-Observer-Critic Model of
Self-Regulation
What's the minimum of self-regulation?
The Three Necessary Jobs or Roles of a Person:
• The Actor
to do it.
• The Observer-Describer
to see what is done.
• The Observer-Critic/Appraiser
to "tell" the actor what changes to make.
A
O
C
This is the classic minimum three part self-regulating feed-back loop
What happens when this goes wrong?
How can it be corrected?
F
T
S
Compare to a home heating system:
• The Furnace
heats it.
• A Thermometer
sees what the temperature is.
• The Switch
tells the furnace to adjust heat to desired temperature.

FIG. 3.4 Actor–Observer–Critic model of self-regulation.

Self-Regulation as Deliberate Action
Actor
Observer
Action Performed
Intentional Action
Cognizant Action (knows the action preformed)
Critic
Recognized alternative ways of seeking goal
Deliberate Action (chooses or corrects the action considering possibilities)

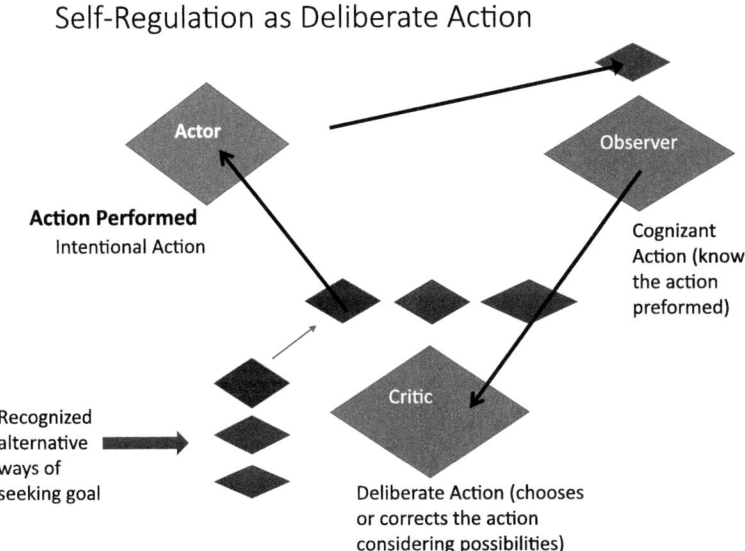

FIG. 3.5 Self-regulation as Deliberate Action.

Observer-Describer, and Critic (AOC). These jobs, roles if you prefer, are aspects of deliberate action and components of the classic negative feedback loop required for self-regulation or self-control. But unlike the automatic feedback of thermostats or homeostatic physiology, there is an actor choosing the change. (The classical way to teach the AOC feedback loop is to compare it to a thermostat, but that has the drawback of suggesting that steps—cycling steps—are necessary. They are not. AOC functions can be simultaneous. If I am acting as a Critic I am simultaneously observing and acting.)

When I introduce the AOC feedback loop to students who've paid attention in Psych 101, they often asked if this is like Freud's Id, Ego, and Superego or, if they are of a certain generation, if it is similar to the Parent, Adult, and Child of Berne's (1964) Transactional Analysis. It is not. Those are impulse-inhibition, conflict-resolution structures. The AOC is a cooperative and synergistic system that works only as well as a person is competent in a particular community. The jobs of acting as observer and critic are not in conflict; rather, they are aspects of what the person is doing when observation and corrective modification occur.

Let's look more closely at the job descriptions—the dramatic roles of Actor, Observer, and Critic—and then at self-regulation.

THE ACTOR AND THE DRAMA
(ALL THE WORLD'S A STAGE)

Within the constraints of their world, the Actor is the author of a life. They may have only so much say, but regardless, they act, finding and creating a world in the wake of their action. The role of the Actor is the spontaneous experience of being themselves, performed with guidance from what they hold personally significant. Informed by hedonic, prudent, aesthetic, and ethical values, desire is expressed as circumstance allows. The Actor's charge is creating and finding opportunity while navigating the dilemmas. This is the dramaturgical pattern.

With no need to reinvent the wheel, Descriptive Psychology uses the theatrical playbook's concepts and strategies for developing and unfolding character and action. The same can be said for the novelist. If need be, we refine their devices for our purposes. Let's return to the dramaturgical vision.

Let's be an audience with permission to go back stage, where the actors are already in character and about to engage in an improvisational tragedy. They have no intention of breaking the fourth wall, so if they notice us, we'd better be ready to engage. Everyone has a place on the stage of the World. The stage has props and actors with rules, policies, and boundaries. The players have statuses assigned by themselves and others as they go about their different roles. Some people are well cast for what they encounter, and some are not. At times people recognize the part they are playing; at times they don't. How cognizant and well-cast is always a matter of "more or less." The director wants the audience to observe this, whether or not it is made explicit. As I've mentioned, the Descriptive Psychologist, as observer and critic, will try to make all of this explicit.

Although there are reality constraints, how the play will unfold is uncertain. Actors improvise within and against the constraints with no "script," except the results that emerge from the interaction. What the Actor has is a set of Personal Characteristics, so the scene is set by *who they are* as they engage the other characters and the objects, processes, events, and relations formed and encountered. The Actors might be told what they should be doing, they might be on a mission and have their plans, but that does not determine what actually happens. The only certainty is that choices are made, and actions ensue: actions that follow from the opportunities and dilemmas that accompany each player's unfolding circumstance as they change themselves and alter the props. As an improvisation, the actors and actions will change as their responses incorporate each other's moves. We've entered a character-driven drama.

The actual "through-lines" are visible only after the play is significantly underway. The game must be afoot. Although the actor knows what is significant, the observer-critic must watch and see. The observer-critic is both an aspect of the actor and the role of the audience.

AUTHENTICITY AND THE ACTOR

A science of persons that keeps its promises must be suited to systematically address the actual nuances of life. Those nuances include creating science of any sort. Bergner (2013) concludes one of his essays on person-centered science quoting Santayana's observation that, "Human life is a peculiar reality in that every other reality, effective or presumptive, must in one way or another find a place within it." How in our world could it be otherwise?

One test of the value of Descriptive Psychology is whether it keeps its promises. As a person-centered science, Descriptive Psychology needs to capture the full scope of the humanities and provide objectivity, coherence, and full interconnection, while respecting their concerns. Similarly, the Person Concept and the IA formulation should provide a place to intelligibly connect any therapy for persons whether Client-Centered, Dialectical or Cognitive Behavioral, Psychodynamic, you name it, provided it works. With this in mind, I think Ossorio's invocation of "the dramaturgical pattern" offers a good way to examine a host of hard to clarify, vital "humanistic" concerns. Consider authenticity.

Ossorio (2006a, b) described authenticity as the ease that comes with being well-cast for the parts one plays. This shows, and is felt, in a flow of action that allows impulse and desire expression, without overconcern about mirroring the expectations of others. This nicely fits Sartre's (1943/1966) existential vision of authenticity contrasted to *mauvaise foi* (bad faith), and the fuzzy psychoanalytic concept of "true self" that Donald Winnicott (1965) offered as an ideal. Sartre and Winnicott celebrated creative choice and spontaneity. Unlike the Freudians, the existentialists never entered the trap of determinism. Winnicott sidestepped the Freudian deterministic stance by beginning with an infant, a mother, a spontaneous gesture, and her response. Accepting creativity and responsibility from the get-go, they began top down with paradigmatic persons. The Person Concept ought to offer them common ground.

Not that you need reminding, but later I'll point out to not misconstrue authenticity with Polonius's advice, "This above all: to thine own self be true, …, Thou canst not then be false to any man." Clearly, there are considerations that prudently trump simply following whim. Winnicott also adds that the "false self" protects the "true self." This protection is better systematized in the self-regulating roles of the Observer and Critic.

I'll return to these themes in the Afterword with Anthony Putman's take about authenticity and satisfaction. Putman (2013) shows how intrinsic values and the experience of satisfaction are intrinsically linked. He takes it an interesting step further, suggesting successful participation in communities that honors those values provides what he calls "ultimate satisfaction." I'll take some issue with how he formulated this idea, but the subject matter he engages is a contribution to "Positive Psychology."

THE OBSERVER-DESCRIBER

The paradigmatic observer-describer is engaging in **Cognizant Action**. My role as Observer provides information as I perform my Actor and Critic functions. In my role as observer what I **Know** is informed by my **Knowledge**, which includes my expectations about myself and my circumstances. Naturally, this includes what I observe about the other actors on the stage. What I observe about you and what you observe about me provides the potential for social feedback and negotiation. The Observer-Describer's observational capacities, sensitivities, and psychological state matters. Observation, differentiation, and description can be misinformed or clouded by ignorance.

THE CRITIC

As the Observer, I describe what is happening. As the Critic, I evaluate how things are going. If good enough, I continue—unless I find something better to do—or decide to do differently whatever I am doing. As critic, I appraise actions and options. The critic is a diagnostician whose job is to evaluate what to continue and how, including the engagement with others. Critic function will guide how appropriate and flexible the improvisations of actions and social practices go. Since so much of life is improvised on the spot, rigid and insistent critics usually make difficult people, persons unable or unwilling to go with the flow.

Where the core job of the observer is to describe, the role of the critic is to appraise. Appraising is different from merely describing. *Appraisals carry motivational significance* (Ossorio, 1986/1990). For example, if I see "a hungry brown bear through a telescope," that does not affect me; it's just a description. But if I see "a hungry brown bear eyeing me," it has motivational significance; it's an appraisal, and all sorts of immediate actions come to mind.

Appraisals guide action and are the defining motivational (W parameter) and cognitive component (K parameter) of intention actions, including nondeliberative emotional and impulsive ones. The Relationship Formula in Chapter 5 illustrates how the pragmatic accuracy of an appraisal determines whether the corresponding behavior is effective and realistic, ineffective, or even irrational. (And I'll take issue with the problematic but typical dichotomy of emotional versus rational. Nothing is inherently irrational about my fear of hungry brown bears.)

Critics judge behavior in light of their values. As judges, critics can be inconsistent, tolerant, generous, prone to "hang 'em high," ill-informed, and so on. The critic role is both personal and social. As a personal critic of my own actions I have first-hand knowledge of my values. As a critic among critics, the degree to which each of us understands and shares the other's values is of consequence in *negotiated* social coordination and regulation. I am distinguishing negotiation from coercion, a matter relevant to the discussion of **Negotiation, Degradation,** and **Accreditation** in Chapter 7.

Here are some relevant maxims:

A person values some states of affairs over others and acts accordingly.
a. **If a person's relationship to something is such that they are in a bad situation, or circumstance, they have a reason to try to improve it.**
b. **If a person's relationship to something is such that they are in a good situation, or circumstance, they have a reason to act to maintain it.**

c. If a person is in a good situation and has an opportunity to improve it, they have a reason to try to do so.

d. If a person is in any situation and it may be expected to become worse, they have a reason to act to prevent that.

A person will not choose less behavior potential over more.

If a person values a specific something, e.g., an object, a circumstance, a behavior, or more generally, a state of affairs, they will thereby also value other specific things of the same kind to the extent that they are relevantly similar to the original.

a. If a person values a general something, they will thereby also value a specific something to the extent that it is a paradigmatic instance or realization of the more general value.

If a person values something general, they will be sensitive to (will tend to evaluate) the relevance of their circumstances to that something and act accordingly.

a. Negative emotional behavior (fear, guilt, anger, shame, etc.) is an attempt to improve a bad situation.

b. Positive emotional behavior (joy, triumph, glee, etc.) is an attempt to preserve, enhance, or celebrate a good situation.

APPRAISALS, FINAL-ORDER APPRAISALS (FOAs), AND ALTERED STATES OF CONSCIOUSNESS

Deep in dark shadowy woods, sensing movement, and fearing hungry brown bears, I drop, play dead, and hope for the best. Wet and covered with muddy leaves, I ask myself if a bear is *really* there. Ordinarily, my implicit, taken-for-granted sense of who I am and what is real lets me judge without second thought. I take things as real, true, or in-character. I don't *think it over*, I just take it to be the case. But fearing bears, I am not in my ordinary state. I prudently act on the impulse to protect my hide. Safe but uneaten, I begin to wonder what's real. Eventually, I get up, glad to make my way to Grandma's. There is nothing irrational in any of this; there's bears in these woods, I think, while knocking on my grandmother's door, "… Grandma, what big eyes you have."

Let's look at how we ordinarily appraise what's real and what we take as fact. Let's also ask if circumstances and psychological states are relevant. And let's begin with an assertion: that what we take to be real or factual involves judging how the answer fits one's self-concept and real world. This context is the available sense of personal, real-world history with its structure of logic, facts, sequences, and duration. Remember, the *real world* is an historically, empirically known place populated by persons and other objects with their particular character. Something is or might be real or true because it actually happened or could happen at a particular time and place. Then ask, what might happen if this structure is violated, disrupted, or unavailable—a place of time and sequence and people and props.

In graduate school in 1970s Boulder, looking for conceptual confusions to Descriptively sort out, mysteries to ponder, and something cool for experimentation, William Plotkin and I tried to make sense of altered states of consciousness. Since we had professors who taught hypnosis, it all seemed to fit. Who isn't intrigued by the mysterious ways of the hypnotist and the hypnotized? Hypnosis highlights questions about "reality-testing," about the real, the unusual, and the anomalous. Bill and I brought this puzzle to Ossorio, wondering, what gives something it's ordinary real-world status. In contrast, what's involved when something appears unreal or untrue? And what about when fantasy or illusion is treated as a matter of fact, appraised as something to act on?

Here's what we decided. Let's call our ordinary appraisals **First-Order**. That's our first say and often the only one needed. We take it things are as they seem, unless we have reason to think otherwise. But what happens when we notice something that does not fit our sense of ourselves or reality? What if we encounter that same stuff and don't consider it weird? We don't wonder how it fits. Bill and I called the appraisals required for "reality testing," how things fit in the world, **Final-Order Appraisals** (FOAs). Our conceptualization suggested limits or disruptions in a person's power or disposition to make FOAs result in the altered states associated with trance, dissociation, delusion, typical dreaming, and certain hypnotic phenomena (Plotkin and Schwartz, 1982, 1985). (These states are also associated with a problematic sense of time and duration. I'll get to that, later.)

Let's consider three hungry brown bears. Noon time, the first bear is chasing me in the forest. Terrified, I consider playing dead, climbing a tree, or running as fast as I can. Not knowing better, I run. Bad choice. This book doesn't get written. Same beginning with the second bear, except this time after a moment of terror, remembering to fly, I lift my arms and float away. Another bad choice because I don't get high enough, fast enough. Fortunately, I wake up. The third bear's a kid's game. You pretend to be Smokey, hungry with nothing to eat but me, and get so absorbed in playing that I end up having to tell your mother how I got theses bites.

In the first case, I realistically appraise my dilemma, but my implementation was lacking. In the second, dreaming without ordinary reality constraints, I employ my well-honed aerial skills, thinking they'd work. They didn't. In the third case, you get carried away in imaginative involvement, but there are real consequences. In the first case, the real-world context was available. The episode ends well for the bear, for me, not so much. In the second, I was temporarily unable or uninterested in making FOAs, hence not inhibited by the actual pragmatics of flight. Dreaming offers me that freedom. In the third, not disposed to make ordinary FOAs, you suspend judgment of what for you is in-character. However, since I know you long and well, I can't help to wonder if your "absorbed" acting was simply or also your excuse to bite. Hard to tell, since that's your story and you're sticking to it.

As an implicit feature of ordinary judgment, FOAs hold our sense of ourselves and the world together. This takes for granted the ordinary is our usual state of consciousness, the way we usually go through the world. When there are FOAs available, anomalies, hallucinations, and fantasy are seen as such. When FOAs are absent, the relevance of FOAs becomes apparent: anomalies, hallucinations, and fantasy are treated as a matter of fact. Observations that could be reality checked aren't—the context of self and world is not available to feel the mis-fit. Urges, impulses, and desires, self-appraised as inappropriate for me in my world, might not be managed as they otherwise would.

The absence of the power or disposition to make FOAs can create a diminished capacity to engage in appropriate Deliberate Action. Bungled, negligent, out-of-character, and psychotic behavior can result. Of course, there is a brighter side to suspending reality checks. Pleasurable dreaming and fantasy, meditation, time spellbound and entranced by the arts, are enhanced by temporary suspension of FOAs. But then, alas, it's time to get real.

HYPNOSIS AS A TEST CASE

Bill and I were especially interested in hypnosis as a target for conceptualization and experimentation given the confusions and apparent mysteries that surrounded it. We wanted to clarify the arguments whether hypnotic behavior was a result of a special state of consciousness (Gill and Brenman, 1961; Shor, 1959; Orne, 1959; Hilgard, 1973) or something more akin to the role involvement of the method actor (Barber, 1969; Sarbin and Coe, 1972). We suspected it could be either or both. Earlier in this chapter you'll remember I bemoaned the confused meanings of behavior and the distinction between a behavioral performance and significance. No surprise, the hypnosis literature often conflated psychological states with their behavioral performance (Plotkin and Schwartz, 1982, 1985). Looking at the performances associated with hypnosis: the apparent surrender of intention to suggestion, the convincing dreams, beliefs, and bizarre actions, we saw no convincing reason it had to be one or the other. But are there ways to distinguish role playing from an altered state of consciousness? After an effective hypnotic induction is the hypnotized subject an excellent role player and/or exhibiting the result of a diminished power or disposition to make FOAs?

The standard hypnotic inductions had the potential to create either a special state or to launch a convincing role. Erickson's (1964) confusion techniques might be an exception, in that intense states of confusion intrinsically involve an inability to determine something's contextual fit. Sufficiently confused, it's not that I am unwilling to make an FOA; I am unable to do so. And frankly, I think the disorienting employment of confusion is ethically problematic unless the subject agrees to being treated this way. But, if you agreed to be confused, how confused would you be?

Trance, dissociation, delusion, typical dreaming, and certain hypnotic phenomena are associated with a problematic sense of time. FOAs and time turn out to be logically connected. This is why, I think, many subjects who score high on the standard hypnotic susceptibility scales are lousy at estimating the duration between hypnotic induction and termination. But absent an induction procedure, the control case, some of these same subjects who had trouble accurately estimating duration, do just fine (Schwartz, 1978, 1980; Bowers, 1979; Kirchenheim and Persinger, 1991). The foundational Person Concept's distinction between Reality and Real World provide some of the explanatory logic.

Descriptive Psychology's concept of the Real World consists of possible and historical **Objects, Processes, Events,** and **States of Affairs.** Here's a relevant part of Ossorio's **State of Affairs System** (Ossorio, 1978/2005) on the structure of process.

1. **A process is a sequential change from one state of affairs to another.**
2. **A process is a state of affairs that has other, related processes as immediate constituents. (A process divides into related, smaller processes.)**
3. **An event is a direct change from one state of affairs into another.**
4. **An event is a state of affairs having two states of affairs ("before" and "after") as immediate constituents.**

A process has a sequence and duration. Real episodes in a person's life take time and have a sequence. When a person's sense of duration is absent or irrelevant, this real-world contextual element is lacking. Under these conditions, questions of reality and truth carry less weight and are harder to judge. Hypnotic induction techniques that rely on confusion, or relaxation and absorption, have this effect. To an extent, this disruption in context carries over to what is felt as in-character. It isn't for nothing that dissociation is also called "de-realization" and "de-personalization."

Standard hypnosis scales measure and equate hypnotic involvement with suggestibility, atypical behavior, and believed-in fantasy (Shor and Orne, 1962; Morgan and Hilgard, 1978-1979). In effect, a performance measure, not a test of state. With this in mind, I suspect poor duration estimation and confusions about sequence might sort out the method actors from the truly dissociated. Both groups can do the weird performances, but those less time bound might actually be entranced.

One last question before moving on. Every hypnotist knows there are boundaries to suggestion, specific to the particular hypnotist and subject. The clinical hypnotist gets different results than the guy on stage. Subjects have boundaries they will not surrender, wherever.

Even under unusual conditions, people recognize themselves by knowing there are no circumstances where they would do, or believe, some out of bounds state of affair. They know it is not in them. When it comes to in-character behavior, a diminished power or disposition to make FOAs goes only so far. Simply put, if a significant enough boundary is crossed, if a person's integrity is truly violated, FOAs might be made. Core values *might* weigh more in reckoning than a diminished range of FOAs.

Humans are complicated this way. Victor Raimy, who taught me hypnosis, answered a classmate's question about hypnotic seduction with, "candy is dandy, and liquor is quicker, but hypnosis is not worth a damn." Raimy pointed out that what happens between hypnotist and subject is within a range of surrender, bounded by the nature of their relationship. The clinical hypnotists and the guy performing on stage have different eligibilities, and implicitly different contracts, with their subjects. A few chapters on, I'll use the Relationship and Relationship Change Formula with their "unless clauses" to systematically clarify Raimy's point. Here's a glance. Notice the use and placement of the IA parameters.

A person has a behavior potential with others based on their individual capacities and their mutual eligibilities and will act accordingly, unless they:

(1) Don't recognize the relationship for what it is. (The K parameter)
(2) Are acting on another relationship that takes priority. (The W, K, and S parameters)
(3) Are unable to act in ways that express that relationship. (The KH and P parameters)
(4) Mistakenly believe their behavior reflects that relationship. (The K and A parameters)
(5) Miscalculate, or the behavior miscarries. (The P parameter)

Outside the range of a person's behavior potential or beyond the hypnotist's relational eligibility to suggest, something else will happen. Of course, relationships and eligibilities change over time, and people might conclude in good faith or bad, "I didn't know I had it in me." Not unlike how I got bitten.

BACK TO THE AOC FEEDBACK LOOP

Actors are able to Observe and Describe their behavior, and simultaneously Critique and adjust their performance accordingly. Adjusting our pace, walking about town, holding hands, crossing the street, all the while negotiating our differences, requires the flexible improvisational functions of the AOC loop. Teaching, coaching, and all our psychotherapies formalize the process with the teacher, therapist, and coach acting as auxiliary observers and critics. They lend their competence diagnosing what needs informing, correcting, enhancing, and practicing; and implicitly or explicitly target the necessary IA parameters. Everyone who is on the same stage is engaged in shared practices and may have a say in influencing the feedback.

If we conceptualize psychopathology as something gone wrong in self-regulation, the AOC feedback loop needs adjustment, with any of the Roles and IA parameters being the target of intervention.

Before we move to the remaining foundational Person Concepts of Language, Culture, and World, there are two conceptual tools missing. They are multitasking inventions that can be modified for all sorts of projects. They employ what we've established about Individual Persons and Intentional Actions. The first is the **Judgment Diagram**, the second the **Relationship Formula**. We've already implicitly used these concepts when acknowledging the complexity of motivation and the flexible but rule-following nature of spontaneity and improvisation. Now we'll make them explicit.

4

The Judgment Diagram, Some Categories of Cognizance, and the Unconscious

Do I contradict myself?
Very well, then I contradict myself,
(I am large, I contain multitudes.)
Walt Whitman, Song of Myself (1855)

How do we reconstruct a person's behavior? The answer is: we have direct access to the two ends. We observe the behavior and we can observe the circumstances in which the behavior occurs. **Peter Ossorio (1977/2015)**

… moral judgment is relevant in three domains: in the assessment of morally relevant situations, in the identification of morally correct actions, and in the interpretation of the intentions and maxims of the moral agent. **Seyla Benhabib (1988)**

People exercise judgment on the circumstances they find, create, invent, and appraise. Appraisals entail perspective, our individually characteristic hedonic, prudential, moral/ethical, and aesthetic concerns. Being who we are, we weigh these perspectives in individual ways. Ossorio built a tool for examining this reckoning.

The Actor-Observer-Critic feedback loop's effectiveness is inseparable from the effectiveness of judgment. We exercise judgment with varying degrees of competence, identifying and knowing how to judge some states of affairs better than others. Since competence is acquired through practice and experience, some of us are more practiced and more experienced than others.

Judgment is another concept that paradigmatically applies to cognizant and deliberate persons. There is little point in "judging" unless it refers to an appraisal of options. Judgment and deliberation go hand in hand, but judgment doesn't *require* deliberation. Whether judgment is immediate or well-considered, some of us, some of the time, can explicitly state the reasons we acted. Sometimes we can't. And what of nonparadigmatic judgment—not cognizant, less deliberate? We'll get to that with a modification of Ossorio's Judgment Diagram.

Using our Parametric Analysis of Intentional Action, this chapter will focus on judgment and the Judgment Diagram (Ossorio, 1977/2015, 2006a, b). The Judgment Diagram (JD) links a situation with a reconstruction of the reasons a person had to act one way or another. In this chapter, I'll examine judgment and decision; bungled and compromised action; and self-deception and unconscious motivation. I will also share some ideas about thinking under the gun and contrast them with the comfort and safety of "free-associating."

Ossorio introduced the JD with some reminders: The JD is a reconstruction of a motivational hierarchy of weighted reasons that informed an action. It does not illustrate a sequence of mental steps. Instead, it diagrams the distinctions integral to a decision—after the fact. The JD starts with a person observed and described acting in some "overall circumstance." This description sets the stage to identify the apparent props and players and what the actor did. Insofar as the behavior was intentional, the actor weighed the relevance of these props and players and decided on a course of action, a summary weighing of reasons that attended their perspectives.

Judgments and decisions are not necessarily a process. Often enough, people simply know what they want to do, their appraisal of a situation is immediate. Ossorio put it this way:

> For most people in most life situations only the most rudimentary process of decision making occurs if, indeed, any does at all. This is because given the circumstances and the social practices in progress the thing to do is obvious and there is 'no real decision to be made.' However, to the extent that there are at least two alternatives that are about equally matched and to the extent that it is important to make the right decision the first time, people will tend to go through procedures visibly related to the Judgment Diagram, including making explicit lists of pros and cons and attempting to weigh them properly. (2006, p. 229)

In circumstances that evoke conflict and ambivalence, when pros and cons are weighed, how we do that tests our competence. If a behavior goes badly, we might stop to reexamine our judgment and list what we considered or should have considered. The Judgment Diagram is not a flow chart of that cognition, but it can be used that way.

In its basic form the JD is only an illustration of the formal relations of circumstances, motivational weights, decision, and intentional action. When Ossorio explained it to me, he said it was initially developed for software to help an intelligence analyst assess a field operative's report. Spy stuff. Different operatives bring different values and competences to a situation and report on it accordingly. The JD provided a format to sort out

The Overall Observed Circumstance

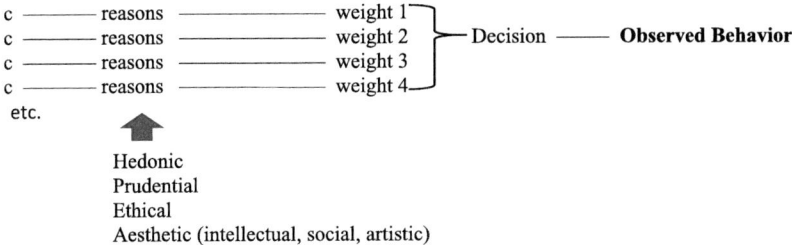

FIG. 4.1   The Judgment Diagram.

what sort of agent would produce *that* sort of intelligence. Or, conversely, knowing an agent's personal characteristics, the light that would throw on the judgments contained in their report. (I don't know why Ossorio was concerned with this. It felt a bit like the "green gas on the moon" question.)

Here's a version of the basic JD (Fig. 4.1). This diagram is neutral about how cognizant the actor is about any of this. Modifications of cognizance are offered later.

Circumstances have a significance—a meaning that carries reasons. (If I appraise my circumstances to be dangerous, that gives me reason to exercise caution.) Circumstances are noticed, appraised, and acted on given their motivational significance and priority. Out of all the circumstances (comprising the Overall Circumstance), the relevant circumstances (the little cs) are picked and paired with their weighted reasons. If listed from greater to lesser weight, it is called a "motivational hierarchy."

On choosing the little cs from the big C (choosing the *relevant* circumstances), we pay heed to some things over others. When I'm thirsty, I'm likely to notice the water fountain whether I was looking for it or not. A motivational hierarchy *suggests* people with appropriate sensitivities will notice certain states of affairs before others. A person's perceptions—infinite in their possibilities—are narrowed by the actor's perspective on *relevance*.

Intentionality and perception were hot topics when Ossorio developed this subject matter. That perception can be *informed and guided by* a person's motivational perspective was an insight shared by the founders of cognitive psychology. Implicit in Jerome Bruner's "New Look" (1973), J.J. Gibson's "active perception" (1979), and Ulric Neisser's "choosing where to look" (1976) is the conceptually inseparable link between circumstances, reasons, and their weights.

Circumstances provide the opportunity to do something to maintain or improve a person's position—their status—from their perspective.

Since behavior requires knowledge and know how, people can confuse, mismanage, poorly consider, or forget what they value. People also change their reasons and change their minds.

When a person's discernible patterns of judgment are sufficiently observed, the through-lines descriptions that identify character emerge. People can be obstinate, stubbornly insistent, wishy washy, inconsistent, even indifferent. Some claim guidance by a "moral compass," playing lip service to a set of values, while hypocritically their actions show otherwise.

The ability to reorder motivational weights is central to self-regulation, to be a person who is an Actor, Observer, and Critic. Dealing with changing circumstances requires flexibility, requires changes in the weighing of reasons, and creates everyday improvisation. Inflexible insistence and intolerance can muck up the work of this daily improv.

The stability and flexibility of the perspectives that actually give a person reasons to act corresponds, I think, to how we judge each other's integrity—their actual commitment to a set of core values integral to their self-concept. Confronting this therapeutically, I ask people, "How much of your integrity is really at stake?" and I'm gratified by how often clients loosen up when they reflect on this.

With those we know well, the JD is usually a reconstruction of our unarticulated knowledge of what counts for them. If we think their behavior was intentional, we take it they had their reasons. In other ordinary circumstances, with those "like ourselves"—members of our communities—we expect that our understanding of their reasons will fit well enough for us to get along. When our intuitive appreciations fail, the JD can be used to sort this out. We can ask questions along these lines if our intuitive or empathetic understanding needs informing.

1. Given their understanding of the overall circumstances, what does this person want and value? (And do we share an understanding of what the overall circumstances call for?)
2. What exactly do they recognize in their circumstances that is relevant to what they want and value? (And do we share a common recognition of the situation?)
3. What do they know how to do given what they see as their current opportunity or dilemma? (And do they have the skill or competence needed to successfully manage the circumstances?)
4. What is the significance to them of how they behave in these circumstances or what significance do they give to their behavior in these circumstances?
5. What personal characteristics are they employing, and what is the importance of these characteristics to them?
6. What is their perspective on how their performance looks?

Reconstructions and interpretations aren't foolproof, but they're the best we can do. Even if we ask a person why they did something, we are still left with our appraisal of their answer.

A DISTRESSING EXAMPLE AND SOME GROUPING OF REASONS

I wrote some of what follows on a Saturday morning in May after another school shooting. Another. This one in Texas. I was trying not to imagine the horror—but I couldn't—so I worked with my preoccupation. Ossorio often taught about emotional behavior by starting with "if a lion enters the room …." I had planned to proceed with that but changed my mind.

A few weeks back in study group one member wondered about the rationality of a mother sacrificing herself to save her child. This is from Clarke Stone's notes:

> Joke: two hikers come across a bear. One of them shucks his boots and starts putting on running shoes. Hiker 2 says, "You can't outrun that bear!" Running Shoes says, "I only have to outrun YOU." So, Running Shoes wasn't ready to make the sacrifice. But what if this story were about a parent and a child. The child says, "You can't outrun that bear!" Parent says, "I only have to outrun YOU." Our competence tells us that's completely wrong. Not a little bit wrong or maybe wrongheaded, but completely wrong. So, when we go back and look now at parents sacrificing themselves for their children, who would they be if they didn't?

Hold this example in mind since I'm going to group hedonic and prudential reasons apart from ethical and social aesthetic ones. This will have implications when I discuss "unconscious reasons" later. I'm going to continue to argue that ethical and aesthetic perspectives are necessarily connected to cognizant and deliberate action, and that hedonics and prudence aren't. Why? Because, at some point, developing an ethical and aesthetic perspective requires knowledge of choice, a recognition of the possibility of choice and renunciation. I also want to remind that these four perspectives inform fully paradigmatic, nonpathological persons—at least of the humane sort. I write "of the humane sort" because the clinical language of health and psychopathology serve different aims than a moral discourse about good and evil. Both ways of talking have a place. Both are relevant in the example that follows.

Here's my imagined observed circumstance: A young man enters a school stalking the halls, shooting. He stops at a classroom where a teacher, who just heard gunfire, braces against the door, loudly telling her students to exit the back entrance. They know the drill, tragically standard in the current American classroom. Orderly enough, they respond.

She'd been instructed to leave, last in line, along with them. She wondered during training if she could barricade the door with her desk, but concluded she wasn't strong enough. Hearing gunshots—with or without second thought—she does what she knows she can do: runs to and braces against the door.

I'm going to use the Judgment Diagram to reconstruct her decision. Perhaps she debated her choices, asking herself, "why am I doing this?" We don't know. Regardless, she votes with her feet, even as bullets pass through the door.

The Overall Observed Circumstance

A teacher hears repeated gunfire approaching her closed hallway door. She's in a large classroom with a hallway door and a back exit. There are 30 students in the room. The teacher yells, "This is not a drill. Exit as you've been trained though the rear door." She runs toward and remains pressed against the hallway door.

The Teacher's Relevant Circumstances (c) and Personal Characteristics (Weighted Values)

1. *Hedonics*: She might be anticipating the pain and anguish of getting shot. Her hedonic concerns are available, perhaps loom large. Nonetheless, she puts herself in harm's way.
2. *Prudence*: She would not ordinarily risk her life, but these are not ordinary circumstances. Her self-interest is conflicted.
3. *Ethical and moral obligations*: She is aware of the principal's instruction for teachers to exit behind the students. But with shots approaching, she appraises there is not sufficient time for her to exit with her class before the shooter arrives. Her duty is to protect her students.
4. *Aesthetic*: She's a Texan and holds "Remember the Alamo!" Her social aesthetic would be violated if she tried to escape with the uncertainty she could do so while protecting her students. Who would she be then? Not someone she could live with.

Decision and Behavior

Her judgment, thought through or not, is summed by her act to stand against the door. Her ethical obligation to her students and her personal–social aesthetic hold greater weight than her hedonic and prudential concerns. I suspect most adults of sound "moral fiber" would act similarly. Our culture holds that "children are to be protected first."

Here are some relevant maxims on reasons and judgment:

Because a person's circumstances are what they are, they have reasons and opportunities to engage in one behavior rather than another.
If a person wants to do something, they have a reason to do it.
If a person recognizes an opportunity to do something they want to do, they have a reason to do it.
If a person wants to do something, they have a reason to create or look for an opportunity to do it.
If a person has a reason to do something, they will do it, unless they have a stronger reason not to.
If a person has two reasons for doing X, they have a stronger reason for doing X than if they had only one of those reasons.
If the situation calls for a person to do something they can't do, they will do something they can do.
If a person wants to engage in a given behavior, they would thereby also want to engage in other behaviors to the extent that they are relevantly similar to the behavior in question.

Here are some maxims on weights of values:

A person values some states of affairs over others and acts accordingly.
If a person's relationship to something is such that they are in a bad situation or circumstance, they have a reason to try to improve it.
If a person's relationship to something is such that they are in a good situation or circumstance, they have a reason to act to maintain it.
If a person is in a good situation and has an opportunity to improve it, they have a reason to try to do so.
If a person is in any situation and it may be expected to become worse, they have a reason to act to prevent that.
From their perspective, a person will not choose less behavior potential over more.
If a person values a specific something, e.g., an object, a circumstance, a behavior, or more generally, a state of affairs, they will thereby also value other specific things of the same kind to the extent that they are relevantly similar to the original.
If a person values a general something, they will thereby also value a specific something to the extent that it is a paradigmatic instance or realization of the more general value.
If a person values something general, they will be sensitive to (will tend to evaluate) the relevance of their circumstance to that something and act accordingly.

Negative emotional behavior (fear, guilt, anger, shame, etc. behavior) is an attempt to improve a bad situation.
Positive emotional behavior (joy, triumph, glee, etc. behavior) is an attempt to preserve, enhance, or celebrate a good situation).
(Adapted from Ossorio, 1998/2012)

THE JUDGMENT DIAGRAM MODIFIED FOR PROBLEMS IN SOCIAL AND SELF-REGULATION

Before getting to the modifications, here's some background for my clinical uses. The JD can be modified to serve other purposes.

When I work with people I wonder about the following:

Their circumstances: How nuanced and well-formed is their construction of their world? Is this a place they can effectively act? (And if not, can they change their circumstances for the better by finding a new place and/or reconstructing the one they're in?) As their therapist—a part of their circumstances—I wonder what I evoke. What does my presence automatically bring up for them?

Their perspectives: How clear and differentiated are their perspectives? How insistent are they about the weights they give the circumstances they find and or seek? (Can they reorder their priorities?)

Their dilemmas: How do they manage ambivalence, conflict, and strong mixed goals? When the dilemmas are acted on without deliberation, how competent are they? (In the next chapter, we will return to this question of "emotional competence.")

Their cognizance, self-reflection, and defensiveness: Are they fooling themselves? Keeping two sets of books, one open to examine, one not so much? I wonder what they are willing to consider and honestly share with me.

My job—my vision of the practice of psychotherapy—means I try for an honest and noncoerced exploration of perspectives. This often involves negotiating motivational weights and reordering them. People get stuck with too heavy a load, or they carry it too lightly. I try to empathically identify and confront insistence, reluctance, defensive intolerance, and what's relevant but unthinkable. I wonder if they dismiss what they should carefully weigh. What is poorly constructed, unconscious, off-limits, or dismissed can throw a monkey wrench in self-regulation and social negotiation.

With these themes in mind, I'm going to add three categories of circumstances and reasons to the Judgment Diagram: (1) those easily cognizant, (2) those a person is reluctant to consider or disclose, and (3) those they are unable to consider. I acquired this ordering from Anton Kris's psychoanalytic volume, *Free Association* (1982), but they are logical possibilities, sensibly independent of theory.

> Nothing is more characteristic of the free association method than the varieties of opposition that are encountered when patient and analyst set about to use it. I find it helpful to consider the forms of opposition under two headings: reluctance and resistance. In doing so, I use the term resistance to refer only to unconscious obstacles to freedom of association, a much narrower sense than is usual in the psychoanalytic literature, and I use reluctance to mean any conscious attitude of disinclination to participate in the free association method or in analysis. Although they may be bound together, their linkage is not obligatory. (p. 31)

Since Kris is writing to a psychoanalytic community, I'll explain some terms of general psychotherapeutic utility. The psychoanalytic method involves inviting a client to honestly disclose what they are thinking while in the company of their analyst. This attempt at honest disclosure *is* the request to "free associate" (Schwartz, 1988). The analyst interprets this narrative with particular attention to how it is shaped defensively—through conscious reluctance and unconscious resistance—and by conscious and unconscious interpersonal expectations—the transference. The expectations of transference create problems when what is expected distorts and interferes with new relational possibilities. Defensive reluctance and resistance shields established expectations from reevaluation. For better or worse, defenses maintain perspectives and serve the person's ordinary manner of functioning. And, perhaps, keep the person stuck in problematic patterns of behavior.

My therapeutic community makes a big deal of clients' transferences and our "counter-transferences." It's a two-way street. To the extent some unexamined interpersonal expectation is implicitly and automatically "transferred" onto a current relationship, it's smart to know whether these expectations are helpful or not. Sometimes we get lucky and the transference—even as distortion—benefits the relationship. That's why Freud (1912a) cautioned to leave the positive affectionate transference alone until it interferes with work. In therapy, it is natural that issues of authority, trust, influence, and dependency get stirred up between therapist and client. As they do in everyday social and intimate life. These expectations have a past and are ubiquitous. My job is to make them explicit and show how the ones that appear in treatment have similarities to what goes on outside.

Transference follows the behavioral logic of these maxims:

A person takes it that things are as they seem unless they have reason enough to think otherwise.

If a person values a specific something, e.g., an object, a circumstance, a behavior, or more generally, a state of affairs, they

will thereby also value other specific things of the same kind to the
extent that they are relevantly similar to the original.
If a person values a general something, they will thereby also value
a specific something to the extent that it is a paradigmatic instance
or realization of the more general value.
If a person values something general, they will be sensitive to
(will tend to evaluate) the relevance of their circumstance to that
something and act accordingly. (Adapted from Ossorio, 1998/2012).

Transference is a particular take on Knowledge. Transference is a concept that shares a resemblance to Jean Piaget's "schema" (Wachtel, 1980)
and Fredric Bartlett, and later, Ulric Neisser's idea of a cognitive "sche-
mata," a term neither Bartlett nor Neisser were completely happy with
(Neisser, 1976). Schemas are a "cognitive package" that shortcuts having
to constantly relearn stuff. Wachtel, echoing Piaget's schema *as assimilat-
ing and accommodating*, describes transferences as "schemas in which assimilation predominates over accommodation to an inordinate degree."
What is "transferred" are relational expectations onto a current relationship evoked by some similarity that fits well enough that it can be as-
similated into the existing schema. Accommodation is the way a schema
changes, accepting what is new to the circumstances. I want to examine
where, to an "inordinate degree," accommodation fails. The psychodynamic concern with transference emphases its potential to problematically
limit and distort a person's appraisals. Having had a beloved, but harsh
and authoritative father, do I automatically engage older male authorities
in ways that bear a family resemblance to what I expected from my dad?

A THEORY-NEUTRAL "PSYCHODYNAMIC" JUDGMENT DIAGRAM

Another psychoanalyst, Joseph Caston (2011), proposed three clinical
markers of personal agency: the ability to stop and change a course of
action, maintenance of adequate self-observation (Observer-Critic competence), and the appropriateness of behavior to the circumstance ("acting
like one of us"). Reversibility, self-observation, and appropriateness are
preempirical distinctions—useful apart from any theory where they are
employed. The following modifications to the basic JD identify what can
impair these markers.

The circumstances of the Three Domain Judgment Diagram (Fig. 4.2)
are decidedly personal—first person. The circumstances are *my appraisal of
my perceptual environment, my sensations, and my thoughts of the moment*, all
of which connect in some way to the rest of my world. But it's personal. If
an observer wants to fill in the diagram's content, they should probably

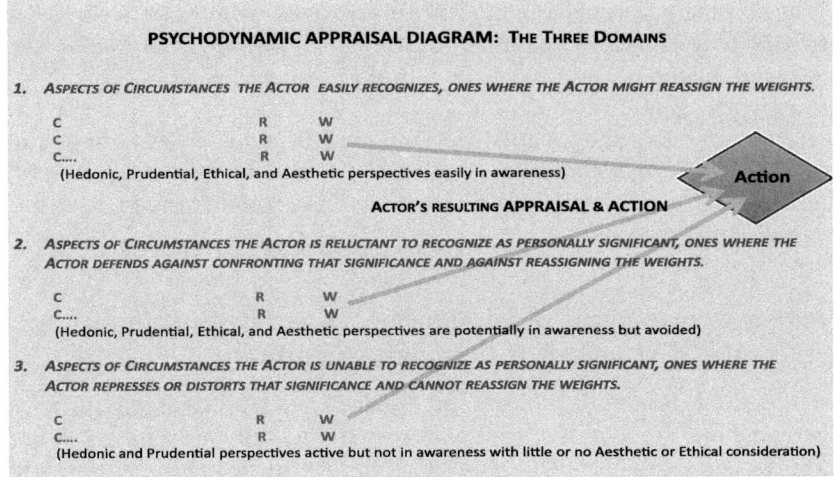

FIG. 4.2 A Three-Domain Psychodynamic Judgment Diagram designed for Actor-Observer-Critic self-regulation (AOC) assessment.

wait for my report to support their reconstruction. I can wear a poker face and do little to reveal what's on my mind. Sitting still and quiet, I might be intensely engaged in action. What can you tell from my performance? How much, how well, and how honest will my account *to you be*?

A THREE DOMAIN JUDGMENT DIAGRAM DESIGNED FOR ACTOR-OBSERVER-CRITIC SELF-REGULATION ASSESSMENT

Domain One: Aspects of Circumstances the Actor Easily Recognizes, Ones Where the Actor Might Reassign the Weights

The weights of Hedonic, Prudential, Ethical, and Aesthetic reasons can range from very high (reflecting core values and first priorities that ordinarily override other considerations) to very low (those that hardly matter). Weights can be more or less flexible to change, from insistent to permissive.

Domain One content is cognizantly available for AOC self-regulation and deliberation. (These reasons I'll admit to myself, if not to you.) Intense desires and taboo—moral concerns and core values—fall into Domain One or Domain Two and are characterized by unyieldingly high weights not ordinarily subject to reordering. In Domain One such insistence is acknowledged as a personal value where it might be reconsidered. Desires and taboos that fall into Domain Two will only be reluctantly recognized.

The pivotal import of Domain One is its place in the AOC self-correcting feedback loop. Within Domain One, we can choose what to think over, talk about, negotiate, and reconsider. In this domain, we are cognizant of our insistences; of our intolerances; and of what matters more and what matters less. With our eyes open, damning the torpedoes, we might go full speed ahead *if it matters that much*. If so, let's hope we're seeing straight; that our vision isn't fouled by under or unconsidered Domain Two and Domain Three reasons.

Domain Two: Aspects of Circumstances and Reasons only Reluctantly Recognized as Personally Significant

Hedonic, Prudential, Ethical, and Aesthetic perspectives might be in awareness but are avoided, thus lowering their availability for consideration, social-negotiation, and reordering of priority. Domain Two content is difficult to employ in AOC self-regulation, hard to admit, and ordinarily won't be shared.

Domain Three: Aspects of Circumstances and Reasons so Unthinkable or Intolerable, the Actor Is Unable to Acknowledge Them as Personally Significant

Hedonic and Prudential perspectives are active but cognizantly unavailable as self-knowledge and cannot be employed in deliberation. What isn't available to cognizance cannot be consciously renounced or chosen. Without awareness of choice, these aspects of the overall circumstance evoke little or no Aesthetic and Ethical consideration. With these limitations, the actor cannot negotiate or reappraise motivational weights so Hedonic and Prudential concerns are static. AOC self-regulation is accordingly hampered. Domain Three content requires an outside observer's interpretation or construction; or self-reflection performed after the act.

The Decision and Observed Behavior

The Actor is only reasonably aware of Domain One and may not acknowledge Domain Two. The Actor's resulting behavior is the response to all the motivational weights, and without reasonable awareness of Domains Two and Three, the behavior may be compromised and ineffective.

Implications and Stray Thoughts

Nonacknowledged priorities can be problematic if their appropriate expression is critical to the person's well-being and place in the community.

If not cognizant of what I value, I don't know what difference it makes. That can lead to problems. These Domain Two and Domain Three unacknowledged reasons for action fall under the various banners of "bad faith," self-deception, and unconscious motivation.

All three domains restrict a person's ability to make an informed choice. Actions can be compromised and bungled when a person's vision of their overall circumstance is restricted, defensively or not.

THE CASE OF TOMMY

Years ago, I worked with Tommy, a 13-year-old only child, who was having difficulty in school. His grades were poor, and at least once a week, without explanation, he would leap from his chair and run from the classroom. On the playing fields, he was taunted as "gay," so he frequently got into fights. He felt being identified as homosexual violated his integrity—his self-respect—and it made him desperate to find a girlfriend.

His home life was unsettled. His manic-depressive mother would occasionally disappear for days, and return bizarrely dressed, declaring plans to leave the family for "the lights of New York." Tommy's father, overworked and rarely at home, appeared in Tommy's descriptions as warm and loving but clueless. I urged his mother to seek treatment and for the couple to enter therapy, but they refused. They did, however, support my work with Tommy and agreed to meet with me from time to time.

Although earlier testing showed Tommy had strong concept formation skills, he had a weak vocabulary, a pronounced stutter, and was reluctant to talk unless he was certain what he wanted to say. As my relationship with him deepened, his stutter became less pronounced. On various occasions, he remarked that if I were his father, his life would be happier. I really liked Tommy and frequently found myself examining the paternal feelings he evoked and the avuncular relationship I offered. Once, seemingly out of the blue, he said I would look better if I used eye shadow. I think he thought he was joking. I told him I'd take it under advisement.

One afternoon, as Tommy entered my office, he slipped and fell. Neither of us thought much of it, although I checked the rug to see if it was loose. It wasn't. Two weeks later, this happened again, but this time he seemed to be looking at my face as he lost balance. We talked a bit about this, but he seemed fine and was clearly not interested in exploring why he fell. He claimed he was not stumbling elsewhere. Running from the classroom was occurring during these 2 weeks.

A few sessions latter, he tripped again as he walked to his chair and again did not want to talk about it. I remember thinking: at Tommy's age, I was reading Ian Fleming's *Goldfinger*: "Once is an accident. Twice is a coincidence. Three times is enemy action."

In my own psychoanalytic session a few days later, I talked about my relation to Tommy, and I wondered about his falling down. I reported a dream I had the night after Tommy's last stumble: I'm playing football in the high school stadium near my childhood home. In the dream, I jump, catch a pass, and slowly, comfortably, fall to the ground. While dropping, I look to the stands where a woman, who looks like my mother, is smiling. As I "free-associated" to falling, I remembered going with my father on a hayride in that same stadium and how I impulsively jumped off the cart. My dad jumped down, picked me up, jumped back in the cart, and we resumed the ride. I think I did that twice. It was a good memory although I remember my father being angry with me the second time.

In that same session, I recalled a series of impulsive behaviors on my part, from when I was seven or eight. I felt compelled to open the back door of our car as my parents drove around the city arguing. Dr. Magraw, my analyst, gently interpreted my wanting to be held and safely contained by loving parents. And, that I was dreaming what Tommy acted out. Adding to the poignancy, my analyst was a year older than my father and attended the same high school; the one in my dream. I ended the hour believing I understood Tommy's symptom as a message needing a response.

The following week, Tommy tripped again. This time I offered my hand and said, "Tommy, I'm not going to pick you up, but as long as you need me, I'll stand beside you. That's a promise." He simply responded, "OK." During that hour, he remembered a time in first grade when he fell on the playground and how good it felt when his teacher rushed over and picked him up.

He never tripped in my office again, and his running from the classroom ceased. I never explicitly explained or interpreted his apparent accidents. I did not believe he would tolerate what I took as the unconscious meaning of his falling. Instead, I spoke in a way I knew he could manage; and I think he felt appreciated and understood. Since he had gotten his message across and achieved his desired response, he no longer needed to repeat it.

Tommy's stumbling symptom was an example of a bungled action, where the weight of his easy-to-acknowledge Domain One motives were set against the weights I've interpreted within Domain Two and Domain Three. (It's hard to tell one domain from the other when the actor is reluctant or unable to say.) I came to see Tommy's stumbling as an intentional action motivated by his wanting to get to the couch while wanting a taboo reassurance of being held by me. For Tommy, it was an accident; for me, it was a compromise of motives that sent an intentional message, a significance Tommy could only show and not tell. (We'll return to Tommy in Chapter 9 as an illustration of an empathic response.)

I started this chapter with some clinically relevant questions. Life is full of conflict and Domain One is not free of conflicting perspectives. How are the normal dilemmas of ambivalence and mixed emotions managed?

ABOUT AMBIVALENCE AND CONFLICT

Conflict and mixed feeling are inevitable about those people and things we value most. Those we are closest to can get under our skin, irritate, and have their own agendas that don't match ours. In intimate life, tolerating ambivalence is a necessary virtue. (When impossible or too difficult to manage mixed feelings, we end up with Domain Two and Three issues.) Here's an example of how ambivalence can work OK in Domain One.

It is natural, at times, to be at odds with oneself, to have values hard to reconcile, where we cannot have it both ways, especially when our hedonics and ethics are at stake (noting that all the perspectives can conflict). One midmorning, I was enjoying the frustrations of fishing inside the elbow below the gut on Cape Pogue. After hours of casting, I reeled in a beautiful striped bass that was a wee bit too short. I love the taste of bass in the morning. There was no one else on the beach but my wife and dogs. My grill was in the back of the jeep. Did I mention I was hungry? Reluctantly, very reluctantly, after measuring the fish and confirming what I already knew, 3 in. short of the legal 28, I eased the poor striper back into the water.

I was conflicted and hungry. I love grilled striper. I could get away with keeping it, but I threw it back just the same. Why? Because I'm a surfcaster who honors the conservation rules. They've worked to restore what had been a dangerously diminished stock. So, I tolerated my mixed feelings: the pleasure in the catch plus the frustration *and* satisfaction in the release. It is satisfying to do the right thing in a tradition I respect. Fishing ethics matter to me. It might be different if I was much hungrier; I can't be sure. So, I grinned at my wife, asked the dogs to stop barking, and had enough bars on my phone to call the Shanty in Edgartown, settling later for their lobster rolls and a Bloody Mary.

I was working from one playbook that morning, motivationally conflicted or not. At odds with myself but not that much. And I knew it. (Plus, I can use it here as an example, and to show what a sportsman I am.)

When some aspects of a complicated circumstances can't be tolerated, some people respond in a pathological manner. They insistently try to maintain a fragile integrity by being unwilling or unable to acknowledge the conflicted complexity they are responding to. Not being able to effectively maintain a coherent perspective, they might panic, might become unable to make final-order appraisals, might dissociate. If they can maintain enough perspective to feel they are reasonably acting, an observer might notice they acknowledge what they can't tolerate, but not as an aspect of their own intent. I'll show how this "splitting" works when we get to Domain Three.

SOME CONTENT AND BEHAVIORAL LOGIC OF THE THREE DOMAINS

Domain One: The World of Easy Awareness

Stuck with "writer's block," I escaped by changing course, and then began writing this on vacation. On vacation, I welcome detours. Unable to maintain attention to the work at hand, I ended up thinking about wandering attention—when it's a gift, not a diagnosis (e.g., Robison et al., 2016). This led to some thoughts about three circumstances of choice and their implications for our sense of satisfaction.

Three Circumstances of Domain One

Circumstance One

Here's my favorite circumstance and one I'd wager is yours, too: being free to follow the whims of the moment. It's a psychological state because it is a temporary configuration of powers and dispositions where the stars are especially well aligned. An interval of flexible, easily revisable interests and choices free of dire consequence.

While surveying circumstances—our environment, sensations, thoughts of the moment—we have the time and the breathing space to think and do as we please. "Do as we please" is key. We're not pressured by the weight of anything we *need* to do, now. We *get* to do what we want but don't have to. The weights of Domain One are flexible, open to spontaneous findings and creations. My experience of this sort of interval is satisfying, time well spent.

Circumstance Two

Here's what I think is our usual state of affairs: most of the time there is something we have to do. It seems there is always something on the agenda. The circumstances have a preassigned weight—a hierarchy or priority. We face these circumstances of the things we *should* do—gladly or not.

Considering the things we should do, I offer this time management advice to students as a learning strategy (and caution them about following my advice): when time is limited, and it's always limited, attend first to what you find most interesting. I'll explain why in a bit. My second strategy—should the task *at the time* be too daunting, and you can get away with it—find another mission with a greater expectation of satisfaction.

Circumstance Three

This one I hate, and it's potentially pathogenic: finding or creating circumstances that distort, constrain, or coerce the capacity to attend to anything else. We feel we have no choice but to attend, are compelled, held in place. This is the desperation—a sense of jeopardy—that comes from inescapable circumstances or unyielding, insistent values. Here, the weights are so high, we *need* to attend as a first priority. If we fail, we expect trouble. If we succeed, we feel relief, with or without satisfaction, but we've dodged the bullet.

I work with people who constantly find themselves in this third condition, people strained and unhappy, relentlessly thinking about things they'd rather not. What they often say is at stake is the requirement of honoring a vital commitment. It becomes a matter of character for them. *They are never on vacation.* Practically, this is not a temporary state but their general status of being in the world. If it reduces their freedom to deliberate, to choose the social practices they let themselves consider, they become unpracticed in fully deliberate action. I think it is reasonable to call this psychopathology. In my practice, I see this state of insistent duty come with depression and somatic complaint.

Realistically, most of what we do is neither freely chosen nor coerced. We look forward to a relaxed agenda and accept the work before us. The choices we have are bounded by the available circumstances and our priorities. We find, choose, and accept one mission after another. Think of being in school, months before summer break.

The satisfaction of following one's whims is a privilege, a luxury similar to Maslow's (1968) recognition that creative growth is more likely after survival needs are met. Although some would like to believe "what doesn't kill us, makes us stronger," desperation and adversity rarely brings out the best in us. They make us mean, anxious, and depressed. It's hard to learn, create, and prosper under the gun.

Examples of Circumstances One, Two, and Three Within Domain One

When I began writing this section, I was on vacation, but I had planned to write something else. My concept of vacation—real vacation—involves a time and place in which I can do more or less as I please. More of my missions are chosen for their potential to satisfy. I've time to play and have fun, just to be. My choices are less instrumental and more of what I like to do. I read, fish, and cook a lot. And I write without discipline and hope for a good editor, later.

Earlier the week before that vacation, anticipating a break from a highly structured schedule, I told myself I'd spend my first Saturday away focused on a less than half-finished chapter on language and verbal behavior for this book. A clock's ticking and I have a contract to fulfill. But when Saturday came, I didn't have the focus to work on my self-assigned chapter, but I reassured myself I'd find time later. Even remembering the fable of the ant and the grasshopper, I chose to hop about. My slogan that week: sometimes be the grasshopper, sometimes be the ant. But don't count on the ant bailing you out.

I woke up Saturday knowing Verbal Behavior would have to wait. After all, it was Saturday, so rather than move to my study, I went for a walk and enjoyed the first of fall's sunlight. Near sunset, I was in the mood to summarize what I'd been mulling over. During the walk, I remembered a conversation with a friend concerning Csikszentmihályi's (1988) concept of "flow," and about the interesting things that might get captured in the current.

The conversation had started with concerns about my teaching. My students are assigned far more than they can possibly read, and they end up reading far less than they should. With that, I advise them to first read whatever interests them most—at least get that done. I suggest they prioritize what they authentically value. This is a variation of telling them to play to their strengths. It's probably good time management advice. They are not going to read all they are assigned, they never do by half, so they should start with what they most want to read. I tell them that strategy might help them assimilate additional knowledge because if they have the requisite competence, what they find most interesting will stick with them better than if they struggle with their lack of interest. The knowledge and skills they actually value will naturally acquire additional knowledge and competence. Remember Piaget's assimilation and accommodation? I'm often right; vindicated when they end up surprised by the unexpected themes that became intriguing because of the themes' relation to the students' initial interests. I offer them the image of a seed crystal that enlarges as it attracts kindred content and a complex rock's fused assimilation of component minerals.

This sort of learning works like a love triangle. When I teach Freud, I point out this is how his Oedipus Complex can be understood. (This and other ways, from the fanciful to the empirically reasonable.) Freud's Oedipus begins with a mother–infant dyad, with a dependent infant enthralled with desire for mother. Eventually, as the infant grows, it notices mother's significant interest in father, and in so doing, learns more about father and what he stands for. It starts with the dyad and then moves to the triangle. (Mothers have their version of this triangle that starts with what Donald Winnicott (1956/1984) aptly called "primary maternal preoccupation.")

Our most vital understandings can begin with a focus on someone that fascinates us and can turn to what fascinates that person. Or we start with something we find compelling, then turn our attention to other things connected to that. I know much of my education happened this way, starting with an idealized teacher and then expanding to learn what that teacher found worthy.

Ossorio framed some of this behavioral logic with the following maxims:

> If a person values a specific something, e.g., an object, a circumstance, a behavior, or, more generally, a state of affairs, they will thereby also value other specific things of the same kind to the extent that they are relevantly similar to the original.
>
> If a person values a general something they will thereby also value a specific something to the extent that it is a paradigmatic instance or realization of the more general value *(Place, 1998/2012)*

For those who do not intrinsically value any of their academic subjects, my advice falls flat. They might as well follow whatever order the syllabus provides.

Now to conditions of Circumstance Three. Consider another truism: coercion elicits resistance or resigned compliance. In my clinical practice, this shows up in "opposional-defiance" and depressive symptoms of chronic exhaustion. The circumstances and values involve ambivalent obligations defied or resentfully obliged. When resentfully obliged, chronic frustrated anger and depression are often part of the package.

Here follow a couple of examples.

I work with a devoted mother who's often exhausted from spending an epoch relearning algebra and studying the life cycle of snakes and snails. It is important to her, and she wants to be generally available to assist her children with homework and idiosyncratic pastimes. She knows this might go on for decades. In an ideal world, she'd be free to think about other things, ideas that intrinsically please her, that challenge and enrich her considerable intellect. But she accepts that her consuming duty to her kids does not allow her the time or energy to pursue much else. At least not now. Her domestic obligations, vital and valued, are performed without fail but are implemented through forced attention to her children's needs. This requires attending some things she'd rather not entertain. This tragic and noble conflict comes with her vision of motherhood. A lot of life is like this. The life cycle comes with demands. But she keeps faith that in the future, she'll return to the other possibilities that also fit her. I expect she'll flourish.

Another person I know struggles with the burden of fulfilling his parents' obligations. In a constant state of demoralization, he's stressed to exhaustion, unhappy, and painfully depressed. He sighs "when can I return to my life." In session with him, at first I didn't understand what was at stake, and unhelpfully thought "this is your life until you do something else and reorder your priorities." It dawned on me finally what he meant and desperately wanted me to understand: "When can I have my own thoughts, the ones that come from me, that I'd turn to if I wasn't so goddamned under the sway of parental ghosts and my family's unfinished business?" Obliged by a trust to hold the family purse strings, he'd become his sisters' keeper; and with that, acquired a conflicted potential for competitive revenge. Despite his sisters' inept and sleazy ways, they were clear parental favorites, and now he has to care for them. He says he would prefer other priorities. Unfortunately, demonstrating to his dead parents that he is the "worthy child" keeps him enslaved. This tangled narcissism is a tough knot to loosen, let alone untie. Here, his sense of integrity is also his disorder. He knows this. This is mostly Domain One stuff of painfully high-weighted, ambivalent commitment and opportunity.

Sometimes out of compensation, revenge, competition, or sheer duty, we value some things so much that when the opportunity or dilemma arrives, we can't attend to anything else. Like a lion in the room, it constrains attention. Some values are an occupying force that colonizes the mind.

BACK TO THE THREE DOMAIN JUDGMENT DIAGRAM AND FEATURES OF DOMAINS TWO AND THREE

Let's start with some general considerations. Domains Two and Three can undermine the awareness of choice and disrupt effective self-regulation. For the outside observer, it is difficult to separate Domain Two from Domain Three. Did Tommy's "motivated stumbling" involve issues he was reluctant to consider or was he actually unable to bring them to mind? For that matter, was the stumbling actually motivated? That claim was my interpretation, and I've no pipeline to the truth.

Can we determine what is really happening when confronting Domain Two and Domain Three? Reasonable uncertainty should attend attributions of agency. We can build a case that something properly belongs in one domain or another, but uncertainty is formally inevitable. In the "two sets of books" examples of bad faith and self-deception to follow, the actors are reluctant to consider the significance of their actions, preferring to believe they were seduced or "unconsciously motivated." One person's "my unconscious made me do it" is another's "the devil, my 'alter ego' or my 'multiples' made me do it." Attributions of unconscious motivation might be legitimate or a handy responsibility dodge. Roy Schafer's (1976) formulation of the unconscious as "disclaimed action" carries this uncertainty.[1] Is the disclaimed really unavailable, or is it insistently avoided? It's very hard to tell.

DOMAIN TWO AND THREE ARE "TRIGGERED"

Consider the "trigger warning" nowadays placed, sometimes mandated, on syllabi to protect students—apparently a vulnerable class—from circumstances they cannot bear. These warnings tag readings, videos, and lectures that might evoke traumatic memories; or elicit anxiety, fear, panic, shame, rage, humiliation, or lust. Envy and guilt, I believe, are less protected by these signs, but could follow a similar rationale. These are the avoided and problematic emotions that can attend Domain Two and Domain Three, except when "triggered." Many of my colleagues are wary of provoking such encounters. (In an early draft, I slipped and wrote "weary.")

Domain Two content is avoided because it conflicts with and violates a Domain One perspective on which circumstances are appropriate to consider as bearably and personally significant—it violates a person's self-status assignment, the dearly held self-aesthetic. Or it evokes emotions and memories a person cannot readily tolerate—they don't have the know how to manage the circumstances.

Domain Three content is completely outside what a person knows how consider. They cannot recognize a place for themselves there. Since know how and competencies are acquired through practice, both Domain Two and Domain Three don't get their required exercise. As a result, the

---

[1] I reference Roy Schafer because of his reworking the mechanistic and deterministic-causal language of psychoanalytic theory into a form compatible with The Person Concept. Mechanistic and deterministic theory colludes with treating action as "impersonal." Some translations of Freud amplified this tendency. In the English Standard Editions, James Strachey Latinized Freud's *Ich*, *Es*, and *Uber-Ich*, translating them as *id*, *ego*, and *superego*. Freud went along, believing this was more scientized and acceptable to the American psychiatric community. These foundational concepts are more adequately translated as *it*, *I*, and *over-I*. Freud's id was an "it"—an impersonal category, his ego was "I," personal and owned (Bettelheim 1983). This is especially unfortunate because it undermines a significant shift in Freudian theory. By the early 1920s, Freud moved from his theory of an unconscious, preconscious, and perceptual consciousness, to a structural theory of id, ego, and superego to allow aspects of ego, this personal I, to be the disowned and defensively repressed but still personal—not an "it." Freud's therapeutic slogan *Es war, soll Ich warden*, usually translated as: *where id was, there ego shall be*, is more properly, where *it was I shall become*. This is consistent with a treatment goal of bringing Domain Two and Domain Three into Domain One where insight and choice is feasible.

observer might see "triggered" actions as immature, inept, primitive, unnuanced, repetitive, and so on. People are very slow learners here, if they learn much at all. I worry about my students.

Empirically Speaking, What Do People Tend to Avoid and Disown?

Domain Two content is ordinarily segregated from self-examination. When this segregation is described as a competence, I hear it reported as an ability to "compartmentalize." Some people, apparently, know how to avoid memories, cautionary tales, and evidence of the contrary. Until they can't. And that might leave them a day late and a dollar short.

People troubled by their ethical and moral transgressions sometimes claim they didn't think they had that in them; they were somehow another person, changed from whom they really are. By some means, they were *overcome* by temptations and destructive impulses they were not able to control or think through, blaming alcohol, "the flesh is weak," and the like. To an extent, they're correct. Intoxication and sexual opportunity are significant factors. The erotic can gather attention and be extremely compelling. Intoxication can diminish the scope and adequacy of deliberation, of ethical and aesthetic judgments in particular. Ever worn beer goggles? And that dream you had you'd rather not discuss and certainly would never act out awake. (It's not just me, right?)

Hedonic and prudential issues: sex, unwanted aggression, and wanton self-interest are the usual suspects and tend to be socially regulated. Here's the Domain Two problem: what is problematic when not adequately controlled becomes especially problematic if it is hard to think over. If something is too shameful to acknowledge, a flexible competence is unlikely to develop.

Here are some illustrations of transgression, denial, bad faith, and keeping "two sets of books."

DOMAIN TWO: RELUCTANCE, BAD FAITH, AND SELF-DECEPTION

Here's the classic of "bad faith" from John-Paul Sartre's, *Being and Nothingness* (Sartre, 1943/1966):

> She is profoundly aware of the desire she inspires, but the desire cruel and naked would humiliate and horrify her. Yet she would find no charm in a respect which would be only respect.... she refuses to apprehend the desire for what it is; she does not even give it a name.... But then suppose he takes her hand....to leave her hand there is to consent in herself to flirt, to engage herself. To withdraw it is to break the troubled and unstable harmony that gives the hour its charm. The aim is to delay the moment of decision.... We know what happens next; the young woman leaves her hand there....

I sometimes work with people who tell me they don't understand their transgressions because they take themselves to have a "strong moral compass." It should be no surprise that the subject is sex. (If not sex, it tends to involve money or violence.) When caught, they act bewildered, maybe panicked, and claim their action was out-of-character, a result of seduction or coercive pressure. Except for those truly coerced, they give lip service to ideals they say guide them while not acknowledging what they'll do when sufficiently tempted. And when the offense is repeated, they act bewildered that it has happened again.

Some claim they don't want out of their marriage, that they love their spouse and family. I believe them. Some feel distress only when caught and tend not to feel much guilt even when sheepishly they say they should. Others become preoccupied, fear loss, and are afraid of destroying their families and hurting their spouses. Often enough, they deny understanding how they got involved in this in the first place.

I'm not talking about the people who betray their vows, want to get away with it, and know damn well if sufficient opportunity occurs that they'll go for it. They are not fooling themselves even if they make excuses or claim innocence. They know they are lying.

Here I am interested in self-deceptive people who don't know they're lying to themselves about their role. With them, I've offered the image of "two sets of books," an accounting of hidden assets. One ledger filled with the ideals they say count heavily, their "moral compass," and the second, usually hidden from inspection, opened only reluctantly but carrying greater weight.

The hidden Domain Two ledger contains intentions that are denied but nonetheless remain in play. These motivations can't be self-acknowledged without unmanageable guilt, anxiety, or shame. With sufficient temptation, these motivations become a loose cannon, not secured by other considerations. All this is made worse when their actual deliberative powers are diminished; "it was the alcohol speaking." Protesting they weren't looking for it, they won't admit their disposition to notice transgressive opportunity and an aptitude to find it. Acting from denied motives, it's unsurprising if the outcome is bungled and unfortunate.

Versions of this common drama are presented as out-of-character by the perpetrator, but given enough time they seem in-character to the audience. Their tragic flaw is the weight they give the erotic and their need to be desired. Feeling desirable is powerfully motivating, especially so when it is compensation for doubt or loss. And are sexual transgressions all that mysterious? For many of us humans, the erotic is compelling, an intrinsic value with enough intensity to temporarily override other concerns. Other primates may feel the same—our Bonobo cousins, for example (Kret et al., 2016).

Why do people do what they do? The simple answer is that circumstances present opportunity. What makes it opportunity is that it is something available and wanted. Of course, the circumstances that provide opportunity have more than a few moving parts. The JD identifies them: we recognize pros and cons—*or we should*. And not all the pros and cons carry the same weight, regardless of what we claim about our character. The actual weights are a central feature of our individual differences, whether acknowledged or not.

Here are some relevant maxims:

Over time, people show their true colors.

If a person engages in an intrinsic social practice, that calls for no further explanation.

A person values some states of affairs over others and acts accordingly.

Here's a maxim that generates through-line descriptions:

If a person finds a given behavior intrinsically significant, they would thereby also want to engage in other behaviors to the extent those behaviors show similarity to the significance of the behavior in question.

DOMAIN THREE: IMPOSSIBLE AND INTOLERABLE CIRCUMSTANCES

Ossorio (2006a, b) developed two models for describing unconscious actions: unthinkability and insistence. I think the Insistence Model fits both Domains Two and Three, while the Unthinkability Model is restricted to Domain Three.

To Ossorio's model of unthinkability and insistence, I've added "the intolerable," a competence concept. **If the situation calls for a person to do something they can't do, they will do something they can do. Or, faced with circumstances that violate a person's conception of themselves and their world, they will see it as something else, and act accordingly.** If unaltered, the unthinkable and intolerable would radically change their perspective of themselves and their world in ways they do not know how to manage. They don't know how to do it without taking it they will be destroying what they take to be the case. To do so, they would be someone they *can't imagine* or *insist they are not*. This, they can't tolerate. To maintain ordinary functioning, they defend themselves from this disruption; something they know how to do in a variety of ways.

Here's Ossorio's framework for the defensive transformation of the unthinkable into thinkable. What is unthinkable does not have a possible place in a person's self-concept and world. What is intolerable does not have a place in their competencies. They can't think it and can't manage it but must do something about it.

It works like this.

THE LOGICAL STRUCTURE OF DEFENSIVE DISTORTION (ADAPTED FROM PETER OSSORIO'S *PERSONS*, 1995)

First, some formal-logical constraints. Used here, "impossible," "unthinkable," and "intolerable" are boundary terms—absolute limits—not degrees of difficulty. Matters of mere difficulty apply to Domain Two, not Domain Three. "Difficult to think" is qualitatively different from "impossible to think." Another reminder: "… the point of constructing a real world is to codify possibilities and non-possibilities of behavior" (Ossorio, 2006a, b, p. 437). **A person requires a world in order to have the possibility of engaging in any behavior at all.** And, **a person requires that the world be one way rather than another in order for him to behave in one way rather than another** (Ossorio, 1998/2012).

The Unthinkability Model

1. The empiricist principle. A person finds out about the real world by observation. The actor has a range of specific concepts and personal characteristics that limit their observations and thoughts about what they observe.
2. For a given observer, the real world is the one that includes them as an observer. For no one is the real world a place where they have no place. This is a formal constraint. For no observer is the real world one that would leave them in an impossible position. A person's vantage point concerns the range of that person's possible observations, descriptions, and critiques.
3. If a situation calls for a person to do something they can't do, they will do something they can do instead.

Conclusions

If, for a given observer, O, the real world is such that it would leave them in an impossible or intolerable position, they will not see it that way. Instead, they will see it as a world that does have a place for them and act accordingly.

A second observer, P, who sees the world differently from O and knows it, can count that difference as O's distortion of reality.

P can account for O's distortion by reference to some real condition that O would find unthinkable (because it would leave O in an impossible or intolerable position) and therefore be unable to behave with respect to it.

Implications

1. Among such unthinkable real conditions would be that O's behavior was a particular behavior or that it had a particular motivation or significance (hence unconscious motivation).
2. Because the derivation above is a statement of logical constraints, the conclusion and the phenomenon are nonvoluntary and automatic (hence one can speak of mental mechanisms).
3. Because the effect of the logical constraints is that the person continues to function more or less effectively when otherwise they would be unable to function, one can speak of the mechanisms as preserving realistic functioning or as ego defensive.
4. The second observer, P, could establish a taxonomy of the kinds of distortions O was engaging in. If the distortions were explained by the operation of mechanisms, the taxonomy could be identical to that for ego defense mechanisms: Denial, repression, projection, reaction formation, etc.

Transference and Resistance Can Be Features of Both the Unthinkability and the Insistence Model

To the extent unconscious transference is relevant, it will show up in the manner the circumstances—usually other actors—are appraised. Ordinarily, transference colors circumstances with a "family resemblance" to earlier relationships. The expectations and concerns that accompanied the earlier relationship are unexamined and applied automatically to the appraisal of the current circumstance. Resistance is an *insistence* that the person's appraisal of their circumstances must be the case.

The Insistence Model

The Insistence Model (Ossorio, 2006a, b) is closely related to the Unthinkability Model with a different emphasis. In the Unthinkability Model the focus is on what doesn't fit because it is unthinkable; in the Insistence Model the emphasis is *on the way things must fit*—the person and their required state of affairs. It can be difficult to tell the two apart. Ossorio described the difference this way: "Clinically there is a simple and observable difference: In the case of Unthinkability you know what my world *doesn't* include, i.e., the unthinkable fact. In the case of Insistence, you know what my world *does* include, i.e., the state of affairs I insist on" (p. 436). In this instance there is not so much an inability to conceptualize an objectionable state of affairs, but an absolute refusal—an intolerance—to consider the possibility of not being a person of a certain sort or living in a world where it is not possible to continue in a particular way. Insistence here implies an absolute refusal to live within a state of affairs, where unthinkability is an inability to conceptualize something as real. Since a person's behavior potential corresponds to their eligibilities to act in the real world, both refusal and inability under possible real-world conditions correspond to restrictions in behavior potential. Accordingly, insistence and unthinkability are hallmarks of psychopathology.

A foundation for the Unthinkability Model and the Insistence Model is a curious status dynamic maxim: **A person will not choose less behavior potential over more**. Ossorio explains this is kindred to another maxim: **if a person has a reason to do something, they will do it unless they have a stronger reason not to**. Here's the relevance to Insistence. In Ossorio's handbook of status dynamic maxims, *Place*, he points out, "If a person's alternatives are formulated in such a way that one represents the achievement of a more valued state than another, the latter will not be chosen over the former. Note that even when the alternatives are formulated in this way, the person may be mistaken about it and thereby choose what he or others will later regard as being of less value. But when I act in error that is not because I have chosen to make a mistake." (p. 52).

Ossorio makes these points to account for the case of the self-sacrificing heroics of the Texas teacher along with those who commit suicide to avoid shame. But what is the sensibility of ending one's life to preserve behavior potential?

In commenting on the Insistence Model, he writes: "Dyed in the wool pragmatists often find it implausible that such 'soft' considerations as 'I have to be a loving mother' can literally result in a different real world for a person. Perhaps the simplest reminder of how powerful such considerations can be, is the fact that death is often enough chosen as an alternative. We noted such cases in connection with the self-concept, e.g., the case of the former politician who committed suicide in preference to living a life of disgrace. One of the alternatives to distortion of reality in a world in which the unthinkable occurs is to choose death instead" (Ossorio, 2006a, b, p. 437).

With certain changed conditions a person might have no potential to be who they insist they must be. In effect, their ability to implement actions of intrinsic and vital significance—essential through-lines—would no longer be possible. Of course, an observer might think they're mistaken. A skilled cognitive behavior therapist might recognize ways they could reformulate their world to allow themselves to continue to be the ways they need to be without a fundamental loss of integrity. The loving mother might find it possible to be both loving and a strict disciplinarian; the disgraced politician might find redemption in combating degradation as a profile in courage. A good slogan for cognitive behavior therapy is another maxim: **the world is subject to reformulation by persons.**

AN EXAMPLE AND SOME CLINICAL IMPLICATIONS

The debater is not interested in getting a good decision; he's interested in winning. So what he does, he defends only his position, and criticizes only the other position. So for him it's a contest, not a negotiation. Negotiations aren't contests.... (*Personality and Personality Theories*, **Ossorio, 1977/2015**).

Negotiation is a key concept in Ossorio's version of clinical psychology and psychotherapy and is a social practice quintessential of persons. Descriptive Psychologists have a particular meaning for the concept. "Negotiations are conducted on at least the provisional presupposition that both individuals have the competence to make the judgment in question, and negotiating is a way of correcting such judgments, not of generating them" (Ossorio, 1969/2010, p. 69). Of course, there's no guarantee of success.

The negotiations I try to practice are not ones of holding cards close to the chest but allowing each player an honest view of what is in play. In Chapter 7, I'll describe a model of psychotherapy that works this way. In short, it involves an honest sharing of perspective so that each participant knows something relevant regarding where the other is coming from. This is akin to the fundamental rule of psychoanalytic "free-association" but not as one sided, since both partners reveal their hand.

Since what can be honestly said resides in Domain One and Domain Two, the three-domain model can be used to sort these matters out. I've conducted couples therapy asking each person to list and share circumstantial factors and their importance; followed by asking each person to indicate their understanding of the other's perspective. As an empathy exercise, I keep them at it until they are able to state the other's position tolerably and accurately.

Where it gets interesting, and maybe therapeutic, is when either of them, or me, doesn't find the information provided adequate to account for what's happening. That's when Domain Two and Domain Three become likely. When the time is right, *when it is safe enough*, the work may hinge on what they were reluctant to address. At times, what they won't talk about is based on a reasonable expectation that their relationship could not survive the disclosure. This limits intimacy but might be all they can manage. That's not for me to judge. When Domain Three issues appear to be wrecking the relationship, my policy is to suggest individual psychotherapy.

I'm going to try to illustrate these themes through a description of supervising a therapist working with a very difficult and potentially hazardous client. The example will focus on a psychological defense, projective identification, chosen because it involves transference and countertransference. Historically, understanding projective identification was important as therapists learned how to use their own emotional responses as guidance. I've also chosen projective identification because it is often presented with the conceptual confusion that attends treating emotions as if they were substances or energies that move about, can be "discharged," or inserted. Chapter 5 will provide a corrective to this view of emotion.

Demystifying Projective Identification

> Projective identification is a process whereby unwanted split-off parts of the self are forced into the object so as to control the object from inside. **Psychoanalytic Terms and Concepts**, Auchincloss & Samberg, ed. 2012

The concept of *projective identification* is often presented in ways that reflect the confusions endemic within clinical theory. These confusions are especially apt to accompany discussions where a disposition or emotion is treated as if it were a substance that can be moved from one place to another rather than an aspect of a relationship. Can people actually *insert* their feelings into others, or is it a matter of conscious and unconscious treatment and response—responses to an action rather than something that literally gets under the skin?

Let's start with an example and try to avoid this confusion.

A supervisee, Jack, told me he found himself feeling hostile and dismissive toward his client, Jill. Their last session had started, like many before, with her criticizing what had gone wrong the previous session, insistently pointing out lapses in his empathy and errors in his therapeutic technique. She said she offered this to be helpful; and reminded him that she had assisted her previous therapists that way. He had come to expect sessions to open like this, annoyed by these critiques, but what especially upset Jack was that she then asked if he was sexually stimulated. At that moment, he described feeling awkward and struggled against an urge to humiliate her. He remained quiet and sat motionless, figuring that was the best he could do.

Jack told me that after Jill's comments he did feel unpleasantly and inappropriately aroused, turned on without being attracted, and that he was angry and felt "held in place," awkwardly self-conscious about his posture. He said it reminded him of his mother forcing him to stand still and silently listen while she berated him. I believe he was honestly surprised by his self-conscious posture and arousal, and after careful inquiry and consideration, suspected he was snarled in a projective identification consistent with both Jill's history and his own.

Jill, a woman in her late 50s, had sat with many therapists over the years. She came to believe all of them found her especially fascinating.

She said her previous female therapist had stalked her and that another male therapist had fallen deeply in love. The available notes confirmed that she had leveled these claims and that they played a role in the termination of each therapy. Unsurprisingly, she said her friendships with women had always ended when her friends turned on her in hostile envy, and with men when they became dangerously attracted. This was consistent with her early family life which included a sexually provocative relationship with her father that informed her combative relations with her mother and sister. The way Jill was valued by her father put her at odds with her sister and mother, a very bad start for Jill's appreciation of sexuality. I think this history is crucial in understanding why projective identification became a defensive strategy that allowed her to experience erotic desire without self-attribution and blame. Her sexuality became a taboo value, a commodity of dangerous worth.

Projection and *projective identification* are forms of *transference* that frequently typify relationships with certain difficult people. In the psychodynamic therapies, it's the job of the therapist to bring transferential expectations into awareness so that they are not unconsciously acted out, or if simply hard to acknowledge, the client cannot claim to be naïve. Projection is a form of transference. A person transfers to another not just an expectation, but also a disposition of their own they find so problematic they defensively disclaim it, while still self-deceptively indulging in the feeling. This is Domain Two and Domain Three stuff. If there is anything mysterious about projection it is the curious inability some people have in recognizing the source of what they feel. It is felt but not owned. This can be the case for both parties. Here is where Domain Two is compromised by Domain Three. Since the problematic circumstance is reluctantly felt but not as something they believe they have their own reasons to feel, it must be coming from somewhere or someone else. What is at stake for the projector is the problematic significance of the disowned feeling. The projector's behavior will correspond to this personal meaning. It might be forbidden to see oneself as its origin, while it is also desired, accepted, scorned, whatever, when felt as coming from someone else. Sex, envy, grandiosity, sadism, and hostility are often involved.

Projective identification is a variation of projection with this additional feature: the projector attempts to manage or control the other person's behavior. The disowned feeling must be controlled and, at times, maintained in the other person. It must be maintained when *in some way* it's crucially valued by the projector such that even if disowned, it cannot be discarded. Sexual pleasure and attraction fit this dynamic well. Whatever enhances self-worth might do. As I mentioned before, feeling desired is powerfully motivating when it is compensation for doubt or loss.

Part of what is uncanny about projective identification is that the target of the projection often reports "inexplicitly" feeling what the projector expects. Jack, you will recall, was unexpectedly and uncomfortably turned on. Projective identification gets its name from the fact that what should be self-identified is instead identified in another person who, in some manner, feels the effects.

Some theories of therapy suggest that if the therapist manages these feeling well, since the projector "identifies" with these feeling but can't own them, the projector can "re-introject" the warded off emotions. There's that funny language of substances projected and introjected—as if they could be absorbed or swallowed. I suspect these theorists would make more sense if they simply noted that people can learn from example. It is useful to be with someone who authentically shows how difficult feelings are manageable.

Projective identification's effects should not be a mystery. Although it has the features of a "spell," it is not an emotional contagion forced inside another's mind as if injecting some voodoo drug. The person "under the influence" may feel something happening to them they did not want to feel. They may claim they are "stuck" with or "struck by" unexpected sensations and emotions. Keep in mind, one way or another, people respond to the way they are treated, and that includes the possibility of acting as a version of what is expected. This is made all the more likely when the issue involves natural responses to a provocation. Raising issues about sexual intent can be sexually evocative. Being treated as having hostile intent will upset some folk.

Consider this unfolding relational sequence between Jill and Jack and how their relationship changed as a result.

Move 1. Jill and Jack's interaction stirs up an unacceptable sexual feeling in Jill that she cannot or will not acknowledge as her own.

Move 2. Jill is aware of this problematic feeling, but finding it *unthinkable* or *intolerable*, attributes it to Jack. He is the only other person present.

Move 3. Since Jill thinks Jack is harboring this problematic feeling toward her, she begins to treat Jack as if he does in her effort to defensively manage the sexual tension.

Move 4. Jack responds to Jill's treatment of him. It matters whether Jill's attribution is consistent with Jack's assessment of his actual feeling toward her. If Jill's projection does not match Jack's conscious intent and feeling, Jack will feel something is askew. In any case, Jack responds in the manner he responds when treated as such. Naturally, this will include elements of his own conscious and unconscious transference and countertransference reactions. In his case, he gets awkwardly and uncomfortably turned on.

Move 5. An ongoing improvisational pattern ensues. Each party responds to the other person's move by incorporating the other's response. And so it continues.

Projective identification can occur with any feeling that creates an intolerably vulnerable position. The mixed emotions normal in complex relationships can be part of this pattern. Feelings of hostility, envy, disgust, or love can be projected when people can't tolerate the ambivalence and engage in what is called *splitting*. In splitting, a person acts as if they can have it only one way or another. If, for example, they are angry with a beloved one, if they can only tolerate affection, they might "split-off" their hostility and resentment and project these feelings onto the person they depend upon and love. Since the toleration of ambivalence is important in sustaining intimate relationships, projective identification is a problematic defense, a minefield for intimacy, producing relations that fluctuate from idealization to devaluation.

Employing projection to clean up an intolerable messiness of a complex relationship can result in exaggerating the desired features. Do any of us really love someone we have no conflicts with? Insisting that's the case sets the stage for an exaggerated benevolence certain to eventually disappoint.

The "splitting" of ambivalence involves a defensive and mistaken attribution. The overall circumstance of Jill being with Jack *is* sexually provocative—initially for her. She *both* desires and fears the stimulation and the implications of being sexually desirable. The stimulation itself is not something she finds unthinkable. She feels it. But it is only tolerable if the initial provocation comes from someone else. She has good reason to insist she is not at fault. She learned this growing up as a target of her father's interest. Her own excitements are now defensively disowned. Sensing her own sexual tension results in her hostile feeling that she's the passive victim of Jack's lust. And as Jack gets stimulated, he fears his own collusion. (And that's why he sought supervision.)

Let's return to the observation that projective identification often produces an unexpected feeling in the targeted person. Remember that projection is the unconscious attribution of one's own qualities onto another person. Since projections can involve problematic characteristics, it is understandable that sexual, aggressive, and competitive urges—common and difficult for many of us—are involved. These feelings are, often enough, an undercurrent in social life but muted by what is more relevant and appropriate to the circumstances. If not brought to the forefront, these feelings might be ignored. Projection brings them to the foreground. After all, when treated sexually, people often get aroused, when treated with hostility or competition, it is no surprise when people react in kind.

People prone to projective identification find targets everywhere. Their vulnerability follows them but does not provide the opportunity to practice better self-control. It's hard to adequately manage what can't be acknowledged. So instead, they try to control the target. The result is problematic for both parties. When both people engage in projection and reactive control, this can produce a *positive feedback loop* of errors compounding errors. Matters get out of hand.

In contrast, if a person's transferences, projections, and identifications are met with a mindful and tolerant response, the relationship may take on features of a *negative feedback loop* and self-correct. The *dampening* of the projection can set the stage for a kinder, gentler set of expectations to emerge. Under these circumstances, over time, the projection might become less necessary. I've seen it happen. This is why therapists understand the importance of reflecting on their own feelings. Fortunately for Jill, Jack knew to sit still and reflect before acting from a state of confusing discomfort.

The engagement between Jill and Jack involved Jill identifying her problematic feelings in the guise of Jack's feelings toward her. It's as if she couldn't recognize herself in the mirror but was transfixed by a reflection that signaled hazard for her. Unfortunately, Jill is unlikely to competently handle what she can't acknowledge as hers to resolve. And this is made more complicated by pressuring Jack.

This is where Jack's job is crucial. Jack's stance toward Jill's projections offers her an opportunity to develop a new perspective. Jack, "in possession" of the projection, is in the position to provide a corrective response that demonstrates that these otherwise difficult feelings can be managed. Jack can engage Jill, empathically and with concern, showing she is valued apart from the commodification of her sexuality.

Jack sought supervision to understand his role in this, wanting to be mindful and not to act it out. His honest attention to what he was feeling and "remembering" (his countertransference), served as a cautionary guide. He showed professional courage describing his reactions with the hope that his natural responses wouldn't be condemned. Talking this over helped. He didn't need to rigidly hold himself in place, nor did he need to discredit or ignore the erotic stimulation. Instead, he needed to be careful and caring in the sessions that followed. He was. Mostly.

Interpretation, Redescription, and a Version of Cognitive Behavior Therapy

Therapeutic redescription is a basic tool in cognitive behavior therapy (CBT). CBT practitioners directly address a person's Knowledge by redescribing the problematic elements appraised in a person's circumstances. The therapeutic redescription provides an alternative image, a thought, that opens up behavior potential. They require their clients to practice with the redescription in various evocative circumstances to make it second nature. This addresses Knowledge and Competence. Practice in varied circumstances verifies the utility of the alternative in place of the old.

When this works, it changes the client's perspective and range of appraisals. Motivations not available with the problematic perspective become possible with the new one.

For example, a depressed client said she felt hopeless and dead inside, and that nothing could change. I asked her to carefully describe exactly how the "deadness" felt. She told me it was like a cold pain, something frozen. I asked if she could imagine that what she took to be dead was instead something very still, cold, and cramped. Cold and cramped because it had been so inactive. She humored me, and said she'd try. As an exercise I asked whenever she felt the deadness to imagine she was feeling painfully still from not moving. My reasoning was that something dead cannot change but something still might. She kept a log of her practice and rearranged the image to better fit her sensations. With practice, she began to feel less hopeless. Things started to move for her.

Therapeutic redescription presents an alternative that fits a client's self-concept, world view, and circumstance. It offers an alternative take on the circumstances, acceptable to accommodate, that opens up options and expands behavior potential. Interpretation is different. Interpretation, as I use the concept, challenges defended perspectives, and that carries a host of dilemmas. Truth be told, most of the time, my work involves more redescription than interpretation. Interpretation is undertaken when Domain Three is the quarry.

ON THE INTERPRETATION OF UNCONSCIOUS ACTION AND SELF-DECEPTION

The interpretation of unconscious activity resembles the dilemmas of gathering and presenting evidence and building a case for judge and jury. Judges and juries should be interested in accountability, bias, and the reliability and significance of evidence—so should the clinician. Unlike a lawyer in court, however, the therapist is not paid to win, convince, or persuade. The job is to expand behavior potential largely through negotiation of perspective.

Therapeutic interpretation is offered in a negotiation toward a shared understanding. This includes accepting disagreement. Disagreement is a reasonable feature of a working alliance. Respecting disagreement serves the potential of revisiting the issue later. Respect can be shown by acknowledging the fundamental inherent uncertainty that comes with interpreting Domain Three content.

Respectfully accepting uncertainty and reasonable disagreement is useful for therapists to model. If reasonable disagreement cannot be tolerated, or if the perspective of one participant violates the fundamental values of the other, therapeutic negotiation will probably not work. This is the territory of the Degradation Ceremonies discussed in Chapter 7. What I am calling psychotherapy is necessarily conducted, I to Thou. Speaking strictly for me, with people I can't tolerate—those I believe cannot and should not be one of us—my impulse is not to show them the light but instead the door. Perhaps you're more generous.

Here is some logic and some dilemmas that come with attempting to interpret or construct Domain Three content, along with the policies I try to follow.

1. Always keep in mind that **people take it that things are as they seem unless they have sufficient reason to think otherwise**.
2. If I say you are acting unconsciously and are self-deceiving, I am saying things are not as they seem to you, that you are distorting or misreading circumstances, or that your reasons for acting are different from what you claim. At this point, we aren't on the same page.
3. Clinicians are in a position to observe, describe, and critique behavior. The purpose of making "the unconscious, conscious" is to identify unconsciously engaged circumstances that impede adequate AOC functioning. Evidence of distortions might be found in transferences observed in the therapist–client relationship. The interpretation of transference is supported by showing that the problematic or distorted manner the therapist has appraised also shows up in other important relationships.
4. It is the therapist's job to build a case that "things are not as they seem" by assembling evidence. (But not as the prosecution where what you say can and will be used against you.) Therapeutically, this might be done in steps: initially, by demonstrating an empathic understanding of the client's current perspective before providing tolerable evidence that supports the therapist's alternative. Further evidence can be gathered showing the client's personal history and current circumstances make their expectations understandable and reasonable both then and now. "Having been treated that way back then, it's no surprise you expect and protect yourself from that sort of treatment now." Further it's a good idea to acknowledge—admit—that something in the current circumstance actually, understandably evokes that expectation. "My being late today and acting distracted when you really needed to be heard, understandably…"
5. To interpret an action as self-deceiving potentially begins an argument subject to all the problems of polemics, authority, and persuasion. A good case can be rejected; a bad case accepted. Therapist interpreters should accept that their clients have defensive reasons to protect themselves. The interpretation of self-deception that targets a pattern of disowned significance—a through-line—is especially trying and inherently contentious. In attempting to establish that a long-standing pattern of significant action has been compromised

by disowned, unconscious motives, a through-line interpretation, the client's character is being questioned. This should be done empathically, gradually building the case. Humans acquire a sense of themselves slowly. The maturation of character takes a great deal of time. This should be respected and is why the classic advice is that interpretations are best offered when the client is close to realizing it anyway. Therapists are paid to be close more than clever. (But they need to be smart enough to appreciate the scope of their client's world (Yermish, 2010).) Attempts to radically change a person's view of themselves and their worlds tend to be traumatic and discrediting. People have to be in a position to accept and effectively use an interpretation. This competence requires practice. Baby steps.

6. The expert status of clinicians can create the illusion that the evidence they gather points to truth rather than possibility. Authentic expert status requires an appreciation of the uncertainty of the evidence. What the therapist in good faith believes is happening may not be what is happening. Uncertainty should be acknowledged.

7. Psychological clinicians should be experts at acknowledging ambiguity and uncertainty; practitioners of possibility rather than truths. Insistence on the part of either therapist or client can be a sign of unconscious defense. The reasonable therapist is careful not to insist on the validity or necessity of any interpretation they provide. The therapist provides a model of noninsistent inquiry. Interpretations are offerings of an alternative, not a truth writ in stone.

8. Before making the case to change or expand perspective, therapists should wonder, "should the case even be made?" what does a change in perspective entail? Is the gain worth the loss?

Relationships, the Relationship Formula, and Emotional Competence

"*...when I was in college, I had a psychology professor who gave a lecture on the nature of human communication. He considered himself an Ossorian, if that means anything to you. He maintained that most promises between people in relationships aren't verbal. His thesis was that promises in relationships, intimate or casual, are often not spoken.*

He believed that the simple act of behaving in relationships—by behaving, he meant being, acting—constitutes a specific promise to the other person. How we behave in a certain situation in a relationship becomes an unspoken commitment to the other person to—I want to say this part exactly right—to act in a similar way....in similar circumstances....in the future." *She took a deep breath before she added, "Unless."*

I was intrigued. "Please go on."

Amanda explained that the unless part was what captivated her. She said that her professor presented it as the most powerful of communication qualifiers, because it was never predefined. It was a wild card. The unless could and did change with each new nonverbal commitment between the people in the relationship. I waited for her to ask me what I thought of the hypothesis. She didn't." **(Stephen White, Line of Fire)**

In this chapter, I'll present Ossorio's **Relationship** and **Relationship Change Formulas** and apply them to emotional behavior. Derived from the Intentional Action parameter's, "unless clauses"—Amanda remembered exactly right—are the qualifying wild cards in Ossorio's formulas. Using the IA parameters, we'll look at emotion as a behavior that expresses a particular relationship—a circumstance the actor appraises and immediately addresses. With that and the Actor-Observer-Critic model

131

of self-regulation, I'm going to develop some ideas about emotional competence.

WHAT ARE RELATIONSHIPS?

Relationships connect something to something else. Relationships have rules and formal operations or they are behavior potentials that govern the expression of behavior. Our relationships to persons and the other elements of the world provides opportunities and reasons to act. The action expresses the relationship.

We have formal and informal ways of considering relationships. Let's start formally with some maxims:

> **A person's possibilities of behavior with respect to any element in their world depends on their relationship(s) to that element.**
>
> **A person's status or place in the world corresponds to their relationship to all the objects, processes, events, and states of affairs that constitute that world.**
>
> **Since relationships confer behavior potential, a person requires that world to be one way or another for them to behave one way rather than another.**

Two dilemmas exist here. Let's use the relation of friends as an example. Even within the limits of a *named* relationship, these maxims allow infinite expression. The manifestations of friendship are endless, but clearly not every act between friends is an expression of friendship. What counts and what doesn't? How do we tell? Try defining friendship, and you'll quickly see the value of Paradigm Case Formulations (PCFs) to sort out whether someone is a friend, is acting as a friend, or is even being friendly. Here's some good news: the Descriptive community has empirically vindicated PCFs of friends and lovers. I'll show them later in this chapter.

Naming is one dilemma—establishing relationship terms that adequately group social practices through shared significance. PCFs are especially helpful when reasonable disagreement about examples is expected. *Place* is the other dilemma—a person's place in their circumstances—their full set of relationships there—carries enormous possibility. Aside from some menus we've fretted over, most of us aren't overwhelmed by this vastness. We value some things over others; some relations stand out. The Judgment Diagram's reconstruction of a person's perspective on their circumstances covered this.

A community and culture's languages—a central Person Concept component—involve explicitly named and ready-to-utter concepts for the lion's share of their social practices with the possibility to generate more as needed. These words and their grammars provide potentially full descriptive access to the subtle, nuanced relationships we enact. (So we've plenty to say about relationships. I'll try not to wear out my welcome by narrowing this narrative to the topics I announced above.)

We can conceptually identify relationships with rules, definitions, or paradigm case formulations. This may have the precision of mathematical and logical relationships or the fuzziness of family resemblance terms, where Paradigm Case Formulations establish negotiable boundaries. Understanding the relationships that mark something as added or subtracted require little more than knowing how to add and subtract. Straightforward, well-defined rules cover this. We know what to expect and how to judge if I tell you I am adding $1 + 1$. But if I tell you I love mathematics, that sort of relationship carries room for disagreement of how math-lovers behave. Sometimes things go as expected, sometimes not.

Let's look at an ordinary social relationship. If I say Pedro is angry with his beloved friend Mike, then without any other detail you have a description that identifies an operating status dynamic. You're in position to appraise whether I'm right about something significant about Pedro's and Mike's interactions: they are friends, they love each other, and that Pedro is now angry with Mike. Since I've told you that Mike is Pedro's beloved friend, you'd expect it to be mutual, but it might be one-sided—and that Pedro is not always hostile toward Mike. If he were, he wouldn't qualify as a friend. Well, *unless* there are other factors in play. "Beloved," "friend," and "angry" identify relationships. Friend and beloved carry a set of expected standing conditions. We'd expect Pedro and Mike have a history that established their loving friendship. The attribution of anger connotes that Mike has provoked Pedro, and the provocation explains Pedro's current hostility. And since Pedro is angry with an important friend, you'd expect him to get over it and not express hostility in ways that destroy the friendship. All this is reasonable.

With time, it might turn out differently. Relationships change. What if Pedro doesn't get over it?

The Judgment Diagram provided a way to reconstruct the motivating perspectives an actor applied in a set of circumstances. It illustrated how the action made sense to the actor. The Relationship Formula gives us another way.

The Relationship Formula employs Intentional Action parameters to describe how an actor behaves as expected *or not*. The formula's "or not" exceptions are found in "unless clauses" that correspond to the parameters of an Agency Description—Wants, Knows, Knows How, Performs, and Achieves. The "unless clauses" indicate how the agent's personal characteristics and performance led to the expected or unexpected result.

The Relationship Formula is a preempirical rule-following device tailored for people engaged in intentional action. When applied empirically, it remains subject to the dilemmas of how actors and their observers might see circumstances differently. The unless clauses are logical constraints and are reminders of possible actor and observer differences.

THE RELATIONSHIP FORMULA

If   X has a given relationship, R, to P.
Then   The behavior of X in respect to P will express P.
Unless:

1. X is acting on another relationship that takes priority.
   This refers to differences between the values of the Want and Know parameters. The actor may be concerned with an entirely different relationship not considered by the observer. The actor's hedonic, prudent, aesthetic, or ethical perspective could be different from the observer's expectations about what is relevant in the circumstances. Any given relationship can be one of many that matter to X.
2. X doesn't recognize the relationship for what it is.
   This refers to the Know parameter and is the observer's construct. X sees it one way, the observer sees it differently *and objectively*, in that the observer's construct is validated by X acting ineffectively toward P.
3. X is unable to act in ways that express that relationship.
   This refers to the Know How parameter. A relevant maxim here being: **if one lacks the relevant competence to act on the relationship, one will do something else instead.**
4. X mistakenly believes their behavior reflected that relationship.
   This refers to the Know parameter regarding self-knowledge and Cognizant Action. Here a relevant maxim is: **a person acquires knowledge of the world by observation and thought**. X's Knowledge wasn't adequate, but X thought it was.
5. X miscalculates or the behavior miscarries. This refers to the Performance or Achievement parameter. A maxim for this being: **behavior goes right if it doesn't go wrong in one of the ways it can go wrong** (Adapted from Ossorio, 2006a, b).

What follows is an example that will introduce issues relevant to emotional behavior.

You and I are in a room. I'm a lion tamer, and you're not. Unexpectedly, a lion enters the room. You jump out the window and make your escape. But I'm a lion tamer. I reach for a whip and chair, and with authority I roar, "Back, Simba, back!"

So, I'm X; the lion's P; and the relationship, R, involves—as you'd expect—my appraisal of the danger relative to my taming skills. The expected competent action is attempting to control the lion to manage the danger. I may eventually jump out the window, but I have choices you do not.

Now imagine the same situation, but I'm a novice lion tamer wanting to run away with the circus. Well, mostly I want to hang out with circus folk and take photos of my adventures to impress people back home. I think I'm more of a lion tamer than I am, but I have the whip and some really fancy boots. Let's take it I'm not all that self-aware of my limitations. What happens or could happen when an unexpected lion enters the room?

You jump out the window and make your escape. But I'm a lion tamer. I reach for a whip and chair, and with authority I roar, "Back, Simba, back!" *Unless* …

1. … *I am acting on another relationship that takes priority.*
   When the lion enters my room, I want an impressive selfie for friends back home, so I grab my phone before taking up the chair and whip.
2. … *I don't recognize the relationship for what it is.*
   When lion enters the room, I don't recognize the prudential implications. Thinking, "Danger? Huh!" I hum "born free," open the window, and point the lion to the great outdoors. Turns out the lion was not looking for an ally relationship.
3. … *I am unable to act in ways that express the relationship.*
   Actually, being a wannabee lion tamer, I suddenly recognize I'm not up to the challenge, I stop humming and I panic and freeze.
4. … *I mistakenly believe that my behavior is an expression of R.*
   I shout "Back, Simba, back! Also, look at my fancy boots!" Really? That's what I think it takes to tame a lion?
5. … *X miscalculates, or the behavior miscarries.*
   When the lion roars and knocks away the whip and chair. I jump for the window. Do I make it? Maybe yes, maybe no. (For completeness on Unless #5, imagine what you and I took to be a lion was actually a kitten. That's a different kind of miscalculation/miscarry.)

THE RELATIONSHIP CHANGE FORMULA

If   X has a given relationship, R, to P.
And   The behavior of X with respect to P violates R, and the behavior of X with respect to P is an expression of another relationship, R1, which is incompatible with R.
Then   The relationship changes from being R to being R1 (Adapted from Ossorio, 2006a, b).

Relationships change. Two maxims are especially salient. The first is a straight forward tautology: **if a person has a given relationship to something, they continue to have it until or unless it changes**. The second, **relationships follow behavior**, is the reminder that whatever behavior occurs, its potential was already there; but if it expresses a different relational possibility, it potentially establishes a different social practice. A friend betrayed becomes an enemy.

How do we account for a change in relationship? Here are a few more maxims: **if a person has a given relationship, and their behavior is an expression of it, that calls for no explanation; but if their behavior violates that relationship, that does call for an explanation.** Similarly, **if a person's relationships or personal characteristics change, that calls for an explanation.**

In Chapter 4's explication of projective identification, we saw Jack and Jill's relationship change as Jill interpreted Jack's empathetic attention as sexual interest and began to treat him accordingly. In the intimate and private environment of psychotherapy, transferential misattribution of a psychotherapist's careful and caring attention as seductive, sexual, exclusive, parental, etc., is a regularly expected opportunity and hazard. For the self-aware therapist, these misattributions provide an opportunity to explore the implications of treating R as R1, for better or for worse. The hazard is obvious: transferences, and countertransferences are fertile ground for a problematic relationship change when one or both parties are unaware of this kind of relationship change.

Perhaps the most useful advice I try with people who want to change a relationship for the better is *treat the other person the way you would if the relationship were already better*. In high conflict couples, this often sounds like I am suggesting a sort of unilateral disarmament. I am. I explain that implementing the Relationship Change Formula takes time. There is no guarantee except that the relationship will change *in some way* in response to the deliberate effort to act outside the existing problematic relationship. I also remind them that no one ever becomes someone else, but a better treatment might bring out a better version of each person. When this advice is applied to a valued relationship, it is predicated on what was valued in the first place is now threatened in the relationship's current, troubled form. In couple's therapy, this can be a contract for each to try to act in ways the other wants, and for the other to acknowledge successful attempts. I'm a fan of the "operant" value of reinforcing desired change by explicitly showing appreciation of the desired behavior. And then to practice, keeping score like a batting average—not expecting perfection but moving a dismal 0.190 to a Hall of Fame 0.400.

The Relationship Change Formula supports the good advice to treat others, when appropriate, as you'd have them treat you; or as Milton Berle said, "Be nice to the people you meet on your way up—you'll meet them again on your way down."

EMOTIONAL BEHAVIOR

Ossorio (1977/2015, 2006a, b) describes emotional behavior as an intentional action—a more or less immediate, nondeliberated response to something the actor takes as real. Others in the Descriptive community, notably Raymond Bergner (1983, 2003), have contributed to this view of *emotion as action*. But before I elaborate on their formulations, I want us on the same page about the words we use.

Emotion terms cover an irregular conceptual terrain that needs sorting out. For example, we have the overlapping ways psychologists use the words "affect" and "emotion." For the sake of clarity, let's see if it helps to separate *emotion* from *affect*. Let's use *emotion* as an *action term* and restrict *affect* to *visceral sensation*. An affect's emotional significance, if any, will come from the relationship of the actor to the sensation—the actor's appraisal of the sensation.

By *action term* I'm thinking adverbs, as in "she angrily approached the bench," or prepositional modifiers, as in "with fear and trepidation, he lashed out." Emotion terms describe *specific* intentional responses to an appraisal. In contrast, affects are simply Knowledge parameter content that acquire meaning by what they tell the actor is happening. An affect or sensation is subject to diagnosis concerning its motivational significance. Is *that* pain a danger? A result of hostile provocation? Or merely telling us a splinter needs to be removed?

I'm fine exempting the technical locution "flattened affect" as a conventional identification of restricted or absent emotional expression. I think most clinicians share a common understanding here. Of course, it still might confuse blunted sensations with restricted emotional expression, and those are not the same.

Then what counts as emotion? When Ossorio (2006a, b) asked his undergraduates to list basic emotions, nearly everyone listed these four: fear, anger, guilt, and joy. I've tried the same exercise with similar results. Most students also list shame, envy, and jealously; and when asked if anyone objected, no one did. (Although rarely on the initial lists, few opposed including grief and despair.)

Ossorio reported that his classes were evenly split as to whether love and affection are emotions. In my classes, most of my students think they are. Since this is the relationship chapter, we won't ignore love. Bergner and other Descriptive Psychologists have developed paradigmatic formulations for romantic love, as we will see below.

In summarizing his class exercise, Ossorio noted an "almost complete absence of 'family member' terms distinguished primarily in terms of intensity … although fear appeared on essentially all lists, uneasiness, apprehension, dread and terror almost never appeared. Likewise, although anger appeared on almost all lists, irritation, annoyance, hatred, and rage almost never appeared. Nor did bitterness or resentment. None of the latter were objected to. Thus, it appears that the students were using the emotion terms 'fear,' 'anger,' 'guilt,' and 'joy' both as specific emotions and as categories or paradigm cases for groups of related emotions" (p. 211). These "intensities" among related emotions will matter in discussing competent emotional behavior.

Do you recall from Chapter 3 the mess Bergner found when he surveyed psychology textbooks for definitions of behavior? When Ossorio asked his students to define emotion, even with their near complete agreement on the paradigmatic emotions, "… a request for a definition of emotion showed no consensus at all. Definitions referred to a kind of feeling, a kind of experience, a physiological pattern, a psychophysiological pattern, an instinctual response, an irrational episode, a state of mind, and a socio-cultural construction, to name a few. The obvious explanation here should by now be a familiar one: we don't learn about emotions by learning a definition or a theory and then applying it. The students' judgments were far more sensitive and sophisticated than their definitions" (Ossorio, 2006a, b, p. 211). Sound familiar? This was akin to presupposing people need some sort of "theory of mind" to act empathetically.

SHARED AND OBSERVABLE RELATIONS ARE REQUIRED FOR NAMING EMOTIONS (SENSATIONS WON'T DO)

Ossorio used the concept of Intentional Action and the Relationship Formula to explicate emotion. Emotions are recognized by what a person does emotionally, not by how their body feels. Actions speak, "feelings" in themselves don't. Felt states and affects are not enough to distinguish emotions. Nor are facial expressions, frowns, grimaces, smiles, etc., as conventionally informative these performances might be, enough. Gestures, postures, and so on, are simply Performance parameter content and not enough in themselves to identify an emotion. We need an intentional action for this.

Forcing a grin is not enough to make you happy (Wagenmakers et al., 2016). You've got to have something to happily smile about.

Employing Wittgenstein's (1953) arguments against private language, Raymond Bergner (2003) built the case that words that identify emotions cannot depend on sensations for their designation. His thought experiment begins with wanting to buy paint that matches a particular color: Take the paint chip you want to match, go off to the local hardware store, and ask a clerk what it's called. The clerk consults a chart, says it's called "autumn gold," sells you a can, and reassures you that whenever you need more, just ask for "autumn gold." Easy enough. Right?

Bergner explains that this easily shared and verifiable name, "autumn gold," cannot happen with sensations or feelings. "Suppose, for example, that I have a novel feeling or sensation. I decide to name this sensation 'arby'. Now clearly there is no way that I can exhibit this feeling, as I did my paint chip, to other persons and have them report, 'Oh, yes, I have just that same feeling.' There is no way for them to observe my feeling and thus determine if they experience one that matches mine." (p. 473)

At the foundation of their meanings, emotion terms cannot be based on sensations, feelings, affects, or anything else that is not inherently sharable and plausibly verified as the same. Bergner points out the implausibility that *"on the basis of the quality of felt experience alone,* we would ever have linked the often vastly different experiences that we lump together under one emotion term." Also, Ray and I both doubt anyone—brain surgeons included—can get inside anyone's head and feel their sensations. None of us knows how to do the Vulcan mind meld.

Are there sensations we *always* feel when annoyed, irritated, furious, enraged, and hateful? These are all varieties of anger, possible responses to provocation. And what of mixed emotional expressions? Bergner asks if there is a common sensation that identifies *just the anger* "when a newly divorced person experiences anger, sadness, fear, and despair all at the same time" (p. 473). Of course not. It's the relationship—the injurious, provoking relationship that attends divorce—that makes the anger understandable.

What about the possibility of a 1:1 correspondence between a sensation and an emotional response? Do we have empirical grounds for this? Pain and pleasure are good examples of visceral sensations. Pain commonly denotes dangerous or damaging contact and is a reason to avoid. Pleasure ordinarily tells us about accord and wellbeing, motivating contact and continuation; "if it feels good, do it." Pleasure, however, is not always welcome, nor is pain always a source of avoidance and dissatisfaction. Consider for a prototypical pain, a sharp blow to the shin, and for pleasure, an orgasm. Coerced and compulsive behaviors that elicit pleasure might temporally relieve tension, but seldom is that relief satisfying. Pleasure connected to forced, devalued, and degrading practices can elicit anger, fear, resentment, demoralization, shame, and guilt. And pain that attends a challenging but valued goal can be taken as part of the territory, affirmation of progress, a sign of getting closer to achievement. Ever been to a chili festival?

Again, the information we get from sensation is Know parameter content. A sensation's meaning—the significance of feeling aches and pains, throbs and pleasures—is its place in the overall appraisal of the circumstances. It's the person's overall *relationship* to the sensation that counts, emotionally. What is P doing by enduring this pain? He won the Habanero Challenge!

If I've been kicked hard in the shin, and it really smarts, it will throb a while and then bruise. If that happens, and you're down the hall, you'll hear me yell. Knowing my temper, you might come running to intervene. But when you appear, do you witness my first punch, or am I holding my assailant and stroking his hair? It depends. Has my shin been assaulted by my nasty uncle or my sister's frustrated 3-year-old? Let me add another variable. You hear my loud painful scream and come running to celebrate my joy, since—whatever the cause—I've awakened from a coma. Damn it hurts, but I'm awake, and I feel my legs again!

A painful sensation could be a provocation for hostility or a reason to celebrate. Or both. I've attended a few child births. Sensations are grist for the mill. If my odious uncle thinks I am dead to the world and kicks me awake, I might celebrate *and* give him a black eye.

FEAR IN ACTION

Let's start with one of the paradigmatic emotions, fear, and something scary. I am sitting quietly at my desk working on this chapter when a zombie enters my study. As we know, I'm sort of a lion trainer but have no such pretensions when it comes to zombies. I'm terrified and immediately want to escape.

Regardless of what I might report feeling—stomach dropping, heart pounding, nearly breathless—what makes this an example of quintessential emotional behavior is my immediate attempt to escape the zombie without thinking it over. This impulsiveness typifies emotional behavior.

Here's the behavioral logic of emotion and its place in the Relationship Formula: Emotional Behavior involves an appraisal of something taken as real that tautologically involves a corresponding motivation. The motivation is implemented by enacting a behavior responsive to the specific circumstances. And there is a learned tendency to act on the appraisal without deliberation. Let us consider an example.

Fear: A real live zombie enters my study. I recognize I'm in danger and
Danger elicits Escape
(without hesitation, I jump out the window)
Unless

a) *I am acting on another motivation that takes priority.*
   As a man of science, how often will I get a chance to study a zombie? So, I set aside prudence and take notes, and additionally I want to distract it so my wife can escape the apartment.
b) *I don't perceive the danger for what it is.*
   I think my wife is again practicing her audition for *The Walking Dead*, and I'll not give her the satisfaction of acting afraid.
c) *I am unable to engage in any such behavior.*
   I freeze in panic.
d) *I mistakenly think that what I am doing is escaping.*
   Forgetting I'm a man of science, I grab my invisibility cloak.
e) *I miscalculate, or my behavior miscarries.*
   With cloak on and jumping for the window I trip over my cloak's invisible fringe.

Let's try an emotion without hungry corpses. What, essentially, is anger? Is it a particular feeling, a tension or heat in my chest? Sometimes I feel that, sometimes I don't. Is it the tightening of my jaw and the gritting of my teeth before I unleash a torrent of invective? Sometimes, I do exactly that, but sometimes I turn away and relax without second thought, I broadcast my disdain with a gesture of dismissal. What makes any of these an expression of anger? Answer: my show of hostile intent. Notice I added "intent" to the last sentence.

Here's anger and hostility using the Relationship Formula.
Provocation elicits Anger or Hostility
Unless

1. *It is too dangerous, morally wrong, not fitting of one's station, etc., to respond with overt hostility.*
   Ossorio aptly suggested that "anger, like dueling, is for peers." Sometimes an expression of anger affirms the worth of the provocateur as a worthy adversary. Similarly, if a counterattack might acknowledge a provocation as worthy, a disdainful absence of response might do the trick.
2. *The provocation, the insult, is not recognized as provoking, as an insult, as insulting,* etc.
3. *The assailed is not just "fit to be tied," but actually tied.*
4. *Naïve as Br'er Fox, Br'er Rabbit is tossed into the briar patch.* And so on.

Here's a sampling of what the actor discriminates in their circumstances that gives them reasons to act emotionally:

- Fear: Danger elicits escape, unless…
- Anger: Provocation elicits hostility…
- Sorrow: Personal loss elicits grieving…
- Guilt: Wrongdoing elicits penance…
- Shame: Getting caught in transgression elicits humiliation…
- Jealously: Losing a valued possession to another…
- Envy: Unfavorable inequity elicits leveling the differences…

And since it's not always bad news,

- Joy: Good fortune elicits celebration…

I've not listed satisfaction or relief as emotions, although you might. I've left out love. You might notice I've listed more negative emotions than positive ones, and this seems the case across cultures. In the delightfully playful volume, *Book of Human Emotions* (2016), Tiffany Watt Smith catalogs 154 "words from around the world for how we feel." Some cultures name "feelings" that others do not. By my reckoning, only 21% seem positive.

Why so few positives and so many negatives? It seems more useful to identify emotional situations we'd like to immediately fix, change, avoid, and get out of than situations we would like to persist—and our emotion vocabulary reflects this. As long as the good times roll, doing nothing more than remaining present may be why we have few terms for our positive feelings and emotions. But, is there really less to do when things work than when they don't? Or, darkly, does the human condition have more to bemoan and less to celebrate?

WHAT ABOUT LOVE?

Does it make the world go around? Is it all you need? Even if you think all's fair in love and war, and even if you recognize that love doesn't conquer all, for us humans, it makes a central difference in how a person's world is prioritized.

We become very emotional with and about those we love, but it is our intimate I to Thou relationship with them that gives love its meaning—not a specific emotion or sensation. Or so I think, and so does Ray Bergner.

Based on the conceptual and empirical work of Roberts (1982) and Davis and Todd (1982), Bergner (2000) describes a Paradigm Case Formulation of Romantic Love—an ideal love—as involving seven attributes: (1) investment in the well-being of the beloved; (2) appreciation and admiration of their qualities; (3) sexual desire; (4) intimate inclusion in their world; (5) commitment; (6) exclusivity; and (7) an actual understanding of them.

Because it is particular to the beloved, having those seven things in full cannot be replaced. One can love another but that is another unique relationship. Given the vital encompassing place a beloved occupies in a person's world, true love lost is profoundly mourned.

STEPS TOWARD A THEORY OF EMOTIONAL COMPETENCE

Emotionally competent behavior effectively restores or enhances a person's status or place in their world. Incompetent emotional behavior is ineffective at restoring or enhancing one's position. I take issue with contrasting the rational with the emotional. Instead, let's ask if any particular emotional behavior is reasonable and effective and, if it is, that seems pretty rational to me. Is there anything irrational about fearfully escaping a lion? A better question: are there competent and incompetent ways of acting while afraid? And that, I think, boils down to how adequately the circumstances are understood and how skilled the actor behaves without deliberation. How well is knowledge and competence expressed in the moment?

What is an *adequate* understanding of a circumstance? Although the map is not the terrain, an adequate map should be reliably scaled, extensive, and have enough detail to serve navigation; thus by *adequate* I only mean pragmatically reliable. It is the impulsive misunderstanding of circumstances that gives emotions their bad reputation.

Emotionally competent behavior requires effective Actor-Observer-Critic self- and social-regulation. Emotional competence involves adequate self-control and some version of "when in Rome do as the Romans do." Emotional behavior has a community and cultural context involving normative values apart from self-regulation. Hence, two sorts of issues arise: how *effective* is the emotional response at changing or addressing the fear, provocation, good fortune, etc.; and how *appropriate* are the values expressed in the appraisal of what is dangerous, threatening, providing reasons to celebrate, etc.

For example, targeted anger is likely more effective and better evidence of competent self-regulation than is unfocused rage. The same holds for fear versus panic. In my case, when I am provoked or threatened, it occurs in my liberal cosmopolitan community. In my town, we value tolerance and inclusion over resentment and exclusion. When my neighbor backs into my car, it is reasonable for me be angry, but not because of the color of her skin.

Emotional competence is also judged by the appropriate *shelf life* of emotional behaviors and moody states. States, you'll recall are nonpersistent, readily reversible systematic differences in a person's ordinary powers and disposition. By mood, I mean an ongoing disposition to remain or reengage emotionally. Do I know when enough is enough, and can I act that way? Of course, when someone tells me to get over it, I may tell them where to get off.

HOW IS EMOTIONAL COMPETENCE FACILITATED?

A sound conceptualization of emotional behavior should offer hints about the circumstances that facilitate emotional competence. For us, with our long periods of vulnerability and dependency, this raises empirical questions. Not just any way of parenting and growing up will do. (Robot persons might be another matter. They might start out already prepared.)

I teach psychodynamic theory to clinical psychology doctoral students. I use an historical perspective informed by the Person Concept. Psychodynamic theories of development emphasize the fundamental dilemmas that infants and children must navigate. For the early Freudians, the central problem was sexuality and aggression. For later and contemporary theorists, attention shifted to the infant and child's ability to handle the complexity of ambiguous or ambivalent relationships, including their "psycho-sexual" and aggressive aspects. The ambiguities, uncertainties, and complexities of emotional life take center stage. In the later theories, the self-experience of spontaneity, authenticity, empathy, and agency are particularly honored. Consistent with these themes is an interest in how values and ambitions are acquired and the conditions that impede or impel their expression. Applying the intentional action formulation of emotion, I'll show how it organizes these issues. I'm interested in the pragmatics of self-experience—its significance in observable actions.

A few more definitions: self-experience in psychodynamic theories often concerns the continuity or discontinuity, the coherence or "fragmentation" of people's relationships to themselves and their world, *given their self-concept* (e.g., Klein, 1976). Their self-concept is a summary formulation of their self-knowledge of their personal characteristics along with their sense of agency and authenticity.

Psychodynamic theories describe development and maturation in reference to patterns—through-lines—with characteristic, "average expected" outcomes. For children with ordinary or exceptional capacities, parenting and environment are relevant in all the theories. Some of the theories are on firmer empirical ground than others. Attachment theories, in particular, seem especially suited for empirical study and have garnered reasonable vindication (e.g., Fonagy et al., 2008).

What do the better vindicated theories suggest about what helps or harms becoming emotionally effective, stable, and empathic; an adult able to engage spontaneously and authentically? From my clinical experience and reading of the literature, the chart below shows major developmental achievements that the *good enough parent* in the *good enough environment* fosters in the *average expected child* in contrast to the results of deprivation and trauma. It employs canonical terms found in the literature descriptive of the "good-enough parent."

In summary, the "good-enough" parent provides adequate empathy and appropriate emotional attunement. They respond, contain, discipline, and celebrate with adequate self-refection. They also know when to let their child "just be." The contrast—the not good enough—is a deficiency of these parental qualities. All this supposes the "average expected" infant and child.

The chart is organized around whether a set of parental and environmental features *foster* or *elicit* an ongoing pattern of life. I use this sort of language to avoid implying causality. There are no guarantees, just understandable patterns where we are not surprised by the result. Whether Officer Krumke buys "I'm depraved on account I'm deprived!", it's a mitigating excuse. The chart is not a deterministic model. It only indicates patterns that make sense in retrospect. To paraphrase Adam Phillips (2014) summary of Freud's theory of development, *childhood informs everything but predicts nothing.*

EMOTIONAL COMPETENCE AND RELATED THEMES

Major issues:

- Toleration of ambivalence or ambiguity
- Toleration of separation and connection with significant others
- Ability to assert, behave authentically, spontaneously, and creatively
- Empathic ability (Fig. 5.1)

Good enough parental attunement, empathy, holding, mirroring, reflexive function, containment	Vs	Deprivation and trauma
Fosters		**Elicits**
Tolerable anxiety		Panic
Toleration of conflict, uncertainty, and ambivalence		Poor toleration of affect, conflict, uncertainty and ambivalence defended through repression, dissociative splitting, and projection
Secure attachments. Toleration of being alone		Insecure attachments, abandonment fears
Accurate empathic appreciation of others. Capacity for I-Thou relations		I-It relations and indifference.
	Emotionally	
Provocation evokes anger	More than	Rage or inhibition
Danger evokes fear		Panic
Loss evokes loneliness and sadness		Aloneness, emptiness, and depression.
One's wrongdoing and transgression evoke guilt and reparation		Debilitating shame, humiliation or attacks on the critical witness (self or other)
Others' success evokes competition, assertion, or admiration		Envy or jealously
Others' loss evokes sympathy		Schadenfreude or gloating

FIG. 5.1   Emotional competence and related themes.

ANXIETY, DEPRESSION, AND OVERWHELMING SENSATION

> Imagine that one of the drug companies has invented a new wonder drug called the Happy Pill. It comes in the form of a small white pill that looks like an aspirin. Its specific value is that it removes anxiety and does it in a flash—just put it on your tongue and bang! Just like that, no anxiety! It has 100% effectiveness and no side effects.
>
> Now imagine that when the lion walks in the room I happen to have a Happy Pill sitting on the seat next to me. Would I be well advised to solve my anxiety problem by taking the Happy Pill? After all, it's quicker, easier, and more certain in its results. Would you expect me, as a normal person, to do that? (*Peter Ossorio, 2006a, b,* p. 319).

I cannot clearly differentiate anxiety as an affect or emotion. For me, it's a disquieting ill at ease sensation of excitement or arousal. If it is especially bad or prolonged, I experience dread and a sense of doom. If overwhelmed, panic. There is always something visceral, something gut felt and clammy. I know others describe something similar. Some characterize anxiety as fear without knowing what to address or without knowing how to change the circumstance for the better. Strung out long enough, this uncertainty and expected absence of competence and knowledge can create the helplessness of depression. Depression is a state of self in a world seen to severely restrict the potential to behave according to one's core intrinsic values; it is living in a world bereft of the important meanings that weave one's most valued through-lines.

What can we do with this conception of anxiety and depression? Anxiety involves problems appraising one's circumstances, an undermined sense of agency. The Agency Description's parameters Want, Know, Know How, Perform, and Achieve are the relevant targets of diagnosis and treatment. Consider:

1. An uncertain or unidentified threat (Knowledge) or a lack of competence (Know How) undermines expectation of an effective Performance and the wanted Achievement.
2. Anxiety as a sensation of arousal or excitement (rapid and uneven heartbeat and respiration, light headedness, whatever) can become the circumstance (K) appraised as dangerous.

The excitement and arousal of the sensation itself can be debilitating. Affects can be overwhelming if they disable or make it personally impossible to attend to anything else. Panic, agonizing pain, and ecstatic pleasure tend to crowd out everything else. (If you are prone to freezing up in panic—to keep loose—taking that daily "happy pill" might be helpful *before* the lion arrives. Or maybe after escaping, if you still can't settle yourself down. Also, keep away from the circus.)

Sensations and worry without a clear threat in the circumstance—"I don't know why I am so worried, no one is threatening me"—can arrive "out of nowhere," a creative spontaneity that does not require a prior trigger (Ossorio, 1969/2010). People generate thoughts from their own concerns given their personal characteristics. And then self-deceive.

The vulnerability that attends Domain Two and Domain Three in the Judgment Diagram is a likely suspect for "out of nowhere" anxiety. This is the stuff we find threatening, try to avoid, but not always successfully. Domain Two and Domain Three circumstances, self-generated or otherwise encountered, can creep in and haunt.

Catastrophic cultural and personal loss and upheaval can disrupt one's sense of what's valued in the world; or leave a place so dangerous that one doesn't know how to manage it; or that there is enough left worth navigating. These conditions are ripe for "generalized anxiety disorders" since threatening uncertainty is everywhere. And with enough demoralizing helplessness, there is listless depression. Anxiety signals that something needs attending, and if the repeated appraisal is, "Why bother?", the actor is depressed.

Even in what is otherwise appraised as a good enough world, one's own body can provide frightening uncertainty. An undiagnosed mitral valve prolapse, a mysterious heart flutter, a sudden bruise or lump, a shortness of breath, all can be appraised as a danger.

The common co-occurrence of depression and anxiety makes sense, as do the common factors in treatment. Medication and self-soothing and calming practices might help address the troubling sensation of physiological or morphological dysfunction. Training, education, reassurance, redescription, and interpretation can change the conception of threat, and expand self-awareness and choice. All these techniques undo the "helpless" features of anxiety and associated depression. When a person is disabled by anxiety and depression, anything that helps restore or enhance deliberate action in the Actor-Observer-Critic feedback is welcome.

Some personal and social losses cannot be restored or resolved. Some leave just too big a hole to fill. If the loss and upheaval is cultural or world encompassing, positive change requires political and community action.

Verbal Behavior, Language, and Linguistic Self-Regulation

*Other illusions come from various quarters to attach themselves to the special one spoken of here. Thought, language, now appear to us as the unique correlate, picture, of the world. These concepts: proposition, language, thought, world, stand in line one behind the other, each equivalent to each. (But what are these words to be used for now? The language-game in which they are to be applied is missing.) **(PI 96)**.*
Essence** is expressed in grammar. **(PI 371) Wittgenstein

Verbal behavior—the deliberate use of language to communicate—is one of the five interdependent components of the Person Concept. People talk. We speak to each other, *and because we are able to do that*, we also talk to ourselves. "Because we are able to do that" is a nod to Wittgenstein's arguments against private language, and his pragmatic stance of meanings tied to use.

Language gives us an edge. The capacity to become competent language users is our superpower. We can deliberately consider and share real and imaginary pasts, presents, and futures. We can explicitly indicate and describe the paths to take, the ones to avoid, how to travel them, and why. We can compare and contrast. Language-enhanced Actor–Observer–Critic feedback makes considering and negotiating consequences easier. "Use your words" may not quell a toddler's tantrum, but I expect it to work for you.

Language in all its forms—ordinary, technical, poetical, mathematical, and so on—provides a fully capable medium for transmitting, preserving, changing, and creating community and culture. Through sound, image, gesture, or other means—our locutions—we can symbolize all the conceptual distinctions we use. This opens up the world. We can get at everything if we know how to play the "language game" with the right concepts and grammar. Language games are ruled by grammar, an *infinitely* generative grammar that coordinates the concepts and provides access to *all* our actions with *all* the objects, processes, events, and states of affairs that constitute our worlds.

149

OSSORIO'S FORMULATION

Verbal Behavior = < Concepts, Locutions, Behavior (IA) as a Social Practice) >

Ossorio's parametric analysis of verbal behavior explicitly ties the meaning of language to its use by persons, interlocking their concepts, locutions, and behaviors. Concepts are the distinctions that have informational value: the distinctions that make a difference in behavior. Concepts are the "operating tools" for our varied and indeterminate actions. They vary the way tools in a tool chest vary, created and employed for different jobs. *Our concepts correspond, one way or another, to all the distinctions we use.* As we become sensitive to new distinctions we want to tell others, we give them names. Locutions are the performances in speech and other symbolic forms that represent the Concepts we use in the Social Practices that constitute our Behavior. Behavior is another Intentional Action (IA), not *per se* verbal, where the Locution's concept is employed in a social practice. The meaning of the Locution rests on the Concepts acted on in this non-verbal social practice.[1]

Verbal behavior is an intentional action. Specifically, it is a deliberate behavior where some of the Know parameter content is the verbalized Concept and the Performance parameter is a Locution that stands in 1:1 correspondence to the Concept. Traditionally, it's the performed utterance, the locution, that is identified as the "verbal behavior."

What about the other IA parameters? As an IA, all the intentional action parameters are more or less relevant for a particular verbal behavior's meaning. For example, the Identity and Personal Characteristics of the speaker and author don't matter much in mathematics or technical formulations where *ad hominem* critique is underhand. But in the status dynamics of ordinary life—conversations, instructions, orders, complements, insults, and so on—they do. A few paragraphs down, *ad hominem* will be shown as intrinsic to the appraisal of an utterance. There are things said that cannot be adequately appraised without knowing who said it. Take my word for it.

VERBAL BEHAVIOR IS OUR DEFINING SOCIAL PRACTICE AND HOW I EARN MY KEEP

The resemblance of Ossorio's approach to verbal behavior and Wittgenstein's *Philosophical Investigations* will thread through this chapter; another thread are the conversations in psychotherapy. I'll start with my day job.

---

[1]But it might be verbal, such as J.L Austin's (1962) performatives where the saying is the doing as in greeting someone with "hello."

I'm paid to read, write, teach, practice, and supervise psychotherapy— good work that doesn't wear out the knees. Much of it takes place in conversation.

Conversations are deliberate actions between individually different persons. Conversations have a *status dynamic*. When I talk with *you*, it is *in some ways* different than when I am speaking to *her*. Even my use of "talking with" and "speaking to" expresses a significant difference.

Our different places in each other's worlds provide a context for how we judge what is said. Consider: "I'd expect her to say that, but coming from you, it means a lot." Or: "She's in no position to ask that of me." The format of the Judgment Diagram applies: the same words are motivationally different depending on the status of the speaker. The speaker and the speech are appraised features of the actor's circumstances.

There are rules to the status dynamics of verbal behavior. Ossorio, resonating Wittgenstein, approached the social practice of verbal behavior as a *form of life* played like a game. Throughout Ossorio's later writings, he moved between a "game model" and a "dramaturgical model." Games were his preference for collections of social practices; drama for dealing with an individual's historical continuity.

My first extended conversations with Ossorio occurred in his usual out-of-office location— the University of Colorado's Alfred Packer Restaurant & Grill. I asked how to prepare for our meeting. Knowing a little of my interests and background, he suggested that before tackling his *Meanings and Symbolism*, I look at Wittgenstein's *Philosophical Investigations*. There, he told me, I'd find an extended introduction to the *social practice* of playing language games. At our next meeting I came back with these, underlined:

> … the word 'language-game' is used here to emphasize the fact that the speaking of language is part of an activity, or of a form of life. *(PI 23)*
>
> For a large class of cases of the employment of the word 'meaning'—though not for all—this word can be explained in this way: the meaning of a word is its use in the language. *(PI 43)*
>
> "Thought must be something unique." When we say, and mean, that such-and-such is the case, we—and our meaning—do not stop anywhere short of the fact; but we mean: this—is—so. But this paradox (which has the form of a truism) can also be expressed in this way: Thought can be of what is not the case. *(PI 95)*
>
> Other illusions come from various quarters to attach themselves to the special one spoken of here. Thought, language, now appear to us as the unique correlate, picture, of the world. These concepts: proposition, language, thought, world, stand in line one behind the other, each equivalent to each. (But what are these words to be used for now? The language-game in which they are to be applied is missing.) *(PI 96)*

Now let's read some Descriptive maxims I've adapted from Ossorio's *Place*. Note their relevance to the status dynamic of language games.

If Jack and Jill participate in a social practice, the fact that Jack participates in one way rather than another gives Jill a reason to participate correspondingly in one way rather than another.

If Jack and Jill participate in a social practice, Jill may anticipate to some extent Jack's choices among behavioral options on the basis of Jack's personal characteristics and relationships to Jill and others.

Jack may participate in one way rather than another (choose certain options rather than others) as a way of letting Jill know what kind of person Jack is.

For each of these maxims, substitute "speak" and the like, for "participate in a social practice," and you'll see what I'm after.

The status dynamics of speech is paramount in psychotherapy and supervision. The knowledge the participants have of each other frames the significance of what they say and what they hear. As a man deep into middle age, I speak from experience. I have the wear and tear that lends me some authority. Sitting in a well-appointed office at a fashionable address, I talk in ways my students probably shouldn't try.

My students are typically in their twenties. As young adults, they necessarily present themselves differently than I do. Even as they attempt the role of "professional" and "psychologist," they manifest a voice and an authority that differs from mine. What is their credibility, *what can they effectively say* when working with a late middle-aged couple who are coping with disappointments in marriage; struggling with their young adult children; silently questioning whether to remain married? Given age and position, I'm usually granted an expertise, but my students are questioned, "Just how old are you?"

My students watch a videotape of my intervention with this couple. When it's over, the discussion begins. Informed by psychodynamic theory, my students bring up transference; countertransference; role enactments; and the "real relationship." They mention the "intersubjective field" among the participants. They try to notice the nuance of what is consciously and unconsciously, deliberately or automatically, evoked in the participants. They sense the couple has accepted me as a paternal or avuncular peer and are open to my way of engaging. But the point of the exercise is for them to imagine that they are sitting with this unhappy couple. What can they say? How might they act effectively?

If my students work with a similar couple, with people more like their parents than their peers, what are they in a position to do? I remind them *they should know their apparent status—and how that might fit their client's world*. First, I ask them to speak authentically in their own youthful voice trained to understand and help. Youth evokes various things for parents and elders, and *that* transference *might* be in play. Second, some people will not believe they are old enough to be taken seriously. I remind them to wait, time will remedy that.

There are ways to engage that help create a therapeutic alliance even across wide status divides. Simply requesting the client's help in understanding this predicament goes a long way toward being helpful. "Can you help me understand what I need to know?" is both informative and respectful. Asking, "How might I be of service?" works, too. This lets the client frame the engagement. It can reveal something about how the client sees the therapist's skills *and eligibilities*. It is always a good idea to know on what footing things start.

Students should be mindful of their personal characteristics and the place those might have in their client's lives. Therapy involves an improvisational assimilation and accommodation of everyone's actions. How well therapy works depends largely on how well the therapist is cast for the therapeutic drama.

WHAT IS THE FUNCTION OF LANGUAGE AND THE STATUS OF THE SPEAKER?

Verbal behavior involves at least these four functions: when speaking, we *identify*, *describe*, *evoke*, and *enjoin* and *instruct*. Those are language games. Let's play some with the taste of an apple, a tart one you've never sampled that happens to be the color "autumn gold." Fortunately, you recognize that color, and know about apples, and how to eat them. We're not starting from scratch. You've just never had this variety. So, if asked to go to the fruit stall and pick one, you know how to tell apples from pears. But which one? I want a big round Autumn Gold. Since you know how to walk, talk, pick, and choose, you grab one you think will do. OK, so we've now got our apple. How do they taste? You've never had one, but we both know you like your apples tart. As do I, a fact we shared at an earlier tasting when we smacked our lips at the "tartness" of good, firm Granny Smiths. But Autumn Golds are different. How so? Take a bite. That's how they taste! Tomorrow, when I ask you to buy another, you might remember the Autumn Gold's flavor by simply hearing the name. The language games here are the social practices of using language to identify, describe, evoke, and instruct and enjoin.

What we identify points out the subject for attention. This is notable because it shows what we think matters. The way we describe provides evidence of our intelligence, sensitivity, nuance, and perspective, and what we believe our listener can comprehend. As such, our ways of speaking— and listening, for that matter—are evidence of our empathy. *All parties in conversation are status assigners.* We assign ourselves a status when we speak and listen. Our place can affirm or degrade, validate or dismiss.

The effect of that status follows from what others take us to authentically represent. "You're not the boss of me," unless you are. "Who are you to pass judgment?" Unless, of course, I am made to succumb to your authority, "your honor." What we evoke is a matter of what the message and messenger bring to mind. The value of our instruction and power to enjoin will follow from whether we are viewed as a trusted source or an authority.

(I suspect this is partly why Ossorio had me read Wittgenstein as an orientation to Descriptive Psychology. He asked other students to look at other texts. He understood I knew Wittgenstein's significance, but correctly figured that I had not heard Ossorio's name until recently.)

With all this in mind, I ask my students to consider the significance of their initial presentation to their clients. I ask how their age, race, ethnicity, speech, gender, attractiveness, manner of dress, and social class might be relevant to how they are heard, understood, and appreciated. This is often difficult. If done awkwardly, it can feel like stereotyping; it can be hurtful. It can be dismissed or resented as abusive, intrusive, and politically incorrect. But many know all too well that stereotyping fills in the blanks before more adequate understanding is achieved. Their work does not begin on a level playing field, is not scored on a blank slate.

In my seminars on psychotherapy and supervision, how we are seen in each other's eyes is center stage. As they do their jobs, I want students to have these questions close at hand:

1. What do I evoke in different people and what do they evoke in me? What versions of this are being played out now?
2. Given my *obvious* personal characteristics, what is a client likely to think I am eligible to do and able to accomplish? If I say something, what will be taken seriously and what will be dismissed?
3. Given my less obvious personal characteristics, what will take *more* time and effort to demonstrate or establish?
4. What about myself *do I need or appear to need* validated.
5. Am I focused on issues that reveal more about me than about my client? Do I appear argumentative, competitive, coercive; or appear compliant, seductive, or something else?
6. What am I unable to hear or address? Does my defensiveness or intolerance look like dismissal, avoidance, or disgust? Is my defensiveness or intolerance degrading and invalidating?
7. Have you *said or done some things that can never be forgotten, forgiven, or undone?* It only needs to happen once; such actions will guide further encounters. Expressions of desire and disgust are especially hard to undo.

8. Are the circumstances of the work validating or degrading? Is my client a volunteer, more or less on equal footing with me; or is participation mandated, forced, or coerced? Volunteers decide if it is worthwhile to continue and can fire their therapists and supervisors. Coerced relationships invite resistance, insolence, and resigned compliance.

With that said, let's turn to the more formal aspects of the place of language and verbal behavior in the Person Concept.

FORMAL ASPECTS OF THE PLACE OF LANGUAGE AND VERBAL BEHAVIOR IN THE PERSON CONCEPT

Ossorio Speaking on Verbal Behavior: A Transcript of a "1998 Rap Session"
From 1978 until a few years before his death in 2007, at annual meetings of The Society for Descriptive Psychology (SDP), Ossorio set aside an evening to respond to questions. The SDP called these evenings "Rap Sessions." Note audience members question what he means but not his authority to mean it.

Ossorio: (reading question) "What is it that makes a set of behaviors language behavior?" That's an interesting one.
Member of Audience: What was the question?
Ossorio: "What is it that makes a set of behaviors language behavior?" Now, one reason it's interesting is that nobody else that I know has an answer to this. Psychologists study behavior; other people study behavior; and they have theories of behavior. And from those theories you would never suspect that there was such a thing as language. You would never suspect that there was such a thing as verbal behavior. Linguists study verbal behaviors. They study language. And from what they say you would hardly know that language was a form of behavior. The ones who are sensitive to this problem have invented their own psychology in order to create a place, a notion of behavior within which language fits. And they are not very good theories as psychology.
[writing on board] $<B> = <I, W, K, KH, P, A, PC, S>$ Now there's the general formula for behavior. It has eight parameters: Identity, Want, Know, Know How, Performance, Achievement, Person Characteristics, and Significance. That's the general notion of behavior. So, what we need to say is "What do you need to have in addition to that so that you have not just behavior but, specifically, verbal behavior?"
Here is the formula for verbal behavior. $<V> = <C, L, B>$. C is a concept. L is a locution. And B is a set of behaviors that consists

of acting on the concept. A slight variation in that is that B is a set of behaviors that consist of treating something as being of the sort identified by the concept. So, for example, "chair." You need a concept of the chair. You need a locution which is the word "chair," and you need a set of behaviors that consist of treating something as a chair. The concept is simply part of the "K" value. "K" [contains] the distinctions that are being acted on. So, the concept here [chair] is simply one of the distinctions that's being acted on. The locution is part of the value of the performance parameter. And these behaviors are simply other behaviors like this, that have this [points to "chair"] as part of the "K" value. And that's all it takes.

Now, what this shows is that to say that a behavior is a verbal behavior is not to describe a certain kind behavior. [It is] to give an incomplete description of a behavior. This description [<V>] is an incomplete version of this [<B>]. So, when you have a behavior that not only is this way [points to <B> = <I, W, K, KH, P, A, PC, S>] but is also this way [points to <V> = <C, L, B>] then you have a verbal behavior. Linguistics is what looks at the performance. What kind of words, what kind of sentences, what kind of structures do you have to have in order for this performance to be the right kind of thing to be a locution? Not any old performance is going to be a locution. So, the field of linguistics is right here [pointing to P]. What kind of performance?

What qualifies as a locution? They have very elaborate theories about that.

Member of Audience: So, you would say that linguistics is the behaviorism of verbal behavior and that it focuses only on the Performance parameter ....

Ossorio: Yeah, there is something paradoxical there. The linguists say *we are not dealing with performance; we are dealing with competence.* In their framework that makes sense. In this framework, clearly, they are dealing with Performance. But notice that since they are dealing with Performance, you could easily say, "Well, since the performance is neither chance nor random, what is implied is a corresponding know how." So, it makes sense for them to say, "We are dealing with the know how." But the payoff is not that they are dealing with the know how. The payoff is that they are dealing with the performance.

Member of Audience: Does anybody deal with the other two?

Ossorio: No.

Member of Audience: Could you say a little more about linguistic theories? I'm not that familiar with them but from what I have read, they seem to say some pretty weird things about competencies in terms of what kind of competence people have. I am not sure how much of it makes sense.

Ossorio: Well, think of how complicated it is to specify what kind of performance is a locution and all of the different possibilities for English—let's just talk about English—for sentences. It's a complex formalism that it takes to lay out the various possibilities of what is an instance of the English language. Now, since that's complicated, you might conclude that the skill is equally complicated. But you might not. If you took this to be a theory of competence, then you would say "That's a tremendously complicated competency." If you take it to be a performance, it may be a fairly simple competence.

Now, what they have done to a large extent is to think "Maybe a lot of this is wired in." You have heard the phrase I am sure. There is one outstanding reason why they say this. And that is, if you were investigating a language and you asked, "What kind of sample of the language would I need to have in order to figure out what language that was, and not merely what language that was, but all of the rules for that language so that I could speak it?", "What kind of data would I have to have?" "How much data?" And the answer they get—and they always get this answer—is what a child gets in the way of input from hearing people talk, etc., is nowhere near the amount and kind of data that you would need if you started out with zip and had to figure out all of the rules that apply to the language that you speak. Therefore, some of it must be wired in. That's how it goes.

Now, there is a fallacy there. Namely, who is to say how much you need to see in order to figure it out? You might argue, "Well, the fact that kids learn without being taught, isn't that evidence that the amount of data you need is really much smaller than these guys think?" You could say that. And in fact, that is what I am more inclined to say than that other..

Member of Audience: ...adequate as an explanation at best...

Ossorio: Not so much that it is adequate as an explanation, because I don't think that either of them is particularly explanatory. It's two different ways of handling the same problem, the same facts.

Member of Audience: Does that apply to music as well?

Ossorio: I would think it would.

Member of Audience: Because, everybody does music?

Ossorio: No, I don't see why all of the stuff about language wouldn't apply directly to music.

Member of Audience: What was the question?

Ossorio: She said, "Would it apply to music, too?" And I said, "I don't see why not." It seems to me a completely parallel situation.

Member of Audience: What about things like [hitting his glass with a knife], meaning "Can I have your attention?" That seems to fit C-L-B. We don't normally call that a word. Is that language?

Ossorio: That's not a locution.

Member of Audience: How come?

Ossorio: It isn't. Remember you have elaborate theories for specifying what is a locution. But behind that we have the native speaker intuition because we are speakers. Any speaker will tell you, "That's not a locution."

Member of Audience: That's a gesture..

Ossorio: It's a signal. Given the right set of conventions, it is a signal. It's communication, but you are not saying anything.

Member of Audience: Could you give me an outline of some kind of theory of the beginnings or development of language… Well, what would a theory of language development look like within the Descriptive framework if you were just starting….

Ossorio: You have to be careful when you say, "What's the Descriptive approach?" to anything. There is no Descriptive approach to anything. Any one of you could use the Descriptive framework and develop a theory of language and language development and they would all be different. It is not that there is a set of answers built into Descriptive that all you have to do is read it off.

Member of Audience: But my question was what would *you* do? [laughter]

Ossorio: The way that I would go is to say there is an age at which kids learn this [pointing to the formula for behavior]. And roughly speaking it is the age where they are going around asking "Why?" And when parents ask them "Why did you do that?" and start getting some kind of answer. And that to me is a very fundamental point in development. Once you acquire the notion of doing something, then there is a whole lot of things, in fact, almost everything else is simply an instance or a variation on that. Because one of the things that you can do is talk. You can say something. So, once you have the notion of doing something, the notion of saying something is simply a special case. So that would be how I would approach a developmental theory. Okay, any more on language?

Member of Audience: I have just a comment that you can comment on if you want. When I was in Saudi Arabia I was told that there were many Arab people who could recite the Koran by heart who couldn't read and couldn't write. I wonder how they do that. They just rattle this thing off.

Ossorio: Okay, the question is that there are people in Arabia who can rattle off the Koran and how long is that? It is about an inch-thick book and they can rattle it off from start to finish. There are people that can do that with a Bible. I bet you that not every Arab can do that. I bet you that not everybody in this country can do it with a Bible. So, what does it take to be able to do that? Well, one thing you can bet is lots of exposure, lots of rehearsal, lots of practice. You don't get it just from listening once unless you are one of these eidetic memory people. So, by listening, by rehearsing, by practicing, if you do enough of that, these people are evidence that you can go that far with it.

Member of Audience: Without being able to read or write.
Ossorio: Yeah, remember the first thing we learn to do is talk, not read or write.

Let's unpack some of this further.

THE DESCRIPTIVE ACCOUNT OF VERBAL BEHAVIOR IS PREEMPIRICAL

An adequate theory of language and verbal behavior must address the full possibilities required by the Person Concept. Descriptive Psychology's job, however, is not to theorize about language but instead to frame the full subject domain and to indicate parameters for sorting out the details. This does not replace the empirical and theoretical work of developmental psychologists, linguists, psycholinguists, grammarians, and their kin. The Descriptive account is logically prior to their difficult and fascinating work.

The value of verbal behavior as a paradigmatic component of the Person Concept is its role in cognizant and deliberate action. Language greatly enhances Actor-Observer-Critic self-regulation, social coordination, and negotiation. Every culture has language that provides this.

There are some features that must be present for language to be sufficiently flexible and creative, that allow verbal behavior to be more than a stereotypic, fixed, or rigid communication. (And that can be hard to tell. Do my dog's barks, sneezes, grunts, and whines have the potential to be meaningfully combined and organized by a grammar?)

A language must have symbols. Symbols that are arbitrary, combinatory, and separate from the object or act allow representation of what is not present. The symbol is not the thing, so to speak. It can be anything from a pictorial representation of the "thing," to a phatic evoker, but, by and large, it is usually an arbitrary symbol that we have decided to use. No part of an apple is an A, P, L, or E. Nor does the word have any taste at all, yet we've agreed to use those letters to make a word, and that word combined with others says something. And says something in some ways because grammar offers an open set of rules that provide the various ways uttered symbols can identify, describe, evoke, instruct, etc., everything.

In summary:

1. The syntactic structure of a language must allow for novel expressions and for varied expressions with equivalent meaning.
2. The semantic structure of a language *may* contain iconic, analogic, and part-for-whole representation, but it *must* contain arbitrary symbols.
3. The meaning of symbols and words cannot require the simultaneous expression of the social practice that gives the locution its meaning. I can say it without otherwise needing to act it all out. (An exception is Austin's (1962) concept of "performatives.")

Images, sounds, icons, and words—what have you—can be symbols for the significance of verbal behavior, including the sort of personal behavior that involves silently thinking with images, symbols, and tunes. But images, symbols, and unworded sounds (think a klaxon's blast), like words, require a grammar when they are part of deliberate thought. (See, for example, Arnheim, 1969.) Simple pictorial or aural representation is not enough. An image or sound by itself does not tell how it is to be used. But for a person who is *already* competent with language, visual imagery and sound without words (think music) can be a part, even the bulk, of a deliberate verbal exchange.

FORMS OF LIFE, SOCIAL PRACTICES, AND SOME MORE WITTGENSTEIN

> What has to be accepted, the given, is,—one might say—forms of life. Wittgenstein *(PI 226)*

Back at the Alfred Packer Restaurant & Grill. After underlining, "… *the word 'language-game' is used here to emphasize the fact that the speaking of language is part of an activity, or of a form of life,"* I could only find three references to "forms of life" in the *Investigations*. On good authority, it turns out there are only three. Hacker (2015) has this to say about it:

> "The phrase 'Lebensform' (form of life) had a long and varied history prior to Wittgenstein's use of it on a mere three occasions in the *Philosophical Investigations*. It is not a pivotal concept in Wittgenstein's philosophy. But it is a minor signpost of a major reorientation of philosophy, philosophy of language and logic, and philosophy of mathematics that Wittgenstein instigated. For Wittgenstein sought to replace the conception of a language as a meaning calculus (Frege, Russell, the *Tractatus*) by an anthropological or ethnological conception. A language is not a class of sentences that can be formed from a set of axioms (definitions), formation and transformation rules and the meanings of which is given by their truth-conditions, but an open-ended series of interlocking language-games constituting a form of life or way of living (a culture)."

Language *is* essentially anthropological or ethnic—"an open-ended series of interlocking language-games constituting a form of life or way of living (a culture)." How else could language have meaning apart from how it is used in social practice?

Language and Social Practice are essential parameters of Community and Culture. That's where we are going next.

Community and Culture

In the square in an old part of town, an itinerant tinker sits on a bench with a tailor, who nods at a young soldier passing by. He wonders why she keeps crossing his path. She's the daughter of the butcher, whose shop sits side by side with the baker's and candlestick maker's—three mates who bathe together, but not with the tailor. They find his accent foreign, so they keep their distance and wager he has a past to hide. The observant soldier, hoping to join the intelligence service, suspects the tailor's a spy; the tinker his cut-out.

In our various communities, we have roles and commitments—some gladly borne, others accepted or resented as necessary burdens. In some, we are so well cast we hardly give them a second thought; others require constant direction and deliberation.

As we move from community to community—stage to stage—some of our roles are openly acknowledged, others kept close to the vest. Some, we play unwittingly. The tailor *is* a spy. The butcher divides his time among work, family, and his two chums. The tub buddies play cricket, but if short of 11, they invite the tailor—an ace bowler—rationalizing he hates the Australians, too. But the soldier is onto him, gathers her evidence, prepares a report that catches the attention of the agency she wants to join. Later, immersed in duty, sharing hazard and ordeal, she falls in love with her Station Chief and they marry. But late one night she overhears him speaking to the tinker and realizes her husband and boss is his handler.

Moment to moment, only some of a person's powers and dispositions appear frontstage; the rest, a behavior potential somewhere in the back. People spend their days playing multiple roles *done the way they do them*. Over time, the contingencies of the mix appear, and the actor's character is revealed. *The contingent relationship of personal characteristics, statuses, and community establishes a status dynamic.* This contingency is value-laden, hence motivational, and played with degrees of interdependence, complementarity, inhibition, and antagonism. As our status in each community and social practice changes, our behavior potential shifts. Imagine the young soldier's condition: profoundly patriotic but harboring a hope and illusion that love conquers all.

COMMUNITY AND CULTURE

People live their lives and find their ways within a society's communities. That's where we learned to speak. That's where we became persons and the sort of persons we are.

Society, here, will refer to the all the people or "peoples" who historically interact, often within a common geography, regardless of whether they share a common culture—although mostly they do. Within a culture resides overlapping and separate communities. Starting with family, we acquire our culture's language and the vernaculars, dialects, jargons, and technical vocabularies of our particular statuses and communities. Within culture and community, we learned and practiced *our* way, with an individual voice. To the established, our locutions mark us as insiders and outsiders.

As people reveal their values and practices, we notice their resemblances as family and kin; townsfolk with professions and trades; coreligionists and heathen; players of sport with fans and rivals; voters with ecumenical and identity politics. We have clubs and cliques and online forums where we share our most crucial concerns, populated by people we will never touch.

Within any community, we find members in good standing and those that hang by a thread. There are communities we aspire to, and ones of no personal relevance. There're ones that if they would have us, we would refuse to join.

When acting as a community member, we are cognizant of our world in particular ways. Distracted or focused, we flit from thought to thought; but while *authentically* acting as a member of a particular community— properly, competently engaged in our roles—some matters take the center stage of consciousness. Within the Descriptive Psychology community, Anthony Putman was a principle architect of the Community Concept. Here's his description of *consciousness of* and *consciousness as*—key distinctions we'll return to in Chapter 8.

> A person is conscious as whatever status he acts as. What he sees in the world around him, in particular what he sees as possibilities and non-possibilities for acting, differs according to his status. ('When a thief looks at a saint, he sees pockets.') What a person is conscious of depends largely on what he is conscious as. To expand a bit: Being a banker, I am conscious as a banker. I look for opportunities to do what a banker does; I pay particular attention to those states of affairs of interest to a banker; I appraise and respond to a situation in one of the ways a banker does. As the third baseman on our softball team, I am conscious of a very different set of things because I am conscious as a third baseman—not as a banker. This is an ordinary, everyday fact about persons: what we are conscious of depends largely on who we are conscious as, and this changes routinely and dramatically as we change who we are in which community. (2013, p. 87).

This chapter is in two parts. First, we'll read Ossorio placing the Community Concept in context, followed by a parametric analysis of

Community, Culture, and **Institution**. Second, I'll turn to topics of social and clinical relevance about the psychological consequences of **Indoctrination** and shunning; **Degradation** and **Accreditation Ceremonies**; and the badly-named but important social concern with **microaggression**. The chapter will close with a Person Concept approach to status dynamics and psychotherapy — **Accreditation Ceremonies** and **Values.**

THE FIFTH MAJOR PIECE OF THE PERSON CONCEPT

Descriptive Psychologists debate whether Community has or should have equal billing with the other foundational components of the Person Concept. I think it should. What follows is from a Rap Session in 2000 where Ossorio addresses the question "What do you think about community being the fifth major piece of the Person Concept or subsuming the language concept?" During the session, Ossorio refers to "the book," which I believe is his *The Behavior of Persons*, unfinished at the time of this Rap Session, and while published in 2006, never fully completed.

Ossorio: (reading question) "What do you think about community being the fifth major piece of the Person Concept or subsuming the language concept?" I'm not sure whether the reference to language is a separate question or a redo of the first. Let me just deal with the first. "What do you think about community being the fifth major piece of the Person Concept?"

That has potential. As I've organized things in the book, there's the four major pieces and then from those pieces, we either derive or introduce a number of subsidiary concepts. But the second major section is *Introducing the Real-World Context*, and that's where you bring in communities, world views, Actor-Observer-Critic, and a whole bunch of things like that.

Well, if you took that whole section, you say "Yeah. If language, person, reality, and behavior are the first four components, then maybe this whole extra section is a fifth component." But it doesn't fit right. It doesn't feel right because you got there via those first four. So, I'd handle them as a derivation rather than a coordinate fifth piece. But as you can see, it's a close cry and if you really want to work it that way, you could probably carry it off.

As I say, what's this about "subsuming the language concept?" Do you mean in place of language?

Member of Audience: Language is a parameter of community, so you could just put the parametric analysis of language into community and have four basic concepts, the fourth of which is community instead of language. Language would be a parameter of community.

Ossorio: I think you'll find that all four of the basic concepts are going to be parameters of community. Remember: Community has a world;

that's reality. Community has members; that's people. Community has social practices; that's behavior. So, you've got those basic components in the notion of community.

Member of Audience: As it is, it tends not to suggest that whole range of study, for instance, that the social sciences cover, which presumably, Descriptive Psychology can encompass, where you're always dealing with things at a combined level. As a matter of public relations ... [laughter].

Ossorio: One of the reasons why I say that you could probably carry it off somehow, even though I doubt that it's optimum, is that you deal with the four basic concepts. They don't somehow add up to community. You need to introduce the notion of community, even though it's a community of individual people. So, you can say "Yeah. There's an irreducible something that's contributed by community. It isn't just derivative from these four." And then work it that way.

A lot of this stuff is simply "This is how *I* feel like doing it." You need to be sensitive to that because it could have been done a different way.

Member of Audience: Pete, I hear you clarifying those distinctions right now. Would you say that what you're drawing upon is the use of those concepts? In other words, ... Let me just put it more basic. What is it you're drawing upon as you make those sets of distinctions right now?

Ossorio: I'm a competent baseball player. [laughter]

(Here, Ossorio is speaking insider lingo, "baseball talk" being a shorthand for a community's technical language. Competent baseball players *because they know how* make their moves and talk about their game in all sorts of ways *because they know how*. These ways are recognized as authentic ways baseball is played—some more winning than others—*because they know how*. Ossorio is making the point that he is a competent Descriptive Psychologist. A point he makes with unquestioned authority owing to his status as originator.)

Member of Audience: And those concepts have a place in the Person Concept?

Ossorio: Yeah.

Member of Audience: And you are clarifying that place?

Ossorio: Yeah. This is how the thing works.

Member of Audience: Isn't it more than that? It's not just that you're a competent baseball player, because not any competent baseball player could do that at all. It's that you know how to write the rules.

Ossorio: I'm a good grammarian, too.

Member of Audience: To me, that's the whole point. Anybody can recognize that "That's a competent baseball player." "Yeah, that makes sense." But only a few people can actually write the grammar.

Ossorio: You know, a lot of it is what I call craftsmanship. No different from being a carpenter and building something where everything fits, and everything is tight, etc. When you're trying to represent a system and it isn't already there, and everybody knows it, craftsmanship is one of the standards. Can you get all of the pieces into the picture that you need? Can you get them to fit together in the way that they need to in order to work the way we know they have to work?

So, when I say, "Yeah. You could carry it off somehow," essentially I'm saying "Yeah. But you'd probably pay a price aesthetically in how the whole thing was put together, in how tight it was." But it doesn't have to be perfect in order to work.

In the previous rap session, Ossorio is asked whether language should be assumed under community. Ossorio's response is that it's dealer's choice but acknowledges, "There's an irreducible something that's contributed by community." The irreducible something is "social practices," and the inseparable connection of language to the social practices of a community. Language is not a private matter. Locutions acquire meaning as *socially recognized* intentional actions. Since both language and social practice are interdependent aspects of the concepts of Verbal Behavior and Culture and Community, I don't see much point in subsuming one to the other.

THE CONCEPTS OF COMMUNITY AND CULTURE

Anthony Putman was the Descriptive craftsman who assembled the Community Concept, work he further extended in a formulation of Organizations and their missions (1990).

Ossorio (1983) integrates Putman's (1981) parametric analysis of community into a formulation of culture. Although they are very similar, let's look at both. The Culture formulation has to deal with the relationships among communities and provide shared domain. Also, remember, there are no restrictions on the form a parametric value must take as long as it captures a salient dimension of information that is conceptually distinct from the other parameters. The only restriction *within a parameter* is that all the content must be of the same logical type. If we're talking foods—fruits and vegetables might fit together, along with the subcategories raw and cooked, but numbers and fruits, being of a different logical type, won't. Ever eaten a 17-bannana? There is no place for a fruit in the number series, nor numbers as a variety of fruit. Numbers are for counting. Fruits are delicious. Counting has no taste at all.

Putman described **Communities** as a set of **Members, Social Practices, Statues, Concepts, Locutions, Choice Principles,** and **Worlds.**

Members

The members of a community are those eligible to participate in the practices of the community. Paradigmatically, members recognize each other as members. At bare minimum, a community has at least two members.

Social Practices

The **Social Practices** are the actions community members engage in when they are doing the community's "done thing." Practices can be *intrinsic* and *core* to the community; or *instrumental*, performed in the service of the intrinsic practices. An ordinary precondition of membership is an ability and interest to acquire or perform the core practices. There are exceptions: some find themselves in a community, born into or drafted. Whether they acquire and value the core practices will be relevant if they are to become "good-standing" members. A competent demonstration of valuing and performing the core practices is traditional in the formal and informal passage into membership. Members recognized as failing to respect the core practices occupy a degraded community status, if they are allowed to remain at all.

The Social Practice Concept is the pragmatic foundation—the "meanings that follow from shared use"—that links culture, community, and language together through recognized intentional actions that people can do individually and together. It's the "done together" that makes it social and provides the possibility of communicable meanings. Given its importance, here's a modified summary taken from Clarke Stone's "A Glossary of Descriptive Psychology Concepts (Appendix Two)."

1. Social practices are a society's patterns of behavior. In general, the patterns include more than one behavior, and most social practices involve behaviors on the part of more than one person.
2. As social patterns of behavior, social practices are learnable; teachable; do-able; and paradigmatically, done. Every society at a given time has an organized set of social practices that constitute "what there is to do" for the members of the society.
3. A person's participation in a social practice is intrinsic if:
    a. the person is participating in that practice without an ulterior motive and without a further end in view, and
    b. the particular behavior is engaged in without an ulterior motive and without a further end in view *other than those which are part of the practice itself.*
4. Viewed as a process, social practices have **stages, options, contingencies**, and **eligibilities**. This process represents every **Version** of the social practice. Every social practice is done in one of the ways it can be done, that is, some version of the process takes place.
5. *In any community, social practices are "what there is to do."*
6. Social practices are patterns of behavior. They are built up from intentional actions, and for a given community, they characterize what is to be done in that community. For example, within the farming community they would include: plowing, planting, fertilizing, irrigating, harvesting, etc.

7. Since an individual is a member of many communities, the totality of social practices of all their communities constitutes their behavioral repertoire.
8. A person may participate in more than one social practice simultaneously.

Social practices are done in many ways and with their own contingent effect. Violation of a core practice can show up in the subsequent way the violator is treated in the practices that follow. Practices can be used to implicitly or explicitly make a point. Consider a family whose husband and wife have an implicit core practice that arguments are resolved before moving on to other things with dinner at 8:30, another important family practice. Ossorio (2006a, b) offered this example:

> Suppose I tell you that last night I got through work at 5:30 and got home at 6:00, as usual. And we had dinner at 8:30 and it was steak, well done. At this point you yawn inwardly and wonder "So, what else is new? Half the people in town could say pretty much the same thing." Then I add a few facts. I tell you that yesterday morning I had a big argument with my wife and we never got it resolved. Also, we usually have dinner at 7:30, not 8:30, and I like steak, but I like it rare – I hate it well done. At this point, you have a very different picture of what was going on. When presented to undergraduate classes, ordinarily about forty percent of the class is smiling after hearing that "we usually have dinner at 7:30, not 8:30" and by the end, eighty to ninety percent are smiling. The reason for the smiles is that indeed they see another picture, namely an expression of hostility on her part. (p. 172).

Statuses

Statuses are the places (roles, jobs, relationships, etc.) a member may have within the community. Having community status is to have a place in the performance of the social practices of the community.

Concepts

Concepts are the distinctions that members are expected to competently recognize and appropriately act on; especially important are distinctions relevant to core social practices. Members can differ in their competences from, for example, novice to master, neophyte to expert, child to adult.

Locutions

Locutions are the verbal behaviors—the general and technical language employed by competent members of the group while engaging in the practices of the community. It's their "baseball talk."

Choice Principles and Policies

The **Choice Principles** typify the decisions usually made when acting as "one of us." When formulating this concept, Ossorio noted an unfortunate potential to misuse the concept of choice principles in formulating culturally deterministic accounts that stereotype people. Choice principles reflect the typical policies and value hierarchies that community members unsurprisingly follow. *Policies are not rigid laws but default guides to follow unless there is a reason not to.* Value hierarchies are subject to an individual's choices when appraising a circumstance. They are the behavioral logic of the "unless clauses" we examined in the Relationship Formula. There are a lot of "unless contingencies," "reasons not to", that competent people recognize in their day to day social interactions. Ordinarily, choice principles *inform* rather than *command*, *influence* rather than *determine*. As an Actor-Observer-Critic, who is acting as a member of a particular community, that community's choice principles—its standards—inform the Critic standards applied when appraising and regulating behavior. People are also members of multiple communities and have many different places in them, play many different roles. All of this informs the behaviors chosen and the way they are performed.

Sometimes, however, choice principles associated with core practices are commands. Prioritizing the choice principles associated with a community's core practices is an important demonstration of community membership. But people don't always choose to march to the drum. This creates conflict when simultaneously acting as a member of two or more communities with different core practices and values. Consider again our patriot soldier and her beloved husband-spy. (See for example, Josiah Royce (1908) on community and loyalty to loyalty, Jonathan Shay (2010) on moral injury, and Anthony Putman (2013) on intractable value problems.)

World

The **World** is the domain of **Objects, Processes, Events, Concepts,** and **Relationships** germane to acting as a member of the community. Ordinarily, members of a community are expected to recognize the distinctions and locutions that pertain to these objects, processes, events, and states of affairs (relationships). We'll look at this more closely in Chapter 8.

CULTURE AS A SPECIAL SORT OF COMMUNITY

Communities require a society's culture for their viability. People are members of multiple communities within an overarching culture. A culture provides a language shared across communities and "ways of living" recognized unsurprisingly as the sort of thing, across communities, many of its members do, even if their particular members don't often or ever act *that way*. Communities within a culture are often interdependent.

Baseball player's need industries to manufacture bats, gloves, and balls. Bankers need other communities of commerce, might sponsor the local Little League, and particular bankers, after closing hours, might want to watch their kids play third base.

Closely related to Putman's parametric analysis of Community is Ossorio's Culture with **World, Members, Language, Statuses, Institutional Social Practices**, and **Choice Principles** as defining parameters. "A culture is a way of living. Archetypally, it is embodied in a society, i.e., a group of historical individuals who live that way … A culture defines a special kind of community marked by stand-alone viability and life-scope. It is the "stand-alone viability" and the "life-scope" of a culture that differentiates culture from other sorts of community. Culture's "stand alone" in the sense that their members "need nothing beyond… to survive and flourish" and typically cover their lifespan (2006, p. 182).

World

World views are overall paradigms for how things are. Cultures—traditional and "modern"—maintain cosmologies, theologies, "myths," "sciences," ideologies, and methods of inquiry pertaining to what is taken as real and normal. This includes (1) the relationships among the various communities inside and outside the culture and (2) the origins, histories, and destinies of the world and the cultures' communities.

More or less set in stone, world views provide the landmarks for what is taken to be the case and what must be managed. The "more or less" marks a difference between *inclusive multicultural cosmopolitan societies* and *exclusive monoculture traditional* ones. When dominant *exclusive monocultures* deem their way of life mandatory within their geographic boundaries, immigration of people from cultures that are sufficiently different poses a threat. Some world views are more open to coexistence and accommodation than others; some insistently resistant. None you can expect will turn on a dime. This has important consequences when an insistent world view is challenged. World views and their associated cultures can be in crisis, reconstructed, or lost. Or, they can be conserved though societal accommodation, isolation, indoctrination, and so on. (Indoctrination and world reconstruction will be topics latter in this chapter and Chapter 8.)

Members

A culture's **Members** are the people, living, remembered, and mythologized, that make up the various communities within the culture. These are the people, alive, dead, and imagined who became a member of the culture by initiating, acquiring and living in accordance with the practices of other members of the culture.

Statuses

Every society has social structuring of distinct **Statuses** that guide the standards, values, and social practices associated with the engagement of the culture's individuals. Members of a culture have statuses that inform their appropriate, usual, and expected social engagement with members within and across the various communities and institutions found within the culture.

Language

Every society has a language or languages spoken by its members distinctively characterized by its concepts and its locutions. Similar to the dilemmas that attend a multiplicity in world views, some members of a society may be more insistent than others about what language is mandatory within a common state of affairs, usually a territory.

Institutional Social Practices

Cultures have important clusters of **Social Practices** we'll refer to as **Institutions**. Common examples are marriage and family life; earning a living in a trade or profession; electing officials; political parties and religions; and the schools, courts, laws, police, and the military. Ossorio (2006a, b) described it this way, "Most institutions are intrinsic in the same sense that some social practices are intrinsic, i.e., they can be understood as being engaged in without an ulterior motive and without a further end in view. In part this is because they are so central to the way of life that no alternative is readily acceptable. In the Spanish culture, for example, speaking Spanish, taking up a vocation, getting married, and raising a family qualify as intrinsic. The pragmatic mark of the intrinsic is that one doesn't need a reason to do it – rather, one would need a reason, and a good enough reason, not to do it. Thus, the ultimate answer to why a person does what he does has the form, 'I'm living the (Spanish) way of life, and this is how it's done (this is how *I* do it).'"

Shortly before he became too ill to continue further, Putman[1] sent me a work in progress that contained a parametric analysis of **Institutions** as a set of **Practices, Roles, Concepts, Locutions, Ethics,** and **Ultimates**.

The **Practices** are the prescribed or required social practices of the institution. These carry specific eligibility requirements with accompanying permissions and restrictions. Rituals such as swearing in ceremonies, funeral processions, graduations, and other formal and informal rites of passage are examples. Institutional practices require **Roles** that have a

---

[1] Personal communication.

specific name and status with associated eligibilities, duties, permissions, and restrictions—ministers, judges, teachers, holders of office, and so on. Performing an institutional role requires the competence to employ the **Concepts** associated with the Institution represented by the **Locutions**— the "baseball talk"—that characterizes the institution. Last, institutions have a common **Ethic**, a set of recognized **choice principles** that prescribe and limit "right" behavior in the service of the **Ultimate** point—the aims, processes, outcomes, etc.—of the Institution's existence.

In a multicultural society, the interwoven status dynamics of **interdependence, complementarity, inhibition, and antagonism** can play out on the cultural level. The problems of hegemony arise when an Institution's Ethics and Ultimates attempt to enforce versions of "right behavior" and the world view on *all* of a pluralistic society's communities. Historically, this has been associated with fundamentalist religions and totalitarian political institutions. Institutions with such all-inclusive concerns attempt to function as independent Cultures.

CHOICE PRINCIPLES, POLICIES, AND VALUES

A culture's choice principles are a broad collection of policies; social values; slogans and mottos; and cautionary tales and guidance myths that identify respected guides to action. The way outside observers take it that choice principles typify a culture's individuals can be informative but can also result in the stereotyping blinders of cultural determinism. *Individual Persons are Deliberate Actors*. Cultures provide many but not all of an individual's options for acting *their way*. Cultural policies and values are relevant reminders and perspectives a person employs in their day-to-day life—an expected or unsurprising motivational hierarchy for their actions; and the "unless clauses" of the Relationship Formula still apply. When in Rome, the Romans don't always do as Romans do. In Mexico, Cuba, and Spain, everyone recognizes *familismo,* but it also might be recognized by its absence in an individual's neglect and indifference. Or, nonnormatively, it just might be irrelevant.

Further, Romans acting as *proper* Romans do, do it their personal way. Ossorio (2006a, b) described a culture's "social controls"—its choice principles—this way: "In general, the availability of social practices, options, partners, and scheduling routinely provides a member with many choices, and there is no way to constrain them so that they are all good (right) choices. A major part of social control is exercised in the form of constraints (i.e., behaving wrongly or badly is not permitted) rather than in the form of specific prescriptions for what to do. Since behaviors are not specifically prescribed, in light of the significantly varied Options available, some coherent set of principles is needed for choosing behaviors in such a way as to express and preserve the coherence of human lives and the stability of the social structure."

SOME BEHAVIORAL LOGIC AND SOME DILEMMAS: MORE MAXIMS

Ossorio offered these reminders of the formal relationship of Individual Person, Deliberate Action, and Culture and Community:

A human person requires a community in order for it to be possible to engage in human behavior at all.
A person requires that the community be one way rather than another in order to behave in one way rather than another.
A person's place in the community provides reasons and opportunities to engage in one behavior rather than another.
To engage in a Deliberate Action is to participate in a social practice of the community.
If a person participates in a social practice, they must do it in one of the ways it can be done.
If a person makes nonnormative choices in their participation in the social practices of the community, that calls for an explanation.
A person may act as a representative of the community or as merely a member.
A person takes it that a member of the community has the personal characteristics required for normal participation in the social practices of the community unless they have reason enough to think otherwise.
When a person is in a pathological state there is a significant restriction in their ability to participate in the social practices of the community.

With this last maxim in particular, let's turn to some dilemmas of community membership, specifically a person's standing within a community and the broadly useful concepts of degradation and accreditation.

DEGRADATION, ACCREDITATION, AND RITES OF PASSAGE: GAINS AND LOSS OF STANDING

I spent my predoctoral internship year at Harvard where I had the good fortune to be a teaching fellow in George Goethals's Life Cycle course. Goethals was particularly interested in the transitional periods of life. When examining adolescence and "coming of age," his lectures focused on Harry Stack Sullivan's (1953) interpersonal theories and Arnold van

Gennep's (1909/1960) *Rites of Passage*. For me, this later resonated with Ossorio's interest in the status dynamics of accreditation and degradation ceremonies—social practices I saw as a model for a person-centered psychotherapy I'll describe later.

Across cultures, changes in the life cycle that involve a clear change in status are often marked by formal ceremonies that Van Gennep (1909/1960) called the rites of passage. In his classic work, he distinguishes three phases to these ceremonies: the rites of separation, transition, and incorporation. Each of these signifies a step in the process of moving from one significant status to another. Some of these ceremonies—accreditation rituals—celebrate the already accomplished achievement. The performance of others is intended to precipitate or accomplish this transition, to actually bridge the social worlds through a demonstration of the appropriate competence, rather than simply to symbolize and memorialize the deed. These correspond to Austin's (1962) *performatives,* where the saying accomplishes the act, as in, "I now pronounce you husband and wife," uttered during appropriate circumstances by a duly authorized person.

Certain classes of performative rites of passage, specifically Degradation and Accreditation Ceremonies are ways a person's place in culture and community can be established, maintained, and lost. These status assignments address the moral place we have in each other's communities. *Are you good enough? Are you worthy of being one of us?*

Writing about the sociology of moral indignation, the ethnomethodologist Harold Garfinkel (1956) described Degradation Ceremonies as formal rituals that remove a person from a valued role within a community. The social practices they were eligible to perform become limited or forbidden. The explicit drama of a courtroom conviction, where a citizen becomes a felon; or the officer dressed down in front of the troops are paradigmatic examples.

I'm especially interested in nonparadigmatic examples. The implicit degradations of everyday life don't look so ceremonial or paradigmatic. Instead, they look like how we treat people *as not one of us,* how we deliberately or inadvertently assign the status that someone is not in good standing with what we believe we represent. But let's start with a paradigmatic formulation.

Garfinkel's has three preconditions and two sets of actions that characterize a *successful* degradation ceremony that serve as a Paradigm Case in the form of a Paradigmatic Social Practice Formulation. The preconditions are:

1. There is a community of persons who adhere to a set of values required for membership in good standing.
2. There are the roles of denouncer, witness, and perpetrator.

3. The denouncer and witness are in good standing in the community and act as its representatives. In any community, there are people who are obviously the real McCoy, who authentically serve as exemplars of what it takes to be in good standing. They are the ones most eligible to denounce transgression and to witness, acknowledge, or enforce a transgressor's removal from privilege. In a paradigmatic ceremony, they have the status to perform these roles in public.

The actions that comprise the degradation are:

1. The denouncer tells the witness the perpetrator has committed an act described in such a way that the act is clearly seen as a violation of community values. For example, the distinctions between appropriation and theft, and killing and murder, illustrate possible options for describing certain actions. Although a community's standards to appropriation and killing may be unclear, ordinarily these actions would be understood as violations if redescribed as theft and murder.
2. The denouncer effectively makes the case that the perpetrator's violation is a genuine expression of their character, and not something to be otherwise explained away or excused. In making this claim, the denouncer indicates that the perpetrator is not now and perhaps never was a good standing member of the community and can accordingly only participate in a restricted fashion, if at all.

Garfinkel's formal paradigm refers to an historical event that can be remembered as the time a person's community status was restricted, but it can also serve as a conceptual device for understanding a variety of related events happening over an indefinite period. Altering the paradigm can illuminate more mundane degradations. When the formal paradigm is successful, there's little doubt the degraded has undergone restriction; altering the paradigm produces ambiguous outcomes. The status dynamics of everyday life involve nonparadigmatic and ambiguous encounters that nonetheless constitute implicit versions of these ceremonies. Moving though the day with welcome greeting and dismissive glance, we let each other know where we stand. Whether obvious, subtle, or intended, our stances and actions can degrade or accredit those we encounter.

Garfinkel's full ceremony deliberately done out loud in public can be accomplished quietly, discreetly, silently, ambiguously, or unconsciously. It can be unintentional and performed by mistake. It can be collapsed to fewer than three principal actors. Two people can do this to each other. Potentially, so can one. Since the ceremony involves social roles, one or more people can play the different parts. People can act this out by themselves and to themselves. I can recognize my transgressions, my own moral failings, denounce myself, and restrict myself accordingly. I might not be good enough for myself regardless of how you see me. The social dynamics depend on the status of the people who accept the new status assignment.

A person might not even know they're the subject of an attempt. People identify themselves with the concepts that fit their self-concept. Some people honestly assert they cannot recognize themselves and their world differently than they do; some may see any significant change in their status as unthinkable given their self-concept. We looked at this back in Chapter 5 under the heading of "insistence."

SOME EFFECTS OF DEGRADATION

The successfully degraded are prone to depression and anxiety. Their social world is now restricted. Their depression corresponds to a lost eligibility—a loss in self-esteem that reflects restricted access to the satisfactions of participating as a valued member of a community. Sadness, shame, humiliation, regret, guilt, "emptiness," resentment, and other kindred moods and emotions are part of the package.

Anxiety corresponds to the insecurity of a loss of personal authority and social support. Members in good standing have each other's back and are expected to be competent players. The degraded no longer can rely on that support or opportunity. When the degraded find themselves in the company of members of the valued community, they understandably suffer the pains of inferiority and rejection. Encounters become awkward. The rhythm of gesture and speech that flows among peers is broken. The recognition of stiltedness intensifies whatever anxiety is present. The degraded may develop a paranoid expectation of harsh judgment, making social contact even more awkward and defensive. No wonder they end up lonely.

A particular style of "outsiders" fantasy may be typical of excluded people. Their degradation may be revealed in fantasies of being lepers, gangsters, untouchables, and the like. They seem more likely to imagine themselves tainted and criminal rather than revolutionary because, in reaction to their values, they see themselves more in terms of personal failure than in terms of political or social rebellion. As a result of the degradation, they might not see themselves as even eligible to criticize the standards they've failed. In not having that option, they are often in rigid agreement with those offended values. In a successful degradation, the denouncer, whether self or other, is held in the perpetrator's mind as correct in the spirit of the denouncement.

Because the degraded see themselves as standing on the outside, it is understandable that their ranks are filled by people subject to disrespectful stereotypes. Those whose sexual behavior is unconventional seem especially vulnerable; chauvinisms of physical appearance, age, gender, race, ethnicity, religion, and class are similarly likely to generate this condition. Further, it is easy to see how degradation can be an "inherited" characteristic: children who recognize their parents as occupying some unfortunate status may see themselves as deplorables, "born to lose." We will look at an example a few paragraphs down.

THE DEGRADED HAVE REASON TO REACT AGAINST THE COMMUNITY

Anger, hostility, and rage can be a move to negate degradation. "Living well" might be the best revenge, but more immediate attempts at revenge are unsurprising attempts at satisfaction. With less at stake, what's left to lose?

Threatened degradation elicits self-affirmation. Attacking the integrity of the denouncer and distracting the witness are reasonable responses to attempted degradation. Excuses that the so-called transgressive performance is misunderstood, not in character, a result of mitigating forces or coercion is an understandable response. "It is not for you to say" and "I had no choice," may counter the threat of being degraded. Mitigating factors can be appealed to as evidence, "don't blame me, I'm depraved on account of being deprived." Psychodynamic and poetic excuses may shift the blame from the repetition compulsion of victim becoming perpetrator to "They fuck you up, your mum and dad. They may not mean to, but they do" (Larkin and Thwaite, 1993). If nothing else works, creating a distracting crisis might.

Redescribing the act as nontransgressive is another defense. In the paradigmatic ceremony, the denouncer describes the act in value-laden terms. Appropriation is theft, death is murder, an absence of assertive response is cowardice, and so on. The perpetrator has reason to redescribe the offending act as something else. "Retreat, hell! ... We're not retreating, we're just advancing in a different direction."

THE CEREMONY CAN BE ACCEPTED AS THE NATURAL ORDER OF THINGS (OR AS HAVING ALREADY HAPPENED)

Degradation can be taken for granted as a community's inherent moral inferiority, as stigma passed through generations. The chauvinisms of sexual orientation, physical appearance, gender, age, race, class, ethnicity, and the indoctrinations of virulent religion and nationalism can convey unquestioned status-assignments of self and others. Children who see their parents as occupying an unfortunate social place may see themselves as "born to lose." And they may be seen that way, regardless of their merit.

For people born into an untouchable condition, a position of shame and degradation can seem the natural order of things. Community chauvinisms establish the additional barrier of people considered inherently ineligible to acquire good standing. *No matter what you do, you are not and will never really be one of us, and that's how it is for all of you.* For some, the rules are unfair from the get-go.

Degradation can provide license for amoral and outlaw ways. Some people simply know their unfortunate place, look around, and say *fuck you.* Some time back, the Boston Descriptive Psychology Study Group discussed the case of a 13-year-old boy that school officials labeled a sexual predator and sequestered from other students. A smart kid, but when confronted by his principal and guidance counselor he offered what they called "elaborate but flaky explanations" for his actions. Most worrisome to the authorities, he appeared unmoved by scorn or guilt.

Some context: he lives on the bad-side of a small New England town. For generations, his family has been considered—and treated—as a clan of deplorables. Well-known and ridiculed, their family name is an insult grade school kids hurl at each other. Getting called by their name starts fights. I knew kids from families like that where I grew up in the South. They never stood a chance. Few did well. Many are now dead. The ones that did OK found redemption in the military, where their competence mattered over background; where their status at home meant nothing to their new community.

The study group thought about the possible consequences of being born into a degraded family. As a Southerner, I am familiar with the lore of Kallikaks and Jukes—not the sociological tale supporting eugenics, but the image of marginal white families in yards filled with soiled diapers, chained mangy dogs, broken car parts, and rusted washing machines. People others treat as trash, uncouth, incapable of civility; ridiculed as inbred, violent, and sexually wanton; considered a danger to society best managed through isolation and arrest.

Such families are rarely happy. Seldom do they have the economic or psychological resources to provide good enough care. Depression and mental illness follow them.

Their children are never embraced, even while sharing the town's dominant ethnicity and religion, they are never embraced. *They could be one of us but aren't.*

This is different from the degradation that attends racism, sexism, anti-Semitism, and Islamophobia. The difference is profound. A member of the study group pointed out that "everyone needs a code to live by," that is, a set of significant values that potentially guides a through-line that can, if enacted, provide a social integrity witnessed and honored.

Communities have their required and honored social practices that people must follow to be recognized as authentically one of us in good standing. So then, what can those who expect disrespect do? *They can turn the table.* With sufficient shared identification, people in marginalized or "deplored" communities may be able to enforce their own values when they have the opportunity. Supported by a charismatic leader, a social movement, an organized politics of resentment is an understandable resistance and antidote to degradation.

The degraded have good reason to turn the tables. Why wouldn't they? They know the dominant culture's established elites and media won't help them feel good about themselves. The Codes—the core values—useful to the disparaged undermines these established institutions. People counter degradation by discrediting those with the power to discredit them.

This is hardly fake news. What was deplored becomes a source of pride, righteous indignation, and opposition. Collectively engaged around shared grievance, antagonism becomes an act of integrity and a source of satisfaction. Chanting "lock her up" affirms good standing membership: a spontaneous shared emotional expression immediately expressed and celebrated. For some, it feels so damn good.

But this only works if there are sufficient numbers to effectively affirm actions that reflect the values of difference and opposition. It helps to see yourself acknowledged by others you don't personally know *as one of us.* In-your-face anger, rage, protest, and indignation can be an antidote for depression and demoralization. But I don't think this explains the boy's predation. He doesn't even have affirmative acknowledgment from anyone.

Communities mutually negotiate and regulate standards. A community can resist degradation more effectively than an isolated family. Parents recognized as a valued part of a broader community can affirm their children and neighbors. An isolated family has only each other; when pathology and degradation are already present, self-regulation is restricted.

Isolation makes it hard to establish codes—choice principles—enacted and witnessed by others who share those values. But for an isolate, one alternative is lawless indifference, guiltless disregard, and license to not self-regulate by what others value. Why not act impulsively on urge? I wonder if this speaks to the boy's predation; his way to manifest the brief esteem of agency, with small regard to how he is observed and judged. We don't know how much he cares what his parents and siblings think. Given their social standing, who are they to judge?

INDOCTRINATION AND DEGRADATION

From time to time I've worked with people who have been shunned by their religious communities. Much of that work involves the "world reconstruction" I'll address in Chapter 8. Earlier, I suggested certain religious and political institutions legislate enough of a person's social practices to constitute a culture apart from larger society. When they self-enforce isolation, they're a type of cult. Indoctrination is part of how they work.

A few years back the study group tried to sort out the behavioral logic of what happens to a person born into a fundamentalist and totalitarian community if excommunicated and shunned. We wondered what they can do with their remaining behavioral potential. What communities are they in a position to join? What psychological states follow their removal? What provides resilience? Central to this inquiry is the concept of indoctrination—enculturation with insistent, not-to-be questioned statuses, social practices, world views, and choice principles. We arrived at a set of principles and maxims:

- A person is indoctrinated when self-compelled to act on an ideology.
- Indoctrination provides its Members with a World, Language, Statuses, and Institutional Social Practices. Its Choice Principles explicitly or implicitly prohibit examining or accepting serviceable alternatives. Awareness is restricted. Accordingly, indoctrination narrows the acceptable domain of cognizant and deliberate action.
- Indoctrination establishes a domain of *taboo* in which alternatives are presented as impure, dirty, shameful, wicked, vile, etc. Contact with taboo results in contamination. Contamination is grounds for an explicit or implicit Degradation Ceremony.
- Indoctrination can be seductive to the young and attractive to those seeking spiritual fulfillment. When indoctrination initially forms a worldview, it provides a required guide to how things are and what to do about them. The young seek guidance. For the spiritual, seeking "ultimates, totalities, and boundary conditions" (Shideler, 1992), there is promise of answers.[2]
- But over time, however, people usually encounter critiques of their views and practices. Serviceable views and practices are usually held fast since they continue to work and are valued without conflict. *But if unserviceable views and practices are questioned or confronted, it can create a crisis of faith that evokes coercive enforcement.* When coercion is applied, it is met with resistance or resigned compliance.

Enforcement met with resistance can lead to a degradation ceremony. The affected community may try to preserve its integrity by

[2] The theologian and Descriptive Psychologist, Mary McDermott Shideler describes the subject matter of spirituality as an intrinsic concern with world ultimates, totalities, and boundary conditions and provides a preempirical conceptual foundation for comparative theology and a doctrinaire-neutral approach to the spiritual.

shunning a degraded–contaminated member. Resigned compliance *might* be treated as a reaffirmation.

- The loss of community will correspond to a loss in behavior potential. The consequences that follow are dependent on whether the indoctrination facilitated or impeded the establishment of the values, knowledge, and skills needed to join other communities within the broader culture. Resilience to the loss is facilitated by already having some grounding in the social practices required to thrive elsewhere.

The shunned also need the disposition to try. Degradation is demoralizing. New community and social practices are needed to compensate for the loss. Unfortunately, for some shunned, the fulfillment desperately sought before may not be promised except though another cult.

MICROAGGRESSIONS

We degrade each other without ceremony. We treat people as invisible, dismissible, inferiors of no consequence who are unworthy of attention. We treat others as commodities worth only our desire and their utility. We degrade strangers with unexamined transferences, typecasts, and stereotypes. We often do so with impunity. If confronted, we act as if we don't have a clue.

Wikipedia's entry on microaggression starts this way: *A microaggression is a term used for brief and commonplace daily verbal, behavioral, or environmental indignities, whether intentional or unintentional, that communicate hostile, derogatory, or negative racial slights and insults toward any marginalized group.* That sums up how I hear the word employed but I don't like the term.

I do not like it because "aggression" is too narrowly connected to hostility and responses to threat; when, I suspect, most instances occur precisely because the "microaggressor" is neither hostile nor threatened, but instead, privileged and ignorant. *They feel safe enough to neglect the implications of their action and act entitled and misunderstood when called out.* Badly named concepts can lead to caricature and dismissal of the degrading social practices at stake.

Microaggressions are versions of the degradation ceremonies of everyday life. More specifically, an unwitting assertion from a privileged position felt as abusive and degrading to the recipient. Why, I suppose, "aggression" has merit is its association with coercive power and a disposition to make nonnegotiated status assignments. When we have the power and disposition to invalidate, we are in a position to degrade.

An educated and reasonable person now living in pluralistic society *knows or ought to know*, microaggressions are an act of negligence.

Here's a Paradigmatic Social Practice Formulation of microaggression. It involves:

- a nonnegotiated status assignment,
- performed *unwittingly*,
- by a person acting *with presumption* as a judge, and
- who, *in effect*, diminishes a person's place in a community significant to the Victim.

1. There are the roles of Status-Assigner, Witness, and Victim. The Victim sees themselves as a member of a marginalized community and sees the Status-Assigner as a member of a non-marginalized community. The Witness can be a third party but need not be. The victim is always a witness.
2. The Status-Assigner treats the Victim so that the assigned status is experienced by the Victim as undesirable.
3. The Victim has not granted the Status-Assigner the right to make such a status assignment.
   Further:
4. The action is not recognized by the Status-Assigner as either aggressive or a response to threat, and the Status-Assigner will deny those implications and allegations

GENERAL CONSIDERATIONS FOR UNDOING DEGRADATION

If a degradation is accepted by the community and the perpetrator, the core problem for the now-degraded perpetrator is regaining status or tolerating a diminished place. Since the paradigm case involves accepting a judgment that the transgressive acts were in character, one path for the perpetrator is to show the unacceptable deeds were not in character or that the character of the perpetrator has changed. Since character is fairly stable over time, this is a barrier to regaining a favorable place. It will take time.

One way to regain favorable status is to show that the perpetrator's actions may have been a transgression of the community's values, but those values are still important to the perpetrator. The community may require acknowledgment of guilt through penance and restitution, accompanied by the acceptance of punishment. Different judges also have different criteria for what passes as sufficient demonstration of dues paid. Nonrecidivism is key but can be difficult to demonstrate since the opportunity to continue in the valued role has been restricted. Time will tell.

It is also possible for the degraded to reassign the significance of what is valued: what was once desirable or transgressive no longer matters that way. This can look like sour grapes to some or affirmations of identity, such as "gay pride" and "black is beautiful," to others.

ACCREDITATION CEREMONIES, PSYCHOTHERAPY, AND VALUES

It matters how the people who matter, see us. How could it not? It especially matters if they see us as one of them. It matters in psychotherapy.

Accreditation ceremonies mark a person's entrance into a new social world. Though ritual and ordeal, accreditation ceremonies affirm new eligibilities and competencies. The properly accredited approach their world differently than before, encountering their world as having options and opportunities that were something else before, if seen at all.

In contrast to a degradation, in accreditation ceremonies the role of accreditor takes the place of the denouncer; the perpetrator is now an initiate or honoree. A person is *eligible* to serve as an accreditor when in a position to effectively reveal or generate an enhanced status in others *or themselves*. Eligibility is in the eyes of the stakeholder community. Paradigmatically, all parties to an accreditation must agree the accreditor is properly entitled to the role and the initiate or honoree is worthy. This is of therapeutic significance because therapists can act as accreditor; their clients, the honored initiate. This is not something accomplished when the participants are viewed with disdain, disgust, or disrespect— inherently degrading perspectives. At times, therapists can be angry with their clients, envious, or even afraid, *but to do this sort of work*, they cannot disrespect them.

Having been trained to identify and promote valued change, most psychotherapists know how to be an accreditor. The methods and stances found across the schools of therapy and consultation—common beneficial factors—are designed to identify and affirm the worth of the client. Roger's (1961) "unconditional positive regard," the "appreciative inquiry" model of consultation (Bushe, 2013), the "acceptance and commitment" approach to cognitive-behavior therapy (Hayes et al., 2012), the psychoanalyst's "analytic attitude" (Schafer, 1983), and the like, are well suited to accreditation. But this only matters if the therapist is seen as a competent representative of the therapeutic community *and that community has merit in the client's eyes*. There are people who want no part of us and what we offer. There are some of us who do not appear to represent what we promise. The contingencies are statuses and eligibilities *mutually* assigned.

Therapy inevitably confronts degradation. A crucial question is whether the degradation is deserved. If the therapist accepts a person's degradation as proper, they'll *somehow* treat that person accordingly. If a degradation is deserved, the therapeutic job is rehabilitation; if that is successful, accreditation.

In the context of a deserved degradation, efforts that smack of accreditation are phony, a sham unless the therapist *successfully presents or represents* an alternative community valued by the client. The therapist must see the client at least potentially belonging in that community and make that clear. *All along you thought you were only an ugly duckling, but you are actually one of us swans.*

To the extent the therapist's life history has common ground with the client, it will inform the therapy. How could it not? The client who suffers degradation has been socially reduced and isolated; afflicted with a strangeness felt in the absence of mutually corrective belonging. Actor-Observer-Critic personal and social feedback is different when excluded or "on probation."

This is the work: challenging the fairness of the degradation while acknowledging the facts—*including the facts of what the therapist values*—creates a new dynamic that invites the therapist's judgments to be judged. It is a show of respect between peers. At times, it is a very good idea to let people know where we are coming from. I am also assuming the therapist is uncommonly self-aware and exercises sound clinical judgment.

I am advocating a disclosure of values that respects the client's place to judge the therapist in ways the standard, asymmetrical stances of nondisclosure do not.[3] This can easily go wrong. Psychotherapy is an intimate conversation. It requires an ethical and prudential concern for what the therapist reveals and evokes. This is all the more reason the self-awareness of the therapist requires considerable supervision and (given my values as a psychoanalyst) a lengthy, personal immersion in one's own insight-oriented psychotherapy; "training analysis;" or comparable practice. People should not do this work without knowing themselves well. It's difficult to confront self-deception by yourself.

Undoing the undeserved degradation is different from rehabilitation. The target of undeserved degradation is analogous to the unfairly punished innocent thrown in jail. The therapist might be the only party who considers the victim not guilty as the "prisoner" loudly commits to a conviction of guilt and general unworthiness.

How is degradation to be undone? As always, therapists must be aware of how their actions reflect their words. The therapist must do more than merely say why the degradation was unfair, incorrect, or no longer in effect; they must *act* accordingly. If a client believes the therapist holds them in esteem and recognizes the therapist as a competent member of a relevant community, the client has an opportunity to practice and test certain social roles they recognize the therapist *also* values. This transformation is no simple matter. At stake is a redefinition of one's place in the

---

[3] I am taking the position that the anonymous judgmentally neutral therapist as a blank canvas for the client's transferences and projects is, *as we should all know*, a myth.

community. The client needs evidence the therapist's appraisals are an accurate redescription of the behaviors previously taken as grounds for self-condemnation; or that the problematic behaviors have been replaced with acceptable social practices. Both therapist and client must substantially agree *about the meaning* of the practices in question.

A therapist's vision of a client's status also changes during the course of therapy. For accreditation to be possible, what must *not* change is the therapist's sense that the client's degradation is somehow unfair, incorrect, abusive, or no longer appropriate. Time served, and appropriate penance and rehabilitation, counts.

A useful method for enacting accreditation can be found in the related social practices of moral dialogue (Cavell, 1969/2002; Pitkin, 1972) and negotiation (Ossorio, 1969/2010). These practices set a stage for status change and acceptance. Although the successful practice of moral dialogue and negotiation can be therapeutic, such encounters between therapist and client have no guaranteed end. The specific issues are complex and sometimes obscure, so they must be accurately identified and confronted. Moral dialogue and negotiation are especially attractive for paradigms of therapeutic exchange because they require mutual respect. The degradation can make the client feel ineligible to initiate or participate in either of these encounters, so it is the therapist's job to foster them.

Moral dialogue is an exchange where persons try to accurately reveal their positions. Negotiation concerns practices of calibrating those judgments through appeal to shared standards. Negotiation is conducted on the presupposition that both individuals have the competence to make judgments about the matters at hand, and that both persons wish to act with a common attention to the relevance of what they say. The Judgment Diagram's multiplicity of reasons to act in various situations offers reminders of the elements that need to be identified. A mutual narrative of how each party identifies them is required for a proper accreditation. I find this practice especially useful when trying to get couples on the same page. At the end of a successful negotiation, both parties know how to proceed.

The not so simple recognition that one is involved in moral dialogue and negotiation can be an accreditation. Learning to engage peer to peer, I to Thou, marks a transition from a world where this is not allowed or invited to one where it is. There are hazards. There is real risk that a failure in negotiation will further the degradation. The client must be able *and* potentially willing to negotiate. There must *be* shared standards and the requisite competence to deal with these values.

In any case, for accreditation to suggest itself as a goal, the therapist must recognize and convey that their client is *in fact* more eligible than the client believe themselves to be. It is the accuracy of this recognition that is up for negotiation. The therapist had better be a keen diagnostician of strengths and vulnerabilities, neither selling the client short or expecting too much. Even with terrible limitations and unfortunately limited boundaries, people remain deliberate actors. Meeting them "where they are" is a start for dialogue and negotiation. All persons can engage in deliberate action; how disposed they are is another matter.

If the client actually engages in negotiation, the therapist is in position to remind the client of the social context they both inhabit and create. This can weaken the client's claim of being outside the valued community. Around and during moments of negotiation, there is an opportunity for therapeutic redescription. Entering these periods of redescription can create considerable anxiety. The client may feel on shaky ground, seeing themselves seen as respectable. Avoiding this anomaly, they might panic and try to undo or redefine the situation. And why not? They have good reason to wonder who will support their bid for respect outside the consulting room. Given what has come of their relationships, who still has their back? Nothing is guaranteed. All of it requires practice to feel natural.

And when the client tries to maintain their accustomed ways, they show how they keep themselves in a degraded place. Here the neurotic paradox intrudes, for despite anguish, people learn to be at home in their *at least* partially self-imposed exile. Any "analysis of the resistance" should take into consideration that acting degraded makes sense to the "victim"; the clarity of degradation is not easily given up. The "initiate" must begin to doubt not the reasonableness of their adjustment to a degraded status, but its necessity *and how it's now become their way of living*. The successful transition from victim to agent-peer rests on the extent to which the client accepts responsibility for actions that undercut accreditation. Accepting responsibility brings the possibility of choice.

When a psychotherapeutic accreditation "ceremony" succeeds, I find the various strands of its development roughly follow the stages of separation, transition, and incorporation that Van Gennep noted as the ritual structure of a rite of passage. Since these stages are a logically sequential description of what happens when a person goes from one social world to another, it is not surprising they can be identified as common features in therapeutic progress. (But don't make too much of them. Keep them in mind as a logical progression, not a mandate to attempt an orderly progression. Change is way too messy for that.)

Here's the correspondence I see in what sometimes happens in therapy. In treating undeserved degradation, Van Gennep's rites of separation correspond to accurately and empathically articulating the client's past and current self-view as a victim; someone constrained by unfortunate and unfair status assignments. Clarifying and redescribing the patient's biography—keeping their behavior understandable—is the goal of this stage.

During this stage, a person becomes reoriented to their past. They must also see this history no longer provides them an unshakable excuse.

This sort of work is common to many psychotherapies—the careful, systematic getting to know a person's manner of narrating history, with attention to the through-lines they identify as destiny. Hearing these, the therapist should ask *how else can these significance patterns be understood and redescribed?* A bit of cognitive-behavioral redescription of the unquestioned circumstances might help. The goal is for the person to see *what already happened* was not inevitable. It happened yes, but it was unfair or incorrect. This can be the beginnings of *the ordeal of reckoning with how it did not have to be that way.* People mourn lost opportunity. Anger and sadness may come with this reckoning.

Having renounced or loosened the aspects of a previous self-understanding, the rite of separation is more or less accomplished, and people may find themselves in transition. But to where and what? In the "rites of transition," a person can face a vacuum of social practices, going from a period of having *found* themselves with self-degrading values and knowledge—the stuff of their previous autobiography—to a period where they must *find* or *create* more useful values, self-knowledge, and practices. With enough support, with an accurate identification of the *necessary competence*, and with *available opportunity*, the "degraded" may be able to explore and practice new ways. This can be an anxious time, experimenting without guarantee of success. Leaps of faith are hazardous without a net. With insufficient support, misjudged competence, and an absence of opportunity—depression, apathy, and recondemnation can result.

Therapists are partners, companions through the rites of separation and transition. With some, in particular those labeled psychotic or borderline personality disorder, an agonizing ordeal can be expected. The clinician-accreditor had better be able to weather the storms with their own safe harbors outside their work. The clinician's job is to be present, empathically tolerant, and willing to confront self-deception—theirs and that of their clients. Mistakes, microaggressions, lapses in attention, and self-interested moves might require acknowledgment and authentic apology. People in treatment are deliberate actors, only more or less owing up to what they recognize they are doing and what is happening. The therapist's job is to expand the accuracy and toleration of that recognition while keeping it I to Thou.

Across cultures, the rites of transition have traditionally been a risky and marginalized domain. The person located there has neither their past routines nor the accreditation of new status from which to generate action and find comfort (Douglas, 1966). During this often troubled period, dialogue with the therapist may be the client's only clear reference point. This is a crucial period of personal experiment, the focus of which is the acquisition or discovery of the behavior potential needed for mastery of more positive social roles. It will take as long as it takes to practice new roles and ways of self-regulation until they have the competence of second nature.

Before an authentic "rite of incorporation," there must be a sufficiently witnessed demonstration of behaving as members of the valued reference group. A therapy of negotiation and moral dialogue offers practice and experience to these ends. But there's no substitute for practice in the appropriate community.

During termination of therapy, one client mentioned a particularly effective method had evolved: pretending he was competent and worthy of respect. He rehearsed for the parts like a seasoned method actor stretching their limits. For months, he practiced "fake it until you make it." At first, he was surprised he got away with it, then marveled at how it became progressively easier to feel respectable. Finally, respectability became an integral enough part of his history for him to feel it authentically.

There was no magic here. He was a man with impressive, well-earned credentials. With support, he risked putting himself where he was not already typecast. Over time, he was accepted there; was incorporated into what he now saw as his place; was acknowledged with a handshake, a nod, and a wish for good luck. We ended with the reminder he didn't need to be lucky, he only needed to continue the values, knowledge, and competence that marked his acceptability.

One more foundational concept to go. *A person requires a world in order to have the possibility of engaging in any behavior at all. That requires the world to be one way rather than another in order for them to behave one way rather than another.*

Reality and the Worlds

... the real world is essentially the world of people and their behavior. All the world's a stage and the non-person portions of it are props which are called for by the drama. (Place, Peter Ossorio, 1998/2012)

"Die Welt ist alles, was der Fall ist.—The world is all that is the case," begins Wittgenstein's *Tractatus Logico-Philosophicus*, a dissertation that's like a fierce prose poem, without a wasted word. He goes on, "The world is the totality of facts, not of things"—a crucial acknowledgment that a world is what a person takes to be the case since every statement of fact is someone's. We don't all agree on what the facts are but there *has* to be a person in there, somewhere. And given the range of people's practices in the world, there also has to be room for the fact that people work with states of affairs that aren't exactly "factual"—yet still have meaning.

What counts as fact in the early Wittgenstein's "logical atomism" are statements asserting something is real or true. "Every proposition has a unique final analysis which reveals it to be a truth-function of elementary propositions" (Proops, 2017). What is absent in the early Wittgenstein is the person and that person's reasons for uttering the fact—the "forms of life" involved (something he will correct in his latter *Investigations*). Every deliberate statement of fact—or anything else—is someone's verbal behavior done as an aspect of a social practice.

In this chapter, we'll look at a world's formal boundaries and possibilities, and how a world's content is found and created. For this, it helps to have a language convention to sort out the possible from the actual. "Reality" will refer to the full range of possibility—the preempirical. "World," "worlds," and "real world" will refer to the empirical—the historical particulars taken to be the case when we observe and think about what we find.

When exactly to use Reality and World was never cleaned up in Ossorio's writing, although in *What Actually Happens* he used Reality as his methodological construct—his preempirical assemblage for all those concepts and relationships that, if fleshed out through observation and thought, make up a person's knowledge of their Real World.[1] I'll also be using Reality as a superordinate over Worlds. This is similar to how we used Culture as a superordinate community that includes other communities. We'll need room for a multiplicity of Worlds. An important difference: Culture is a boundary, that is, you can see what's on the other side of it. Reality is a *boundary condition*—we can't see what's on the other side of it. Boundaries and boundary conditions are *categorically* different.

You might notice that World and Culture cover much of the same ground—as do all the foundational Person Concepts. Worlds and cultures contain everything needed for a person's life, but with a subtle difference in emphasis. The conceptualization of a World has as a central focus the current, former, and potential characters, props, their relationships, and their place on the person's stage. In contrast, the Culture concept emphases institutions and choice principles, their members and roles, and when and how the props are to be used. As an overarching guide to behavior, Cultures frame ways of life and define their member's shared worlds. As cultures change, the worlds of its members change. That said, much of this chapter could have just as well fit the last.

Another point. A physicist, chemist, and physiologist *might* prioritize the distinctions of World and Reality as more germane to their practices than a concern with Community and Culture. When physicists, chemists, and physiologists are asked, "what is reality?" they answer in their way, respectful of their subject matter's institutional mission.[2] As a psychologist, so do I.

The Person Concept's preempirical formulation of Reality and World must provide for their mission and mine without distortion. It must also allow *any* refinement required in a subject matter's account of reality as

---

[1] Truth functions are only one way among others that people judge statements as effective or ineffective guides to behavior. Knowledge, pragmatically speaking, is a more inclusive category than fact. The "logical atomism" of elementary facts doesn't account for the full range of action. One knows one's facts in the sense of asserting something is true, but people know and act on other things as well. The pragmatics of the latter Wittgenstein's "meaning follow from use" and the social practices of Ossorio's Verbal Behavior and Intentional Action employ the more inclusive category of what people Want, Know, and Know-How to do and the Significance of what they are doing.

[2] An institutional goal of physical sciences is to establish what Rom Harré (1964) calls a General Conceptual System. Such systems indicate the classes of independent individuals, the properties of those individuals, and the relations between individuals or properties. Each of the central interdependent Person Concepts—Individual Person, Behavior, Language, Culture, and World—are general conceptual systems of their domains, and each contains the other. The Community and Culture of the physical scientist has as a parameter the special and limited world of physics, chemistry, and so on.

long as that alteration does not violate the paradigmatic requirements of the Person Concept. The subject matters of physics, chemistry, and physiology cannot be constructed from elements and processes that rule out the person choosing to study those elements and processes. If an account does, it needs to be replaced by one that doesn't. The World must have a place for the person who observes, appraises, formulates, and reconsiders.

The Person Concept is a superordinate General Conceptual System that contains all other conceptual systems. Rom Harré (1964) calls a General Conceptual System, a system that indicates the classes of independent individuals; the properties of those individuals; and the relations between individuals or properties. Each of the foundational interdependent Person Concepts—Individual Person, Behavior, Language, Culture, and World— are general conceptual systems of their domains and each contains the other. A general conceptual system of Reality and World should address such questions as: What is its composition? What are its limits? What are the relationships among the conceptual elements that make up the world? And given we are interested in a world of people and their behavior: How is the world real? Is it found or created?

I'll start with the preempirical conceptualization of Reality—the concepts that make up a World—and then turn to world construction, reconstruction, and consciousness.

Consciousness is consciousness of one's place in a world, an awareness that comes from our stable, changing, vulnerable, and resilient status. The world can shock and surprise. An appraisal of its aesthetics can satisfy and evoke wonder.

PERSONS AND THE ELEMENTS OF THE WORLD

Where Ossorio's explication of language, ethics, and aesthetics bear family resemblance to the latter Wittgenstein's pragmatic emphasis on *use* and *forms of life*, Ossorio's construction of the Reality and World concept resembles the logical form of the *Tractatus*.

Wittgenstein worked it out this way in the 1922 *Tractatus*:

1. The world is everything that is the case.

1.1 The world is the totality of facts, not of things.

1.11 The world is determined by the facts, and by these being all the facts.

1.12 The totality of facts determines both what is the case, and what is not the case.

1.13 The facts in logical space are the world.

1.2 The world divides into facts.

1.21 Something can be the case or not be the case while everything else remains the same.

2. What is the case—a fact—is the existence of a state of affairs.

And from Ossorio's (1998/2012) *Place* (slightly amended). Notice how the world is addressed as real, found, and created:

A1. A person requires a world in order to have the possibility of engaging in any behavior at all.

A2. A person requires that the world be one way rather than another in order to behave in one way rather than another.

A3. A person's circumstances provide reasons and opportunities to engage in one behavior rather than another.

A4. For a given person, the real world is the one which includes them as a Person, and as an Actor, Observer-Describer, and Critic.

A5. What a person takes to be real is what they are prepared to act on.

A6. A person acquires knowledge of the world by observation and thought.

A7. For a given person, the real world is the one they find out about by observation.

A8. A person takes it that things are as they seem unless they have reason enough to think otherwise.

A9. A person takes the world to be as they find it to be.

Also,

D11. The world is subject to reformulation by persons.

WHAT ARE THE ELEMENTS OF THE WORLD?

Descriptive Psychology's concept of Reality and World consists of the concepts and facts concerning the **Objects**, **Processes**, **Events**, and **States of Affairs** (OPESAs) that have a place in Behavior. OPESAs are the conceptually distinct elements we act on. I (a state of affairs with object properties) have a telephone (another object) that starts ringing (an event), and then goes to a voicemail (a process) that I avoid (a state of affairs). All this is real. No single element of the OPESA is enough to make up a World. The entire package is required with the addition of Transition Rules to take these elements apart and connect them together.

The computer scientist and Descriptive Psychologist Joel Jeffrey[3] sums it up this way, "What kinds of things are there in the world? Objects, processes, events, and states of affairs. Everything you ever see in the world, as you look around you, will be one of those. What are concepts? Distinctions people can act on." That's the whole kit and caboodle.

---

[3] As a clinician, I'm writing about the World concept's relevance in my community. Jeffrey, a computer scientist, has employed it to present a mathematical definition of structure and structural similarity (2010), an explication of cognition and consciousness (1998) and with Anthony Putman, a broadened motivational base for rational economic behavior (2013, 2015).

And how does the world seem? The Descriptive Psychologist and blockchain wizard, Greg Colvin, tells this story. "After my first undergraduate class with Pete, he left on sabbatical and I was left trying to make sense of *What Actually Happens*, sitting for hours in the library where the single manuscript was available. When Pete returned I told him, 'I just don't get this Reality concept.' And, of course, he said, 'Let's take a walk.' All I recall of the walk is him taking a pencil and asking me, 'What is this?' 'I dunno, two pieces of wood pressed around a graphite core, rubber and a metal band to hold it together.' 'It's a pencil, damn it.'"

Ossorio developed these transition rules for the composition and interrelations of the Reality concepts. Where the maxims resemble the early Wittgenstein; the transition rules reflect Ossorio's reading of Gottlob Frege—a starting point he shares with Wittgenstein (e.g., Green, 1999).

STATE OF AFFAIRS SYSTEM TRANSITION RULES

Here, made explicit, is our implicit understanding of how Objects, Processes, Events, and States of Affairs are composed, can be taken apart, put back together, and relate to all the other Reality and World Concepts.

1. A state of affairs is a totality of related objects and/or processes and/or events and/or states of affairs.
2. A process is a state of affairs that is a constituent of some other state of affairs.
2a. also, is an object, so also is an event, so also is a state of affairs.
3. An object is a state of affairs that has other, related objects as immediate constituents. (An object divides into related, smaller objects.)
4. A process is a sequential change from one state of affairs to another.
5. A process is a state of affairs that has other, related processes as immediate constituents. (A process divides in related, smaller processes.)
6. An event is a direct change from one state of affairs into another.
7. An event is a state of affairs having two states of affairs ("before" and "after") as immediate constituents.
8. That an object and/or a process and/or an event and/or a state of affairs has a given relation to another object and/or process and/or event and/or state of affairs is a state of affairs.
9. That an object or a process or an event or a state of affairs is of a given kind is a state of affairs.
10. That a process begins is an event and that it ends is a different event.
11. That an object comes to exist is an event and that it ceases to exist is a different event.

Here's Ossorio in a 2000 Rap Session discussing Transition Rules.

Ossorio: "What led you to start developing the Person Concept?" In a sense, the answer is very simple, namely, total dissatisfaction with the state of the art in psychology. Total dissatisfaction with the nature of the explanations … Total dissatisfaction with the research methodology and the rationales for it. And when I say, "total dissatisfaction," I mean I sat there and laughed. [laughter] I simply couldn't take it seriously. And I said, "There's got to be a better way." Out of the dissatisfaction came …

And as you can see, in terms of being a competent player of the game, which we all are, one of the major things is you need the motivation to go do something like this. If you have it, lots of people could have done it. Without that motivation, you just go along and do things the way they've been done. So, I would count that motivation as the major thing about how come I got into the business.

Member of Audience: Pete, I don't know how/if others can tolerate this, but you had mentioned to me that you hold a little bit on Frege, and some of your thoughts about Wittgenstein's early work. Were those pieces that you had laying on your desk, that kind of inched you toward making something like the Person Concept?

Ossorio: No. They were influential at certain points in *why* I did it the way I did it, but they weren't what got me started. I was started before I ever read Wittgenstein. Not before I read Frege, but before I read Wittgenstein. However, Frege was more directly responsible for a piece than Wittgenstein was. The piece that he was responsible for is the Reality Concept. The Transition Rules in the Reality Concept were explicitly, consciously patterned after Frege's Axioms of Set Theory. Remember those axioms that start with "a = a," "a + b = b + a?" What I thought was, "We need something that simple and fundamental having to do with the real world in order to have the piece we need." So those Transition Rules, I hope, have that same simple quality, but fundamental. That was very conscious.

Member of Audience: And could you tell us …

Ossorio: By the way—I did it in about an hour.

Member of Audience: I was just going to ask, could you place it a little bit? Where were you sitting at the time you did it? [laughter] I'm just curious. Did you have Scotch on the desk?

Ossorio: No.

Member of Audience: Before you leave this one, since you brought up the massive dissatisfaction, do you have any explanation for why this massive dissatisfaction has not occurred to more people? This specifically bothers me because I've been reading a lot of the science and religion literature, and why the same sorts of dissatisfaction have not cropped up among these people who are concerned with the place where they need it …

Ossorio: Yeah. In a word, I think there is that kind of dissatisfaction, but it takes a different form. And it takes the form of being victimized. I was never a victim. Lots of people feel the burden of that. Lots of people are hurting from it, and they know it. But what they don't have is that fighting spirit that says, "Go kill the bastards." [laughter] Now it isn't just a matter of fighting spirits. I had a lot of background in a lot of things. I spent 17 years in college. And a lot of it was just auditing classes of various sorts—lots of philosophy, some linguistics, some math, lots of psychology. And some of it, a fair amount of it, I learned from experts, so that I wasn't about to be browbeaten by second hand guys in psychology who were simply retailing what the real guys—the philosophers, the mathematicians, the linguists—were saying as original work. Because of that, I wasn't stopped by the usual borders where most people would say, "Well, I don't know anything about that. That's linguistics." "I don't know anything about that. That's mathematics." "That's philosophy." I said "To hell with it. Here it is."

WORLD CONSTRUCTION: THE WORLD FOUND IS THE ONE CREATED

World is an aspect of the overarching Person Concept. There is no world *as such* without persons. (There might be something, but who's to say?) As an ingredient of the Person Concept, the World requires distinctions to be made, and that requires a person's values, knowledge, and competence to establish, vindicate, and maintain. Every world is someone's world—the full set of OPSEAs subject to appraisal and action.

Concepts and practices construct the World. The Real World is the *single whole* that contains a place for a particular person (as Actor, Observer, and Critic) and all that is in that whole, no matter how large or small. Reality provides the boundary conditions on a person's world and behavior potential. But here's a kicker: we have our limits, but one of our limits is we can't know those boundary conditions. There is no practical way to foreclose on possible deliberate action. It's a matter of trying and seeing if the effort is vindicated.

The world stage changes as the props and characters change. It changes as observational sensitivities, motivational perspectives, and social practices change. Fundamentally, it changes as different concepts are applied to observation and thought that in turn create the potential for new behaviors and social practices. And since a person's world is a social construction, it is subject to destruction and reformulation.

A PERSON'S PLACE IN THE WORLD PROVIDES
BEHAVIOR POTENTIAL

The world of Persons is discovered and created—found and invented. The improvisational encounters of people and circumstance set the stage. We discover, invent, and create through action and interaction. The limits cannot be determined a priori.

Although every world is someone's world, worlds do not exist in solipsistic isolation. Meanings are established publicly through social practice. Worlds, like languages, have the potential to be shared. However, since action requires knowledge and competence, not every world is completely sharable with everyone. A person has to be in an appropriate position, must have the requisite *status*, to engage in the actions that validate a world view. Without the necessary math, I remain blind in the world of physics. Without some sense of soul, I am numb to the experience of the spirit.

These distinctions are embodied in the Descriptive concept of status.[4] A person's status is their place in the world. Here, status means more than a conventional concern with rank and prestige, although these notions are features of a person's overall status. Rank, for example, is a form of status that says who gets to go first, who has the final say. Ossorio's concept of status involves all the relevant distinctions that provides a person's behavior potential. At different times, under varied circumstances, some aspects of a person's status are more relevant than others. Consider the drill sergeant who directs the march in lockstep but looks like she's herding kittens when attempting to get her kids up and ready for school (although you'd not be surprised to see something similar in the way she does both).

Here's Ossorio in a 1996 lecture talking about Status and World:

"Recall the relationship formula that we went through—that a person's potential for behavior depends on his relation to the things around him. And the heuristic example is the geometric relations between my being here and things in other locations in the room.

Then we extended it to not merely geometric relations but human relations, that things are possible if you have a friend than if you don't have a friend. Things that are possible with a friend may not be possible with a stranger, or vice versa. Things that are possible if you mistrust somebody

---

[4]The Descriptive concept of status resembles the ecological notion of *niche* formulated by G. Evelyn Hutchinson (1957). Hutchinson's niche is an "n-dimensional hyper-volume" consisting of all of the resources and environmental circumstances relevant to an organism's way of life over the course of that organism's lifespan. Ossorio's "status" and Hutchinson's "niche" define the boundaries of world and habitat, respectively. They both concern the full behavioral context with its possibilities and constraints. A difference is that niche is concerned with a class of organism—a species—range of resources and influence, whereas status is concerned with an individual person's behavior potential.

will not be possible if you don't. So, all of the kinds of relationships you have with the people in your life will provide you the opportunities and give you the reasons for anything that you might do. Except, of course, we have to include not merely people, but non-human objects. I commented that dealing with things in terms of relations can get very, very tedious, in fact unmanageably tedious. I gave the example of all of the things in this room, and all of my relations to every single one of them, and then all of the relations of any one of them to any one of the others. I said we have ways of handling that kind of thing, namely, we have what amounts to a map. In this room, we place different objects in different places, and once we do that, their relations to each other are determined, and we don't have go to through this long, long, long list of my relations to everything in the room; and then its relation to everything in the room; and then its and its and its and its and its. Instead, we have a very parsimonious way of getting at that whole set of things simultaneously, simply by talking about the location, the place of a given thing in a given domain. I said that notion of place, if you extend from geometry to human relations, is the Descriptive notion of status. A person's status is simply his location, his place, within some domain, and if there's no specification, that domain is simply the whole world. That notion of status is what corresponds to Being-in-the-World. It's simply your place in the world, where place is considered not as geometry but as the network of relations, of opportunities, of possibilities, of pushes, pulls, etc., that come from being related to the world and the things in it in just the way that you are. That's where your behavioral potential comes from." (Ossorio, 1977/2015, pp. 498–499).

CONSCIOUSNESS, FINAL-ORDER APPRAISALS, AND WORLD MAINTENANCE

> Worlds are not once and forever things. Once formulated, the overall structure of a person's world and the states of affairs that make up that world have to be maintained or they may be lost. Thus, in general, a person alternates between maintaining his world as a whole and dealing with the particulars of his world.
>
> When a person engages in behavior involving some particular part or aspect of his world, he is maintaining that part but simultaneously ignoring other parts and aspects of his world, including its overall structure. (Mary Roberts, 1985)

Given our psychological state and status, we go through our day *conscious of* a world and *conscious as* ourselves in that world.[5] Joel Jeffrey (1998a, b) provides this parametric formulation of consciousness:

Consciousness = <Individual, Status, World>

---

[5]Compare Timothy Leary's (1961) aphorism "set and setting" as fundamental variables for a person's experience using psychedelics.

> The real meat of the parametric formulation … is the third parameter: World. Worlds are vastly and profoundly larger and more complex than their constituents. As a result, saying *A* is conscious *of a world* and *as a particular place in that world* [status] is saying a tremendous amount. (Jeffrey, personal communication)

The consistency of the world as a whole is that it is someone's world maintained by their power and disposition to act on the OPESAs—the props and their relationships encountered on the way. Our actions, our social practices, and our verbal behaviors—uneven, inconsistent, logically varying—correspond to the differences in the communities where we engage in our affairs. The terrain of consciousness reflects this stability and variability. We act on ideas in the context of one community that would be out of place in another. People recognize, ignore, accept, and struggle with all sorts of contradictions during their daily practices. A person's Real World holds all that. Its coherence—if we want to call it that—is not so much a matter of consistency but a matter of how a person manages transitions from one community's state of affairs to another. Consider the evangelical paleontologist. How old is the world? This version of two sets of books has different texts for different communities and social practices. Never the twain shall meet? As conscious actors our first-person experience is our own measure of world consistency. Are we true to our community? Can we manage the dissonance?

Our actions reflect our appraisal of opportunity and dilemma, and this changes with our psychological states and circumstances. The world *we take to be the case* changes as the person *as appraiser* changes. In Chapter 3, I introduced Final-Order Appraisals (FOAs) and reality testing. FOA's are Critic appraisals involved in "world maintenance" and reformulation. A person with the power and disposition to make FOAs can detect anomalies—props out of place, unusual ones and those they've never encountered. As an implicit recognition of how things are and *should be*, people make an FOA of OPSEAs that violate the implicit coherence made explicit in the State of Affairs Transition Rules. FOAs are simply the appraisal of whether something fits the world as a single whole. Ordinarily, it's just the recognition that things make sense. And what makes sense can be bounded by the practices and expectations of a community.

Only when things are out of place or don't make sense, do questions ordinarily arise: is what is seen and heard real or true? When asked, such questions are answered with an FOA. In the absence of the power to make FOAs, anomalies are not treated as anomalous but simply what is there. When the disposition to make FOAs is relaxed, some people might approach anomalies in a new light, less concerned that they don't fit their "ordinary" world, freer of the assumed constraints. This carries a creative potential of world transformation (Schwartz and Godwyn, 1988).

While imagining we sometimes suspend our disposition to make FOAs; while dreaming, dissociated, and in similar states, we have less power to do so. More open to accepting anomaly, such altered states of consciousness provide opportunity and hazard.

CONSCIOUSNESS, IMAGINATION, AND THE OPPORTUNITY OF THE DREAM WORLD

For humans, our Real World includes the special domain of imagination and dream. We work the world differently while asleep. We create and encounter OPSEAs with less regard to practical waking consequence; are freer to entertain the representations our *personal imagination* provides.[6] In the safety of sleep, many of us are less deliberative than while awake. The pragmatic constraints that attend wakeful Actor-Observer-Critic feedback, loosens.

For me, it's less necessary to "reality-test" asleep, safe in bed.[7] Only dreaming do I dare leap tall buildings and soar. Having listened to people's narration of their dreams for many years, I believe my experience of dreaming is neither typical nor fundamentally different than other people's, just a bit more lucid. I've worked at it. My dreaming has been shaped by practice and experience.

As an experimentalist, I was once part of a group that empirically demonstrated that one's current *problems, dilemmas,* and *opportunities* are basic units of dream content and connect dream experience to waking life. We found that the dilemmas and opportunities represented during dreaming are similar to those we have while awake but fleshed out by our individual imaginative capacities and interests (Greenberg et al., 1992; Schwartz, 1993a, b). Dreams continue our conscious concerns, constructed with the powers and dispositions available while asleep. For some, if they remember their dreams at all, they report producing fragmented and incoherent scenes, others produce well-formed and lucid dramas.

Every dream is personal, shaped by the dreamer's characteristics relevant to the circumstances the dream world offers. The imagination of the dreamer can astonish both the dreamer and others. "Where the hell did that come from?" While dreaming, intentional actions are portrayed, but normally without the full Actor-Observer-Critic feedback that informs

---

[6] I am going to take for granted that I am the imaginative author of my dreams. They are not visitations.

[7] I doubt this would be case while asleep in a foxhole. Even asleep I remain alert to personally significant events in my environment. I can sleep through thunder but not through the sound of my children or wife crying.

waking life. There are exceptions. Some people know they are dreaming. Lucid dreamers may be as cognizant and deliberate as they are in waking life but with the additional potential to direct the drama (Schwartz and Godwyn, 1988). The skilled lucid dreamer is conscious of a stage imaginatively found or created and is conscious as a dreamer with whatever freedom that provides. Since there is less social consequence to what we do when asleep and less A-O-C deliberation, this contributes to dramatizing impulsive and immediate desires that might be thought over but not acted on when awake. *We do not need to look before we leap.* What I represent and do in my dreams doesn't get me in the same sort of mischief that my waking action would.

As I get older, my dreams provide more opportunity to play. I am not someone else when dreaming, but I go places and do things not otherwise possible. When asleep, I am very skilled at flying. It took some practice, but I'm good at it now. As a child, I'd sometimes crash, but now I soar. When I say I am not someone else, it occurs to me that I have sometimes dreamt I was one of my dogs. But no one who knows me well would find that out of character.

WORLD'S CHANGE: RECONSTRUCTION OF WORLDS AND CULTURES

Given our Hedonic, Prudent, Aesthetic, and Ethical perspectives, we construct in our Social Practices, a World of Objects, Processes, Events, Concepts and Relationships (OPESAs). We reform, reconstruct, replace, and create worlds as our OPSEAs, social practices, and perspectives change. Some change as observational capacities and sensitivities change.

Loss, Mourning, and Reconstruction

When we acquire or lose social practices, our world changes, accordingly. Since a world is maintained through social practice, our partners in practice are involved in our world maintenance. The death or loss of a person's most significant companions—lovers, spouses, parents, children, friends—creates heartbreak, a gap in a person's world. Such loss restricts the satisfactions of mutual participation. It can alter the power, disposition, and eligibility to engage in the world as it was before. Knowing John has my back lets me participate in his world and enlarges mine. If John vanishes, I may lose that. Recovery requires a sufficient world for engagement. Resilience requires sufficient resources to return to shape.

Some people never recover. Some have lost so much they find no way to regain sufficient satisfaction in the world that's left. When a person says their world is empty and life is now meaningless, I suspect they refer to the absent core practices they performed with the lost or deceased.

Others—most I hope—have sufficient remaining relationships to maintain, regain, or create new footholds in the world. *And among the remaining relationships are ones with the lost and deceased.* Here's a key point: *Relationships don't end. They remain behavior potential.* We remember and evoke their voices. If we know their through-lines, understand their character, we can continue the relationship in our imagination, accurately authoring their part in our continuing dialogue. Novelists, playwrights, screenwriters, all of us to an extent, can represent someone else's perspective. If we are empathic, we have that potential.

Mourning is the rite of passage from the world where they lived with us to one where they do not. Cross-culturally, mourning rituals create the safety to practice acknowledging the loss while tolerating a close hold on the memory of the deceased. Practicing profound engagement with the memory of the deceased sets the stage for some of their characteristics becoming our own. With sufficient practice, we become competent representatives of aspects of what they represented to us. In the past, we practiced their perspectives with them, but now we do this by ourselves. This was Freud's insight when he noticed loss may be resolved though "identification" with the lost object (1917).

Cultural and World Transformation and Reconstruction

The props and practices of a world are only so durable and stable. Mountains and oceans last longer than cultures and communities. For humans, the body is fairly constant while cultures come and go. Social practices and technologies shift fast, evolution of human embodiment is very slow.

Concepts and technologies that enhance observation and thought open the door to new social practices that can reveal anomalies in the expected world. And what is to be done about them?

Three strategies come to mind. The first is not caring at all. The second is discovering it was never an anomaly in the first place (it fits there, not where you were trying). The third way transforms the world as a whole to a context where the anomaly has a reasonable place with all the other OPSEAs. The systematic explication of the structure of the new context, its new General Conceptual System, is the paradigm shift Kuhn (1970) calls a scientific revolution.

Some communities and institutions tolerate change more than others. Some seek it. The sciences in particular have *negotiated resistance* and *reasoned acceptance* of paradigm shifts built into their methods and mission. Other institutions, notably fundamentalist religion and politics with "the final word" are reactive against any change that challenges their existing paradigm.

Trauma, Resilience, and World Reconstruction

To the extent the world does not seem broken there is little reason to fix it. To the extent a world is stable and desirably so, one only has to maintain the concepts and their social practices. Most of my time is spent where I am prepared to make my way. I'm very practiced at that. My familiar world is a very safe space. But sometimes it's not.

MONDAY APRIL 15, 2013, MARATHON DAY

From a note and blog posting. "I was coming out of Trader Joe's, hungrier than interested in the Marathon, rounding the corner of Bolyston and Gloucester, when the first bomb went off. The smell of gunpowder, some sort of black powder, moved up the street. When the second bomb exploded, I started running. My office was around the block. When I got there, three children, who minutes before were cheering their mother, huddled with their dad—frightened and confused on my steps. The best I could offer was cold water, and then their mom came running down the street more concerned about her children's fear than her own injury.

In the midst of this I had the weird thought that black powder is local." Later I wrote,

"Tonight the Boston sky is painfully beautiful." It was the end of what started as a beautiful April day, but everything—everything was both familiar and eerie.

Painfully beautiful is not how I ordinarily respond to the night's sky. My safe world was partly exploded. People I know lost limbs. In the week that followed, everyone *in my neighborhood* felt the world had changed. The only exception was an emergency room nurse, a first-responder, experienced and well trained to respond to malicious death and dismemberment. I am not. That week the usual and benign became threatening: women in burkas, discarded suitcases, anything associated with a reason to think things are not as they used to seem. And we were under curfew, SWAT vehicles and package checks, suspended due process, the sort of conditions that would in other times make a Bostonian's blood boil. In contrast, a cop I know telling me he was getting so much love you'd think he was a fireman.

Restoration Is Participation

Later, summarizing what was happening, I wrote along these lines:

When the stresses of life are ordinary and manageable, most of us feel we have it together. We have a cohesive sense of ourselves and the world. Things are in place and we understand how they connect. But under the strain of trauma, this cohesiveness can be replaced by a feeling of fragmentation and anxiety, nothing safely fits right. The world is disrupted, suddenly dangerous and unfamiliar, and a dissociation, a spaciness sets in, replacing the usual order and sequence. We startle and don't exactly know where we are or what is happening. For a time, we look to ourselves and others as out of character.

Trauma disrupts, cuts and entangles the through-lines that organize the drama of our lives. The patterns we were following, the improvisations we could enter, are torn. Flexibility ends and for a time we are stuck. We need these through-lines to be reknit, restored, rerouted. Our sensible and navigable world requires reconstruction. When the trauma has been imposed by malevolence, the desire for justice, revenge, and retribution appears and is confounded by a helplessness left in the injury's wake.

How do we get it back together? What are the parameters that define resilience and reconstruction after catastrophe and trauma? Sleep helps, finding time to retreat and regather is a good idea, love and work help restore meaning. Seeking community is vital.

For some, a return to the normal is rapid, hours or a day does the trick. But for others, especially if a previous vulnerability, an unresolved injury is touched, it can take longer, at times, much longer. Old traumas feel fresh. Sleeping dogs wake up and howl.

The problem with reconstruction, *of being made whole*, involves the extent that our relationships, social practices and memories are entwined with the damage and the loss. How significant is the damage to the person's basic values, knowledge, and skills? The basic questions of significance and extent are fundamental. How extensive and how important is the damage to the person's status, their world-view, and self-concept? These are at stake in grief and mourning.

One way or another, everything in a person's life is connected to everything else. These connections create a dynamic. Disruption in relationships entwined in a person's intrinsic practices creates change throughout a person's life, in some cases to the extent that our actions no longer appear to be our own. This is akin to the world paradigm shift required to account for anomalies. Terror is an anomaly in my world. I am glad I was unprepared in my expectations. But just how does a trauma, a terror, fit into and reconfigure a world?

After significant damage and loss, we often ask, out loud or through action, *what can I still do* and *what must I do now?* When we grieve, we ask, *what can I do with this terrible gap in my world? What is left to value? Who can I still depend on? Who can rely on me?*

Adversity elicits resilience to the extent a person's remaining attributes are sufficient to regain a worthy world. Many would like to believe adversity makes us stronger, but we should know too well how often it makes us mean, depressed, and anxious. Resilience involves the remaining values, knowledge, and competence a person can bring to a reconstruction. To recover, we eventually assess what remains intact—what wasn't damaged. Do we still value enough to have faith in our potential to reconfigure our world without undue distortion? Will there be anything left to notice besides the scars?

I sit with a lot of people who are grieving and in mourning. For some, the distinction between mourning as a temporary state or a more stable status is blurred given the time and work required to reconstruct their world. It complicates matters if they find they need to create a significantly different place for themselves. It can take considerable time to grow this place and mature into it. It takes as long as it takes to practice and become competent with the new status and to find that place satisfying. Reconstruction is reengagement.

9

Empathy in Practice:
A Demonstration of Some
Person Concepts

The concepts of Individual Person and Intentional Action provide distinctions we can use to untangle empathy, that family of ideas central to what makes persons humane. I'm going to construct a Paradigmatic Social Practice Formulation (PSPF) and Parametric Analysis (PA) of empathy as empathic action, a practice where (Fig. 9.1):

- one person communicates to another their recognition of the significance of the other's actions,
- does so with an appreciation of that person's perspective, and
- does so respecting that person's toleration for being seen in that light.

But first, let's survey how empathy appears in ordinary and technical talk. Any PSPF or PA should cover these uses.

WHAT DO PEOPLE MEAN BY EMPATHY?

When I ask people what empathy means, they usually respond with something about feeling other people's feelings or seeing from their perspective. They agree, in general, it's good to be empathic, bad if you aren't. Also, bad if you have too much empathy—"my biggest problem is that I'm just too sensitive to other people's feelings." Some believe they're empathic when they say something like, "I feel your pain." Others when they catch your eye and nod in mutual appreciation, with or without a word spoken. My psychology students may mention something I believe: narcissists and sociopaths lack sufficient empathy; that when these troubled and troubling folks were infants and children, they didn't get enough.

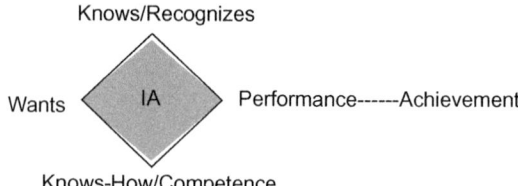

We recognize others as empathic when we feel they
accurately acknowledge our values and
motivations, our knowledge of what we recognize, and
our relevant competence, and especially as they recognize
the significance of our intentions in a manner we
can tolerate.

We tolerate what we feel competent to manage.

FIG. 9.1   Empathic action.

THEORY OF MIND

Graduate students, offering their technical expertise, might add something about "Theory of Mind." They've been taught that empathy requires
having some sort of theory about other people having minds, perspectives,
subjectivity, what have you. If I have time, I subject them to a 3 minute lecture
on the absurdity that anyone needs a theory that anyone has a mind. I note
we don't need to theorize people have minds lurking behind their actions;
we simply treat people as we have come to know them without inference,
hypothesis, or theory. Why would I need a theory that you, the reader, have
a mind? I simply take it to be the case. If I had reason to believe otherwise,
I might theorize, but day-to-day, what we have isn't some variety of theory,
but a competence developed by acting as a person in a world of persons. Do
I employ theory when I know that hitting you hard with a big stick hurts;
that there will be consequences? (On the other hand, for people who utterly
lack an adequate understanding of others, a list of reminders—not a theory—grounded in a formal conceptualization of intentionality might help.)

Naturally, with due diligence, given my questionable authority, grad
students want a good reference. I offer P.M.S. Hacker's (2018), *The Passions:
A Study of Human Nature*, where he describes "Theory of Mind" as unfortunate scientizing, and blames it on W.V.O. Quine and Wilfred Sellars:

> Within philosophy, in the United States, ordinary psychological words were held
> to be a theoretical vocabulary belonging to a primitive theory of the mind denomi-
> nated 'folk psychology' … It was not long before philosophers were advancing the
> view that our ascription of psychological attributes to others presupposed possession
> of a theory of mind. The mental attributes of others being unobservable … they have
> the status of *theoretical entities* postulated by a theory.
>
> This idea was seized upon by psychologists, ethnologists, and cognitive neuro-
> scientists. It seemed to many that this was the only way to explain what was referred
> to as 'mind-reading'—even though what is read, is not the mind, but expressive
> behavior. (p. 380)

The expressive behavior Hacker refers to is intentional action. A quintessential Wittgenstein scholar, Hacker knows a thing or two about conceptual confusions and "language on holiday." Driving his point home, he states "the problem of knowledge of other minds ... is a tangle of purely *conceptual* problems that can be resolved only by conceptual means, that is, by systematic connective analysis of a whole field of interlocking concepts." (p. 385). The Person Concept's interlocking fields of Individual Person, Intentional Action, Verbal Behavior, Culture, and World supplies those concepts.

I also suggest to my students, Peter Fonagy's (2002) concept of mentalization. Mentalization covers similar ground without the conceptual confusion of a "theory of mind"; without requiring us to understand others via hypotheses and inferences—tested, vindicated, or disconfirmed.

MIRROR NEURONS

My grad students sometimes also say, "What about mirror neurons? Aren't they responsible for empathy?" Let's consider some nonreductionist biology. When some critters observe another critter's behavior, various cortical neurons activate the way they do when the critter itself performs the same sort of behavior (Rizzolatti and Craighero, 2004). But is this "mirroring" empathy, or simply potential information based on shared anatomy that might inform an empathic response? Do patterns of stimulation mirroring another's action account for empathy? Or is it grist for the mill, simply data, empathically informative only if recognized about the other's sensations and action patterns?

This works across species. Well, let's test. Yawn, and your pup yawns with you (Romero et al., 2013). Around my dogs, if I smack my lips, they'll lick their chops and look to see if I'll share my lunch. Are Hart and Banjo empathic? Check them vs the PSPF that follows.

Mirror neurons are parts of the body that contribute to a human's empathic potential. They contribute to but are not the understanding; for that, we need a person. By analogy, without eardrums to resonate to sound, it would be hard to hear music. But do my ears appreciate the music? No. For that, we need a person.

HOW IS EMPATHY DESCRIBED IN THE WORK OF MAJOR PSYCHOTHERAPY THEORISTS?

Empathy is a defining feature of effective psychotherapeutic, nurturing, and healing relationships (e.g., Meissner, 1991; Shedler, 2010). Here are definitions from three theorists who offer similar versions of the therapist's empathic stance and its effect on their clients. Their views inform mine and are fairly representative of the field at large.

Carl Rogers (1975)—empathy involves "entering the private perceptual world of the other," "being sensitive, moment to moment, to the changing felt meaning which flow in this other person." Empathy requires assuming a nonjudgmental stance, careful not to uncover meaning that the other finds threatening.

Heinz Kohut (1984)—empathy is "the capacity to think and feel oneself into the life of the other person," as "vicarious introspection." Kohut also underscores that appropriate and therapeutic empathy is "attenuated empathy," a diminished response that is not overwhelming to either party and protects both from becoming too defensive or "walled off."

Roy Schafer (1959, 1983)—"empathy is sharing and comprehending the momentary psychological state of another person." For Schafer, empathy is a central feature of the analyst's attitude from which the psychoanalyst constructs a mental model of the analysand and expresses this with care, working hard not to "mortify" the client. Schafer (1983) writes about empathy as empathic activity, a form of intentional action; this is a position I find particularly useful. My conceptual analysis will correspond in significant ways to Schafer's "action language" mental model.

All three authors describe empathy as:

- an accurate understanding,
- attuned to the present interaction, and
- tolerable to both people.

The requirement that empathy is experienced as tolerable separates empathy from mere understanding or an exploitative "psyching out" of the other.

A VERY BRIEF HISTORY OF THE CONCEPT OF EMPATHY

I am especially interested in empathy as revealed in action, particularly when empathic actions require thoughtful attention. The word "empathy" has roots in such effort. Hacker's (2018) etymology does not begin with easily shared perspectives. The path toward "empathy" joins "sympathy," a much older word, with a more recent, entirely deliberate approach to understanding foreign and ancient literatures. It takes careful deliberate effort to grasp these literatures and the minds that produced them. Using empathic methods in psychotherapy can involve similar challenges.

Theodor Lipps was an influential German philosopher in the second half of the 19th century. He brought the concept of *Einfühlung* (in-feeling or feeling into) from aesthetics into the social and human sciences.

Empathie was Herman Lotze's 1858 Greco-German alternative to *Einfühlung*, a term Johann Gottfried Herder then used for the scholar's imaginative immersion into a culture's way of life and history. Herder's view was that a people's history and culture, the content of their real worlds, is idiosyncratic enough that historians and ethnographers cannot rely on what is familiar to them to make relevant judgments about other cultures. Alien cultures have to be understood in terms of their particular worlds, practices, language, and values. Something similar is required of the clinician who wants to maintain an empathic stance in less than ideal circumstances and with clients from unfamiliar backgrounds and circumstances.

This takes us back to the empirical and conceptual/preempirical distinction. The concept of Person is preempirical. If well-formed, it should be applicable to all people; however, its empirical-historical particulars are not. We might all be persons, but we are not otherwise all alike. What remains familiar, because constant, is our implicit knowledge of the meaning of persons and action. This implicit knowledge can misinform if it is treated as something whose historical particulars are constant. An explicit, well-formed PSPF and PA exposes the dimensions where individual and historical differences can occur. The formulations I'm going to offer should correspond to the ordinary empathy we expect from those close and dear and help the clinician navigate more difficult social terrain.

A PRACTICAL EXAMPLE FROM THERAPY

Here are some more considerations. Among those one knows intimately, empathy can be easy, until it is not. With some others, it's never easy. With some people, empathy is hard work. We all have stuff we want to hide or obscure. We don't always want to be known—although we might appreciate an empathic recognition of that. Don't we?

I am especially interested in those hard-work circumstances that call for an empathic stance. The work of psychotherapy can require empathy with insistent, troubled people and those whose personalities and worlds are outside the therapist's comfort and experience. When empathy is lost, careful deliberation might aid or restore it, and it helps to have a map. The parameters of Intentional Action (IA) can provide the coordinates for such a map.

TOMMY REVISITED

Let's revisit my work with Tommy. After my training analyst, Dr. Magraw, interpreted my "catching and falling" dream as wanting to be safely held by loving parents, I thought I understood what Tommy was signaling with his stumbles. So, I offered him a hand and said, "Tommy,

I'm not going to pick you up, but as long as you need me, I'll stand beside you. That's a promise." Subsequently, he stopped tripping in my office and running from the classroom. As I mentioned, I never explicitly explained or interpreted his apparent accidents since I thought he couldn't tolerate the meaning of his falling. Instead, I believe I spoke empathically, and he felt understood.

Let's unpack this with the IA parameters—Wants, Knows, Knows How, Performs, Achieves, Significance, and Personal Characteristics (PC). I came to see Tommy's stumbling and classroom behavior as having significance, an intentional communication and a compromise formation that involved conflicting motivations. What Tommy wanted (**W**) was support, to be picked up and held, and he wanted that from me. His problem was that placed him in an intolerable position since he felt only women or mothers are proper for that sort of contact. It would be too "gay" for him to recognize that he wanted to be held by me. I think this is why, making me more like his mother, he joked I'd look better with eye shadow. Tommy was very concrete this way.

Consciously, Tommy recognized (**K**) that I provided an opportunity for support and he knew how (**KH**) both to stand and to fall. Of course, only the falling required explanation; Tommy's competence in standing was not in question. He also knew (**K**) that falling results in being picked up and held, but given his fears, he could not directly ask for that support. Instead, he noncognizantly demonstrated his dilemma by his stumbling performance (**P**). In the form of a compromise formation, Tommy achieved (**A**) both asking for my support and the avoidance of his homophobic concerns. Given his concerns with appearing gay, the significance (**S**) of Tommy's stumbling and his classroom flight represented his wish to be held. But that was intolerable directed at a man. I, too, understood those feelings but was not nearly as homophobic as my teenage client. By telling Tommy I would stand with him as a comrade, rather than hold him as a woman, I answered his request, empathically, in a way he could tolerate, though he remained without insight.

Was my understanding of what Tommy was unconsciously asking, correct? Absent a pipeline to the truth, vindication came from the behaviors and memory that followed. Tommy's behavior changed, and he remembered his first-grade teacher's care. Magraw's interpretation felt right, too. His message affirmed what I wanted from him and my father, and implicitly acknowledged my concerns with Tommy. What I said to Tommy came from what I thought our relationship could bear; Magraw's from our tacit agreement that in a training analysis, insight is the goal and interpretation is explicit. In both cases, a relationally appropriate understanding framed the intervention.

Psychotherapeutic interpretations and interventions clarify meanings and offer support. Properly done they also carry the reminder, "you are not alone, your perspective is worth careful and caring attention." Caring and accurate attention to perspective, explicitly stated or otherwise shown, is empathy.

EMPATHY AND EMPATHIC ACTION

Empathy is a social competence. It is an attribute of engagement and cooperation. It is notably relevant in intimate, vulnerable relations and in improvisational play. Why? Intimacy and play hinge on feeling safe enough to engage; that one's moves will be well-enough understood. If we need to respond, "Sorry, I was only joking," it's because we've crossed a line.

Empathy is not easy without common ground. When hurtful misunderstanding is likely, it may not be safe or appropriate to play around, let alone take understanding for granted. This can make playing with strangers difficult if nuance is important but shared perspective is uncertain. Still, there are some things we can usually take for granted *since we are likely to treat them in similar ways.* For us humans, we are fortunate to have our primate body. It ordinarily provides us with sensations of pain, pleasure, and the like. This holds across the vertebrates, too. I write "treat" rather than "experience" because, unless *I* have reason to think otherwise, when you slap that mosquito on your nose and scratch the bump, you are doing more or less as I would. You are scratching an itch.

But what if you don't? My dog always likes a scratch behind the ear; my box turtle, not so much. I don't know about you. I can fail to understand the perspectives shaped by a stranger's communities and culture and likewise fail to appreciate the differences of a nonhuman's body and niche. And no matter how similar I take us to be, you might have your sensitivities and reasons to treat that mosquito differently.

Pondering whether we share joy and celebration can be as thorny as wondering if you feel my pain or if I may scratch behind your ear. Empathy and toleration connect through knowing how to present understandings in manageable ways. From jokes to world view, what can't be tolerated elicits insult, attack, and defense. If you respect the value of I to Thou, be mindful there are differences in what we tolerate; to what violates the integrity of our core values. Offering Tommy my hand was fine, picking him up or offering a hug was not.

Let's change course some. Consider those whose empathy is defined and guided by "when you're in pain, I'm in pain," in contrast to "I see where you're coming from." So, what is actually shared if I say, "I feel your pain," and you agree? I'm not going to approach this as a mind-merger, but from the pragmatics of observable engagement. I understand what you feel through my thoughts and observations of what you do and your personal significance to me. What validates this understanding? It's my treating you as a person; as an intentional actor whose behaviors tell me what is significant to you—the perspective you're coming from.

About that "shared pain": my self-concept and sense of well-being incorporates the strengths and vulnerabilities, the very personal characteristics of those I actually love. For example, as a father, I cannot separate my well-being from my children's. As a husband, I cannot fully separate my sense of well-being from my wife's. We are joined that way. A version of what happens to them happens to me. With my children, for example, I can honestly claim to be pained when they are hurt. I share their joy when they celebrate.

But while pained or joyful I still might misunderstand, "where they're coming from." People tell me I'm a bit thick and I believe them. Feeling, correctly or not, what they are feeling leaves "where they are coming from" unaddressed. If I'm not sure or want to know more, I can ask.

But what to ask? A Paradigmatic Social Practice Formulation of empathic action and a Parametric Analysis of that paradigm can guide us when empathy is hindered by unshared values and knowledge, unknown circumstances, defensive preoccupation, or just the inherent difficulty of getting on the same page with a stranger and those we know well but still misunderstand.

I use these two formulations when I sense I'm poorly attuned to someone and don't want to be; or when listening, to better *understand what they understand* about someone we are discussing. An explicit analysis of empathy can structure an interview with these goals, so these formulations come in handy in psychotherapy, consultation, and supervision. Since I am paid to train doctoral students to put what they know into words, I can offer them a systematic method.

EMPATHY, PARADIGM CASE FORMULATION, PARADIGMATIC SOCIAL PRACTICES FORMULATION, AND PARAMETRIC ANALYSIS

Paradigm Case Formulations (PCFs) in the form of a Paradigmatic Social Practices Formulation (PSPF) are useful when conventional definitions prove too limiting, various, or ambiguous. Empathy poses this problem. A PSPF of empathy should make sense to everyone, and where it doesn't, the disagreement should be easy to see. An adequate PSPF of empathy, coupled with its PA, can distinguish *if, how,* and *how much* a person is behaving empathically.

In Descriptive Psychology, we understand something by looking at its implications, by the difference it makes in behavior. Since empathy is often described as shared experience, we might ask: how can we tell? Seeing from another's perspective is a fiction of sorts. I can only walk in my shoes and see from my perspective. What I have are my observations and thoughts about my interactions with others. I observe other people's actions, but only from where I stand. There is no way around this fact. Instead, I'm asking how we sense that someone is empathic. What are they doing when they act empathically with us? The answer comes from appraising how we feel treated. "Feel" here is relational, whether it is my immediate appraisal of my sensations, or my appraisal of how we are getting along.

While an empathic person acts with an immediate belief they see and feel another's perspective, the other can only recognize this from the empathic actor's performance. The PSPF and PA that follow concern the significance of an observed performance. Both the PSPF and PA respect what an empathic actor feels, but focus on how that feeling is vindicated from the observed person's perspective.

A PSPF OF EMPATHIC ACTION

In earlier work, I developed a PSPF of empathy as empathic action. Empathic action communicates an accurate understanding of the significance of a person's behaviors and circumstances in a way they can tolerate (Schwartz, 2002, 2013). This requires appreciating their current perspective by understanding their active motivations; their relevant knowledge of themselves and their circumstances; their relevant know how; and the significance, to them, of their performance. This PSPF of empathy allows alterations that capture the concept's ordinary meanings. For example, although I have described this as a two-person interaction, the number of participants can be increased. The accuracy of the understanding can be recognized by all or just assumed by one ("I'm being empathic even if you don't realize it."). A practical use of the parameters is that disagreements, deficiencies, and misunderstandings can be identified and potentially remedied (Fig. 9.2).

A PSPF Formulation of Empathy as Empathic Action

Empathic Action is Deliberate Action where one person observes the Performance of another person and communicates to them an accurate understanding of the Significance of their behavior in ways the other person Knows How to tolerate.

Transformations

T1. Change the Observer's Intentional Action from Deliberate to merely Cognizant. (From a choice to communicate to merely aware that one is communicating.)

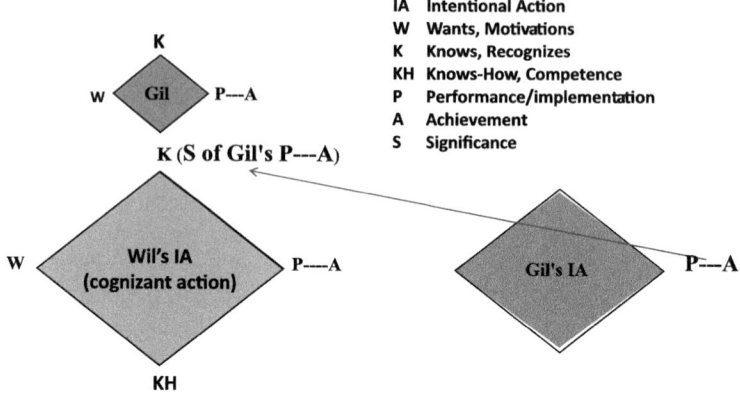

IA   **Intentional Action**
W   **Wants, Motivations**
K   **Knows, Recognizes**
KH   **Knows-How, Competence**
P   **Performance/implementation**
A   **Achievement**
S   **Significance**

Wil's recognizes Gil as a Deliberate and Cognizant Actor

All   Cognizant Action content may be more or less present, uncertain, unclear, and/or distorted.

_{wrs}

FIG. 9.2   Wil's cognizant and empathic recognition of Gil.

T2. Change the Observer's Deliberate Action to merely Intentional Action. (Merely communicating without choice or awareness.)
T3. Change the number of observed participants (empathic action toward a couple, a family, a community, etc.)
T4. Change one or more of the persons to nonparadigmatic persons. (Nonhuman companions, pets, etc.)
T5. Change the accuracy or recognition of the parametric content. (This formulation values Significance over the other parameters, i.e., appraisals of Significance are more paradigmatic than mere appraisals of performance or implementation.)
T6. Change the degree to which the empathic actor communicates their understanding in ways the observed actor can tolerate, i.e., the ways the observed Knows How to manage being understood.

An Example and a PA

I'm drinking with my close friend, Joe, whose girlfriend, Sharon, just left him over a serious misunderstanding:

> Joe, it sucks watching you bite your tongue, still loving her so damn much, swallowing what she thinks. It pisses me she can't handle it. I don't know what else you could've said. I feel so fucking bad for you. For what good it does, you're a good man and did the right thing. I'll buy the next round.

Give me the benefit of the doubt and accept that Joe felt understood. We know each other well and have our way of talking; well enough that I might have accomplished the same by merely listening, nodding, shaking my head, patting his back and with a half-smile calling for the bartender. Empathic action is not limited to verbal behavior. With empathy, it's not the words so much, as how the words express the relationship.

The significance of what I say to Joe occurs within our idiosyncratic relationship. I talk this way with him. If you suffered a similar loss, that way of talking might not be a good idea. Empathy occurs as a feature of a social practice reflecting the status of the individuals' relationships to each other.

In a moment you'll get to a breakdown of my comments to Joe where I employ the IA parameters as reminders. Unlike a formal articulation of an IA, I'm using the parameters as a guide to help me sort out relevant issues that might facilitate or interfere with my empathy with Joe. (Think of the IA parameters like a favorite Swiss Army knife with its nifty tools, good for improvisation.)

Here's the PA:

Behavior = Intentional Action = <I, W, K, KH, P, A, S, PC>
I   The identity of the actors: Wynn and Joe.
W   What the actors Want to accomplish. I want to comfort Joe, but that only matters if Joe recognizes that I understand his actual dilemma from his perspective—that he wants to reconcile, but even more significantly, he wants to protect Sharon from what he thinks would hurt her more if she knew.
K   What the actors Know, distinguish, or recognize in the circumstance relevant to what the actors Want. I communicate that I know how this all looks to Joe and that I see it that way too. Joe loves Sharon, but he wants to protect her from the truth.
KH   What the actors Knows How to do given what they Want and Know about the relevant circumstance. I know how to speak in ways that express my bond with Joe. Joe doesn't know how to tell his girlfriend what really happened in ways she can manage, but he knows how to bite his tongue and tolerate his frustration. He knows how to talk to Sharon but not about that. Joe and I both know how to drink to dull the pain.
P   The procedural manner or Performance of the action in real time. Our drinking together and my stating my understanding of Joe.
A   The Achievement of the action. My communicating, in ways that reflect my caring relationship with Joe. Joe feels understood. We both get comfortably drunk.
S   The Significance of the action for the actor. What the actor is up to by performing the act in question. Both of us recognizing and

sharing the painful intensity of a love lost out of misunderstanding, and in Joe's case, to protect his girlfriend from a mortifying truth. **PC   The Personal Characteristics of the actors expressed by the action.** Joe, a hurting, drunken friend in love, who will sacrifice the appearance of integrity because his actual integrity rests on being the guy that accepts loss over causing more hurt to someone he loves. Makes me want to drink another round, too.

A PRACTICAL CHECKLIST OF EMPATHY REMINDERS

Here's a list of questions, corresponding to the IA parameters, that serve as my checklist for empathic action. They help when somethings gone askew. If appropriate, I can ask these questions of myself or of the person I'm attempting to empathize with. Given my density, I try to remind myself that I only know so much and should not presume to know more.

1. **Given their understanding of the overall circumstance, what does this person want and value?** And do we share an understanding of what the overall circumstance calls for? (The W parameter.)
2. **What exactly do they recognize in their circumstance that is relevant to what they want and value?** And do we share a common recognition of the situation? (The K parameter.)
3. **What do they know how to do given what they see as their current opportunity or dilemma?** And do they have the skill or competence that is needed to successfully manage the circumstance? (The KH parameter).
4. **What is the significance to them of how they behave in these circumstances?** (The S parameter).
5. **What personal characteristics are they employing, and what is the significance of these characteristics to them?** (The PC and S parameters).
6. **What is their perspective on how their performance looks?** (The P parameter and the K parameter).
7. **Can they tolerate, i.e., know how to manage the way I express what I understand about them?** (The KH parameter).

THE IA PARAMETERS AND SOME REMINDERS FOR PSYCHOTHERAPY

When close relationships go well, easy understanding and empathy go hand in hand. This is implicit in the flow of a comfortable social life. Psychotherapy is a deliberately protected, sequestered departure from the ordinary. The confidentiality, the exclusive attention, and the other policies of engagement are designed to ensure the possibility of an empathic exploration of what would otherwise challenge the patience of intimates and others.

On good days, therapeutic dialogue offers insight and a comfortable appreciation of being understood; on very good days, desired change. Until it doesn't. Perhaps there's the boredom and awkwardness of disconnection. Or suddenly the crunch of ruptured accord that echoes misunderstanding and indicates where hard, important work needs to be done. Psychotherapy is sought out of difficulty. When the therapeutic encounter is boring or grows awkward; when anxiety, rage, or panic appear; when the topic of concern is repeatedly evaded; therapists have reason to question their empathic understanding. It helps to have methods to address this. The IA parameters can organize reflection.

Identity

Every action is someone's action, and that someone has a name or title or some individual status marker. The identity parameter is a reminder of this. The identity parameter is a name; but consider how naming reflects a person's status. The name one person calls another suggests the named person's place in the namer's scheme of things. One of the first questions clients often ask is what to call me. Dr. Schwartz? Wynn? And what should I call them? What do they want to be called? What will be the significance of using names or titles that express socially different meaning? Is the naming personal and intimate? Paternal, maternal, or patronizing? A reminder of roles and boundaries? What does it mean if the means of address changes or a name is mixed up or forgotten?

Wants and Values

We have *our* reasons for what we do in any given circumstance, even when responding to coercion, accident, or reflex. Or while intoxicated, half-awake, or even while dreaming. What we attempt in whatever state we are in reflects an appraisal of our situation with the values, knowledge, and competence available to us. People's individually different hedonic, prudent, moral-ethical, and aesthetic "weighted" values inform their appraisals. My reasons in any apparent circumstance might not be yours; the situation I see may not be how you see it. Behavior that appears strange, inappropriate, irrational, or self-defeating from my position could make complete sense to you. When a lion enters our room and you make for the door, you're confused why I sit relaxed and continue to polish my nails. Have you forgotten my earlier life as a lion tamer?

People's actions reflect their values. Some values are easier to recognize than others; some values are more agreeable to claim than others. Some of what I want carries a burden of guilt, shame, and sanction. Even if I believe it shouldn't, I might gather you do. We have reason to carefully hide the bodies and not want them dug up. We hide from ourselves as well. In my work, I rarely confront unconscious motivations. Rather, I help people consider the implications of what they have done or might do; or the motivations and actions they are reluctant to recognize and own. What's hard to face is difficult to change. What's troubling to think is hard to share—and reconsider. In Chapter 4 we used the Judgment Diagram to illustrate how this can result in undersocialized, "primitive," insistent, and compulsive thoughts and actions that hobble the Actor-Observer-Critic feedback that regulates individual and social selves. When problematic "wants" are unexamined, choice is narrowed, and actions get bungled.

Approaching what a person is reluctant to claim requires empathic tact. I was taught to "blame the environment" before asking folks to look at their contribution to the mess they're in. That's not always a good idea, but the gist of this policy is to avoid making people defensive before touching sensitive nerves. Starting with the circumstances makes it easier to approach how that situation was an understandable provocation, entrapment, enticement, temptation, attractive nuisance, or whatever. *I see why it made sense to do what you did.* While I don't buy the devil made anyone do it, I appreciate why a person might make such a claim.

Being kind is part of the therapeutic process; appearing less than overly judgmental is another. We play to the audience, to how we understand the values of others. Like it or not, we dance like people are watching. I think I mentioned before that few days pass before someone says to me, "I shouldn't care what others think." I respond with a version of, "Bullshit, of course we do." with an emphasis on "we." We live in communities where our standing is not independent of how we appear. Even claiming we don't care, we usually do. But, if it helps us practice, pretending no one is watching is sometimes a good thing to do.

Social engagement and judgment are inseparable. The degradations and affirmations of everyday life also happen in psychotherapy. Inescapably, we judge, but how we act on our judgments—how we implement our complex recognitions of what is helpful—is another matter. We can neither excise our values nor give up judgment, but with self-aware constraint, like Joe, we can learn when to bite our tongue. And, as I suggested in Chapter 7, when we are in the position to offer an accreditation, we might reveal shared values.

Knowledge and Knowing

Along with the basic question of why a person does something is why they are doing it now. The answer is some version of finding an opportunity or dilemma in the current circumstance. What can be found is something known and more or less competently discerned.

We have—but sometimes forget—our particular knowledge of concepts and facts. Sometimes we act on distinctions without cognizance of doing so or without being able to verbalize what we recognize. We can be wrong about what we know, and this has consequences. Our knowledge can be more or less clear, certain, and serviceable. Our observers might think we aren't recognizing an opportunity when it stares us in the face. And sometimes our sensitivities are heightened or dulled. Hoisting another one, Joe and I had this goal.

Acquiring knowledge has a learning history. Our capacities differ, as do the circumstances that provide opportunity. Same goes for our interests. Given where and how someone grew up, what are they expected to know? Do they match these expectations? Plus, in the same families, communities, and schools, what is acquired is idiosyncratic. Underdeveloped, diminished, and deficient capacities make a difference.

The empathic observer knows that if a situation calls for a person to do something normally expected of members of a community, if that person lacks the relevant knowledge (or values or competence), they will do something else instead. A person can only act on the values, concepts, and skills they have available, unless they suddenly acquire it by luck or accident. We're creative; this happens, but don't count on it.

Knowledge and talent vary. I often have the good fortune and dilemma of sitting with brilliant, extraordinarily talented people. Here's a caution for the therapist: some people are more discerning and knowledgeable, are just plain smarter than you. They recognize and understand nuances you don't. This is a problem when the people you see act and comment on actual features of themselves and their worlds you can't see. Without adequate reflection, this might evoke defensive competition; a diagnosis of intellectualizing; and dismissal. I know this for a fact. So, after I quell my defensive, competitive, and dismissive urges, my best move is to ask my client to help me understand what I'm having trouble following. This is an important part of the job, anyway—having people clearly communicate—using *their* words—to be understood.

This is a tactic when supervising people whose work involves expertise I don't have. I have faith in my capacity to tell when something has been presented well. (When a physicist client is stymied in rage and envy over a colleague's critique of her work, I can help her articulate the significance of her feeling. Her emotions aren't rocket science.) For many years, I've run a supervision seminar for fourth-year doctoral candidates. They practice with first-year trainees and often end up assigned one whose interests and field experience is very different from their own. Often, fourth-years worry they don't have anything to offer if they don't know much about what their "supervisee" is supposed to accomplish. I give them the same advice I give myself: they know enough, or should, to recognize when something is described adequately; its implications spelled out. Since doctoral-level clinicians ought to be able to verbalize what they understand (or don't), asking their trainees to carefully describe what they are doing *until they both understand* is a good exercise. It also tests the empathy of the fourth-years as they help their first-year trainees (who want to appear professional, and to cope with anxiety and confusion). They're the new kids on the block, wanting to look tougher than they feel.

Know How and Toleration

An empathic observer implicitly notes what the observed is appraising, i.e., what they see that is of motivational significance. Inextricably tied to what a person knows and wants is what they know how to do. Not everyone has the capacity, practice, and experience to know how to do what we might take for granted; while some people are so talented, so well-practiced, their performance look like magic.

Once competence is achieved, behavior going well enough does not call for explanation. When it goes wrong, it does. Tommy's walking toward the couch and sitting down raised no questions, but his repeated stumbling did.

How people evaluate their competencies is essential to what they try to do and how they account for failure and success. When people believe they don't know how to perform what their circumstances demand, it should come as no surprise if they are anxious or avoidant. In the absence of knowing how to do something valued, what looks to the observer as opportunity can be taken as a threat. Anger, fear, guilt, envy, worry, anxiety, and panic might be felt in situations where a person takes it that they lack the relevant competence to handle problematic or desired states of affairs. If it matters, and you think you can't do it, you have a problem. If this happens often enough, Seligman's (1972) insight that "learned helplessness" is a path to depression makes sense and may follow. This is why the Know How parameter is of special relevance to what a person can tolerate. We approach and tolerate what we know and know how to handle.

What we assume about our and others' competencies is part of the degradations and accreditations of everyday life. If unexpectedly "I didn't know I had it in me," but I succeed, my bet is I'll more likely feel relief instead of satisfaction. Phew. Satisfaction attends the competent achievement of desired goals, a different but kindred state to visceral pleasure. Accordingly, "I didn't know you had it in you," is not usually praise, but insult.

We are limited in what we can tolerate, how we can manage being seen, and what we let ourselves consider. We protect ourselves from what we think we can't handle. People have self-concepts and defensive styles that limit and shelter awareness. We sometimes engage defensively, even when we've outgrown the need. We may not know that what was good to defensively avoid in infancy and childhood can now be managed. Some of the fits and starts of maturation work this way. The empathic clinician keeps this in mind: people engage defensively if they don't have strong enough reasons to think it is safe to behave otherwise. To help a person tolerate more than they believe they're able requires careful gathering of evidence, empathically presented. If a therapist correctly recognizes a client has grown capable and provides room and support for them to practice, they might shed unneeded defense. Here I use "might" because humans can be fixated and very stubborn.

Psychotherapy is sometimes an exercise in learning how to sit still. It takes practice to know how to sit still when strong feelings are evoked. An empathic companion helps make it safer for the client to examine the unconsidered and the avoided. Slow down and think it over. Except when immediacy is necessary, it's good to know how to look before you leap. Looking at a dilemma together can build tolerance by modeling how difficult circumstances and their attendant feelings can be approached. Patience and practice are required, sometimes hand in hand. This is the love in the work.

SIGNIFICANCE, THROUGH-LINES, ACCREDITATION, DEGRADATION, AND THE DEVELOPMENT OF CHARACTER

Degradation and Accreditation Ceremonies are social practices that involve judges, witnesses, and the judged, and concern the standing of the judged person in a community. These practices identify how the significance of a person's actions define something essential about their values, character, and integrity. At their heart, these judgments are about whether someone is "one of us." Since empathy involves shared perspective, our perspective, the presence or absence of empathic action is a way of treating another as one of us—or not.

A reminder. What a person's behavior means to me can be quite different from what it means to them. Regardless of how compelling I find the evidence, they might not appreciate how I see the significance of their behavior. There are no guarantees I have it right. Right or wrong, it will figure into my treatment of them and their response. Right or wrong, it will also reflect the power each of us have to maintain our credibility within a community and to establish which values matter most. The power of the judge is maintained by their controlling the agenda (Lukes, 2005). Many of us grew up with parents, teachers, and others whose authority allowed them to tell us what is important and required us to listen to them when they wanted us to think it over. Therapists should pay heed to this as a source of transference when they attempt to direct the work. Is their direction welcome guidance or is it coercion that will be met with resentment, resistance, or resigned compliance?

When communicating an observation about the significance of an action (especially when this involves interpretation of something problematic), all the dilemmas of trying to make the unconscious cognizant, all the problems of trying to get someone in touch with what they're reluctant to see, come into play. It calls for tact, enhanced by recognizing people can tolerate only so much. This is not so different from the vulnerability that attends intimacy. Lovers, friends, and therapists need permission to test the boundaries of self-understanding. Serious breaches of empathy and its restoration can occur around this.

Empathy might set the direction for through-lines. For example, Heinz Kohut (1984) saw parental and peer empathy as crucial for the development of a child's ambitions and talents. As a setup for an implicit accreditation ceremony, he emphasized that empathic parents should be worthy of their child's idealization; and, in turn, admire their kid. Kohut is describing the sort of parent-as-judge a child would want to validate goals. *You're cool, and you think I'm pretty OK, too.* The child's talents, accurately recognized and admired by the parents, are further developed through play and practice in the company of the child's peers.

What would this promote? Donald Winnicott's (1971) position is that the good-enough parent needs to celebrate their child's "spontaneous gestures"—their assertions and creations, in empathic cognizance of their child's intentions and initiatives. Winnicott and Kohut offer a formulation of how parental and peer empathy affirms values, validates character, and points to through-lines worth developing. The child is offered support and guidance for roles they might be well-cast to grow into. (Here's a thought experiment: if we reverse the parental and peer attributes and make the parents unworthy of idealization, dismissive of the child, and prevent practice with peers, what do you suspect might happen? It's hard to be sure. Children find ways to invent themselves apart from the obvious circumstances, but I would not expect a good outcome.)

Empathic action communicates an understanding of the significance of an action from the actor's perspective. *I see how you look at things and their significance to you.* If it also carries, *I see it that way, too,* likely, it is felt as sympathetic. If it also identifies a through-line, it's commentary on character and integrity. Judgments of worth and place are core status assignments. This is tied to being seen as one of us and having shared community. Trying to see another's perspective is attempting to share and value something in common. This is how empathy connects and builds community. Accreditations are enhanced by empathic acts, degradations by indifference to whether a judgment is tolerable.

PERSONAL CHARACTERISTICS

People's behaviors are an expression of their personal characteristics. Some of them are more valued than others. I might not give a damn about qualities you want me to possess. Behaviors seen as out-of-character do not create the conditions for degradation or accreditation that they do when treated as in-character. Whether we offer praise or give people breaks, depends on this distinction. It gives us wiggle room.

The more familiar we become with the other's values, knowledge, and competence; the more harmonious social life feels; the more we can ignore empathy or simply take it for granted. When relationships feel attuned, cooperative, and effective; when we don't feel unfortunately judged; we have little reason to question whether empathy is present or needed. In contrast, when engagements feel awkward, broken, ruptured, or breached then deliberate attention to the Intentional Action parameters points to targets in need of repair. When culture, gender, age, embodiment, mental state, social class, etc., confuse; when differences in status are large; when we know we don't know much about the other, attention to the parameters can be very useful. Given how frequently psychotherapists find themselves with people who seem initially strange, deliberate attention to these distinctions can guide self-refection and inquiry.

Afterword and Summary: Satisfaction and the Construction of Worlds or, At the End of the Day, How Does It Feel?

For the clarity that we are aiming at is indeed complete clarity. But this simply means that the philosophical problems should completely disappear.

The real discovery is the one that enables me to break off doing philosophizing when I want to. The one that gives philosophy peace, so that it is no longer tormented by questions that brings itself in question." **(Ludwig Wittgenstein, Philosophical Investigations, 133)**

But he, Herzog, had committed a sin of some kind against his own heart, while in pursuit of a grand synthesis.

What this country needs is a good five-cent synthesis. **(Saul Bellow, Herzog)**

Getting closure is challenging: what to put in, what to leave out. What's enough to be satisfied that the story has been told and the subject matter properly represented? And consider the subject: the Person Concept's interconnected place for everything! Fortunately, I've not been alone. While writing, I engage in silent dialog with Peter Ossorio and Anthony Putman. To maintain authenticity, I've relied on members of the Descriptive Psychology community: Raymond Bergner, Keith Davis, and Joel Jeffrey in particular, but especially Clarke Stone—my constant, critical reader and active contributor. All of them could have written a version of this, too.

Am I satisfied with what I've said? Several years ago, after rereading Saul Bellow's *Herzog* I wrote the following. I'm back, looking at the same water. Read it as a summary of what I've been trying to say before.

What is it to be satisfied? What kept Herzog and Wittgenstein in torment? (But Wittgenstein also said, "The delight I take in my thoughts is delight in my own strange life.")

Sitting at my table facing Poucha Pond, it's a mid-July morning on Chappaquiddick. My wife is reading while our dogs doze and sniff the humid Atlantic air. The saw-grass that bounds the property hides a weathered plastic blue bulldozer and orange dump truck, sturdy remains of summers past. I'll write a bit more and then take the Jeep to Wasque. Maybe the storm last night improved the fishing. There is nowhere I'd rather be, nothing I'd rather be doing.

A man I know, entangled in his family's affairs, complains constantly about the endless tasks he angrily undertakes. Few people would have the focus or competence to manage what he toils at daily. "When will I get back to my life?" he asks. When his week finally ends, he doesn't look forward to the next.

Both of us are deliberately engaged in activity that significantly expresses our particular personalities. He's certain he'll get the job done. It will be unassailable, with every document examined, understood, and in place. Nearly perfect. Me? I've no guarantee I'll catch anything.

Both of us can state our intentions with an important difference. For the moment, I'm comfortable and have no further aim in sight. He's not. I'm unsure what I'll be doing later, except that I'll want to edit this, so it might be clearer to you. Knowing him, by early evening he'll be absorbed in his body's painful tensions and want relief. He'll take for granted no one will understand or really help. His pain will frustrate him. He'll go to bed even more angry and determined than when he first awoke.

I am describing two different patterns of intentional behavior that underscore a through-line of satisfaction and dissatisfaction. Intentional behavior is an expression of our values, knowledge, and competence. The weights we give these values, our motivational priorities, correspond to what we want to accomplish in any given circumstance. What we actually do depends on what we recognize and know how to perform given the conditions at hand. This is all organized by the significance of what we are trying to achieve. We may be only more or less aware of this significance, but it will establish a pattern, a through-line, central to how our worlds feel.

All of us, in our own way, live our lives engaged in the social practices of our communities. Our actions express our personal characteristics and our participation in the institutions and communities that constitute our culture, our way of living. What we create and value, we find here. This will be the source of our satisfactions.

Not everything we accomplish provides satisfaction. Much of what we do is *instrumental*, done because it provides access to something else we want. We work in the coal mine for money and fuel. We need to buy groceries and pay the rent, but we'd do something else to keep the lights on if we could.

Some of what we do is *intrinsic*, done just for the doing. We do it in expression of our core values: hedonic, prudent, ethical, and aesthetic. Successful performance that expresses this is satisfying.

How does this work? Hedonic pleasure speaks for itself. The prudent or self-interested enhancement of one's place in the world should be a source of satisfaction (or, at the very least, relief).

Ethical and aesthetic actions are especially significant since they are deliberate and involve the recognition of choice in a way not required when simply seeking pleasure or behaving with prudence. The ethical choice of "the right thing," done for the sake of justice and fairness, can be its own reward.

Aesthetics involve the appreciation of how things fit together, how they make sense. The artistic, scientific, conceptual, or social engagement with beauty, truth, rigor, elegance, objectivity, and closure is profoundly satisfying for those who are competent to engage in such pursuits.

Some of our values are complementary and work well together. Some are relatively independent or noncontingent. And some of what we want conflicts and antagonizes in unsettling ambivalence. Life is complicated.

The weights we give our values, core and peripheral, are fundamental to what we take as opportunity and dilemma. We build our worlds this way and are satisfied or dissatisfied with what results.

Satisfaction is rarely achieved by accident. Authentic accomplishment requires competent participation. This is a matter of choice, of selection, and is deliberate.

Here is the gist of my thesis: recognizing a sufficient link between the instrumental and the intrinsic and having sufficient faith the connection will hold is vital for satisfaction. I also think it is an aspect of general happiness. Feeling satisfied accompanies an instrumental act when we know it has a significant connection to something we also value intrinsically. This connection can be a self-aware appreciation or simply felt. I am going to follow this idea because it will clarify why some people are generally happy and some are not. I know people who can't find this connection and I know people who defensively resist where the connection leads. In general, they are unhappy.

When I am sufficiently satisfied and see my circumstances as my good fortune, I'll feel happy. But not all satisfactions bear good fortune, coming as they may in the wake of a tragic or ironic undertaking: settling a score; paying off a debt; finally making it right; going down swinging.

Again, my thesis: the feeling of satisfaction ties the instrumental to the intrinsic and is a function of the awareness of the tie. Mindful recognition of how the instrumental connects to the intrinsic is fundamental in establishing satisfying and unsatisfying through-lines in people's lives. I suspect a life lived without sufficient recognition of this connection will be depressive, anxious, frustrating, and narcissistic. It may also involve a sense of helpless repetition, a feeling of being compelled to do things again and again without satisfying closure.

It complicates matters that connections are not always recognized and felt. The connection is there, its significance to the observer may be clear, but the actor is defensively unaware. Some refuse the price of insight when it brings more guilt, shame, sadness, or anger than they can bear. In avoidance of these bad feelings, a person may compulsively and unconsciously repeat a performance, devoid of satisfaction or closure. If unaware of an action's connection to something of compelling and intrinsic significance, it becomes especially difficult to renounce the act, or choose a more adequate implementation. Under these conditions, desire feels futile, meaningless, becomes a sort of shadow boxing. Nothing solidly connects or ends.

Ultimately, the significance of doing something rests on its intrinsic foundations: hedonic, prudent, ethical and/or aesthetic. When an act is performed with awareness of its connection to something's intrinsic significance, it provides some sort of satisfaction. The experience of satisfaction is a motivational aspect of the awareness of this connection, whether the act is intrinsic or instrumental. Satisfaction is the feel of the connection. Some satisfactions provide closure, and some provide reasons to do it again.

My friend, Anthony Putman, takes this further. He writes that the experience of a certain satisfaction, what he calls *ultimate satisfaction*, holds a person's world together. A person's world has at its foundation intrinsic social practices. People construct their worlds from what they find and can do. Every world is someone's world, and someone's shared world. Worlds involve a community's practice.

Some practices, that Tony calls *ultimate practices*, affirm the particular coherence or sensibility of a world; to engage in these practices is an affirmation of that world. This makes it all the more vital for the instrumental to be tied to the intrinsic. Creating a well-formed formula is one of these ultimate practices for a mathematician, but the ritual of selecting and sharpening a number four pencil can provide satisfaction as an instrument of that act.

(Notice I am distinguishing the varied worlds where a person participates from a person's overall status in their "world of worlds." Tony writes about a mathematician's ultimate satisfaction in recognizing the elegance of a proof. He's felt it himself. But every mathematician participates in more than just the world of mathematics. We all engage in varied and irregular roles in the institutions and communities that make up our worlds. Still, worlds have some sort of coherence. They fit together the way a person's life fits together. In some way, it all connects. This is not to say that this coherence will necessarily be seen and felt. It may not feel to people that their worlds make sense, separately or together. As Peter Ossorio pointed out, we can't count on this to be simple. The terrain of a world varies irregularly as does the relations among worlds. This is why we have and need complicated grammars and varied sets of conceptual tools to sort this out.)

Tony writes:

"Every community has a shared world that makes sense to its members. The sense it makes is particular to each community's world. This *"making sense"* is inherent in participation in the community's core practices.

Every community has a set of ultimate practices, participation in which affirms their world and is accompanied by ultimate satisfaction.

Ultimate satisfaction is a strong basic human need. Persons are powerfully, inherently motivated to seek it.

The specific experience of ultimate satisfaction differs from community to community. Its importance to maintaining the community and its world does not.

In short: ultimate satisfaction holds the world together." (2016)

Knowing how to regularly participate in the core practices that provide ultimate satisfaction seems wise, perhaps spiritual. I appreciate the wisdom of those who do. I suppose this is why I find spiritual practices daunting. The late theologian Mary Shideler described the spiritual as the domain of *totalities, ultimates,* and *boundary conditions.* A synthesis or feel for the totality requires a stance and perspective beyond my reach. It would be pretentious for me to say I even try.

Spiritual practice requires, I think, an appraisal of the totality of worlds. There are philosophers, theologians, adepts, and disciples who attempt explication and entrance to this totality, wanting to know the awesome dimension. Can you *grok* it? I can't.

Spinoza's state of *beatitude,* suggesting recognition of God's love and understanding of the whole is, I gather, this type of experience beyond my means.

I've stopped trying to imagine the Zen state of *Satori* involving the wholeness of dissolved paradox and attachment.

More accessible is Aristotle's practical wisdom, a version of *eudaimonia,* described in his *Nicomachean Ethics* as an effective comprehension of how friendship, pleasure, virtue, honor, and wealth fit together. This seems closer to what is possible for many fortunate and ordinary lives. This practical understanding requires acting on the intrinsic practices of *the good.* This, I can attempt. It resembles Tony's concept.

Tony's ultimate satisfaction is situated in the core practices of particular communities and their worlds. This less than grand synthesis is achievable and vital, at least for some.

Tony's ultimate satisfaction, if I understand what he is saying, has a limited and reachable scope. He's hypothesizing a basic human need to participate and feel how things fit together. This is an aesthetic recognition even if it also involves pleasures, self-interests, and just pursuits. To call ultimate satisfaction a basic human need implies that if not met, pathology will result. I think this helps us understand some of the pathologies of narcissism.

But perhaps he's overstated it as a universal need. I question Tony's claim that "Ultimate satisfaction is a strong basic human need. Persons are powerfully, inherently motivated to seek it." I think to say persons are "powerfully, inherently motivated to seek it" overstates its place in the lives of most people. I think it makes more sense as a desire for a sort of optimal satisfaction for those who both *know* and *want* to seek it. For those folk, if not achieved, their worlds may feel fragmented, empty, or broken. Norman Normal doesn't know what he's missing, but Wittgenstein and Herzog painfully do. What brings sufficient satisfaction for Norman may be insufficient for those on a more demanding aesthetic quest.

But if Tony is correct, he is pointing to a pathology of ordinary life and providing a key to the diffuse pattern of malaise that is frequently part of banal existence.

The problem is that although unmet needs will result in some degree of pathology, what is needed is not always known. The needed must in some way be known for it to be intentionally sought.

What, then, are the implications of an absence of ultimate satisfaction? Will the center not hold? How does the absence of sufficient satisfaction affect a person's experience of themselves and their worlds? What happens when a person cannot see how their actions connect to what they intrinsically value? What if they almost never feel the connection? Or, alternatively, what if their sense of the intrinsic is underdeveloped or underutilized, an insufficient mix of the hedonic, prudent, ethical, and aesthetic? Some of these perspectives are harder to develop than others. I suspect that ethics and aesthetics fall into this camp.

There is an underdevelopment of aesthetics and ethics in the narcissistic character. Instead, compensatory hedonic and prudential concerns fill a void and become the foundation of their worlds. Despite the narcissist's apparent pursuit of beauty and perfection, an intrinsic appreciation of aesthetics seems less core to what they are about. Their quest seems mostly compensatory, a matter of self-interest. Beauty and perfection are salves applied to their questionable self-worth, providing needed attention and admiration, trophies valued for purposes of display.

A poverty of ethical behavior is often how the narcissist gets diagnosed in the first place. A version of the *Diagnostic and Statistical Manual of Mental Disorders* describes the narcissistic personality as exploitive, lacking a "moral core." They act out an aggrieved entitlement where self-interest trumps intrinsic concerns with justice and fairness.

Most developmental explanations of malignant narcissism begin with a child who has been damaged by inadequate parental empathy and an over or under indulgence that meets the parent's needs more than their child's. Akin to Maslow's recognition that survival needs have to be met before optimal growth can occur, the narcissist is constantly hungry for

attention and affirmation, vulnerable and exploitive in attempting to satisfy a self-interested craving.

Some narcissistically damaged people have talents and appearances
that provide them considerable hedonic and prudential success. They
crave and celebrate what they possess and appear untroubled by what's
underdeveloped. But most narcissists are not so lucky, they won't achieve
celebrity, fame, or fortune. They know misery, instead.

Are there limited satisfactions clung to in lieu of optimal satisfaction?
Might someone seeking ultimate satisfaction, but failing to competently
achieve a workable insight, enact a pattern of frustrated action, a repetition compulsion, or the problematic satisfaction of an addiction? One's
reach might exceed one's grasp.

The man I mentioned at the start of this entry has very little he experiences as done for its own sake. Mostly, he acts from an unresolved
ambivalent duty to his dead parents, who never understood nor loved
him enough. His childhood involved trauma and the absence of adequate
parental empathy. All this is complicated by his hostile and competitive
relations with his siblings, better loved and more disabled than him. He
works hard and constantly to gain the love and respect it is too late to
achieve from his mother and father. Instead, he is haunted by a confusing ambivalence and unappreciated duty. He has no time for play and no
one he really wants to play with. Fortunately, what saves him from total
despair is his highly developed sense of ethics. This and his considerable
intelligence may see him through if he can separate from his compulsive
enactments of hostility, fear, and guilt. He wants to "return to his life"
but his inability to a find valued intrinsic connection to what he feels he
is required to accomplish leaves the end of each day a disappointment.
This is his life, a world that hangs together as disjointed tasks discon-
nected from a fuller appreciation of their significance. His dead parents
will never provide what he intrinsically values and can't find. For now,
a fuller realization of the meaning of his action is too painful for him to
tolerate. The connection of the instrumental to the intrinsic is either unavailable or too much to bear. Unconsciously and defensively he is stuck
in the instrumental.

I know I can't connect it all together. Wittgenstein saw method and
conceptualization pass one another by. Herzog, his grandiosity finally
passing, stopped writing his never-to-be-sent letters and made ready for
dinner with Ramona, thinking he'd light candles because she was fond
of them. I didn't catch a damn thing today, but for a good 30 seconds,
thought I'd hooked the biggest fish of my life. I needed to tighten down
the drag because my line was running out faster than I could reel. But then
the jerking became a steady pull east with the current. Afraid something
would snap, I flipped open the bail, saw what had hit, and released a

log floating a few feet under the surf, 70 yards out. The guys around me laughed, but I didn't lose my lure.

Over the course of this writing, struggling to find time and clarity, punching above my weight, more than once my wife was disturbed by my attention-seeking torment. But every time she noticed, I could honestly respond there was nothing I'd rather be doing.

Chappaquiddick Island, Massachusetts
October, 2018

Appendix One: Ossorio's Status Dynamic Maxims, Behavioral Logic, and Reminders for Proper Description (*Place*, 1998)

The work of the philosopher consists in marshaling recollections for a particular purpose.

If someone were to advance theses in philosophy, it would never be possible to debate them, because everyone would agree to them. (Wittgenstein, Philosophical Investigations).

In Descriptive Psychology, maxims are primarily warnings and reminders (or encouragements) to an observer describer of human behavior. They are addressed to the issue of how not to go wrong, how not to do it wrong—where 'it' refers to describing people and their behavior. In contrast to axioms that are impersonal and emphasize truth and universality, maxims are designed to be used by a person in addressing another person who in general already knows but who in that context, for a given purpose (etc.), may benefit from such a warning or reminder (or encouragement). The thrust of this set of maxims is "Don't violate the a priori requirements that stem from the fact that we're talking about people, not about, for example, material objects, egos, organisms, consumers. Not surprisingly, roughly 90% of these maxims could also be used directly as tautologies, although that is not their raison d'état and I don't recommend it." (Ossorio, 1991).

A. Person and World

A1. A person requires a world in order to have the possibility of engaging in any behavior at all.

A2. A person requires that the world be one way rather than another in order for him to behave in one way rather than another.

A3. A person's circumstances provide reasons and opportunities to engage in one behavior rather than another.

A4. For a given person, the real world is the one which includes him as a Person, and as an Actor, Observer-Describer, and Critic.

A5. What a person takes to be real is what he is prepared to act on.

A6. A person acquires knowledge of the world by observation and thought.

A7. For a given person, the real world is the one he has to find out about by observation.

A8. A person takes it that things are as they seem unless he has reason enough to think otherwise.

A9. A person takes the world to be as he has found it to be.

B. Behavioral Choice

B1. Because a person's circumstances are what they are, the person has the reasons and opportunities that he has to engage in one behavior rather than another.

B2. If a person wants to do something, he has a reason to do it.

B3. If a person recognizes an opportunity to do something he wants to do, he has a reason to do it.

B4. If a person wants to do something, he has a reason to create or look for an opportunity to do it.

B5. If a person has a reason to do something, he will do it, unless…

B6. If a person has two reasons for doing X, he has a stronger reason for doing X than if he had only one of those reasons.

B7. If the situation calls for a person to do something he can't do, he will do something he can do.

B8. If a person wants to engage in a given behavior, he would thereby also want to engage in other behaviors to the extent that they are relevantly similar to the behavior in question.

B9. If A has the relation R to C the behaviors of A with respect to C will be an expression of R, unless…

C. Value and Behavioral Choice

C1. A person values some states of affairs over others and acts accordingly.

C1a. If a person's relationship to something is such that he is in a bad situation, or circumstances, he has a reason to try to improve it.

C1b. If a person's relationship to something is such that he is in a good situation, circumstances, he has a reason to act to maintain it.

C1c. If a person is in a good situation and has an opportunity to improve it, he has a reason to try to do so.

C1d. If a person is in any situation and it may be expected to become worse, he has a reason to act to prevent that.

C2. A person will not choose less behavior potential over more.

C3. If a person values a specific something, e.g., an object, a circumstance, a behavior, or, more generally, a state of affairs, he will thereby also value other specific things of the same kind to the extent that they are relevantly similar to the original.

C3a. If a person values a general something, he will thereby also value a specific something to the extent that it is a paradigmatic instance or realization of the more general value.

C4. If a person values something general, he will be sensitive to (will tend to evaluate) the relevance of his circumstances to that something and act accordingly.

C4a. Negative emotional behavior (fear, guilt, anger, shame, etc.) is an attempt to improve a bad situation.

C4b. Positive emotional behavior (joy, triumph, glee, etc.) is an attempt to preserve, enhance, or celebrate a good situation.

D. Stability and Change

D1. A historical individual acquires a given individual characteristic by virtue of having the prior capacity and the relevant intervening history.

D1a. A person acquires a given person characteristic by virtue of having the prior capacity and the relevant intervening history.

D2. A historical individual having a finite history has some nonacquired characteristics during some part of that history.

D3. If a person acquires a given person characteristic, he acquires it in one of the ways in which it can be acquired.

D3a. If a person acquires a given relationship to something, he acquires it in one of the ways in which it can be acquired.

D4. A person acquires concepts and skills by practice and experience.

D5. What a person takes to be the case about the world is the outcome of his observation, thought, and action.

D6. If a person has a given person characteristic, he continues to have it until and unless it changes.

D7. If a person has a given relationship to something, he continues to have it until and unless it changes.

D8. Relationships follow behavior.

D9. If a person knows something, he continues to know it until and unless he forgets it or changes his mind.

D10. (A9) A person takes the world to be as he has found it to be.

D11. The world is subject to reformulation by persons.

E. Person and Community

E1. A person requires a community in order for it to be possible for him to engage in human behavior at all.

E2. A person requires that the community be one way rather than another in order for him to behave in one way rather than another.

E3. A community is characterized by a common world, a language, a structure of social practices, statuses, way of living, choice principles, and individual members.

E4. A person's place in the community provides reasons and opportunities to engage in one behavior rather than another.

E5. To engage in a Deliberate Action is to participate in a social practice of the community.

E6. If a person participates in a social practice, he must do it in one of the ways it can be done.

E7. When a person is in a pathological state there is a significant restriction in his ability to participate in the social practices of the community.

E8. If a person makes nonnormative choices in his participation in the social practices of the community, that calls for an explanation.

E9. A person may act as a representative of the community or as merely a member.

E10. A person takes it that a member of the community has the personal characteristics required for normal participation in the social practices of the community unless he has reason enough to think otherwise.

E11. Reasons for behavior (Deliberate Action) are states of affairs.

F. Interactions of Persons

F1. The behavior of one person with respect to another is a participation in at least one of the social practices of his community.

F2. (B9) If C has the relation R to Z the behaviors of C with respect to Z will be an expression of R, unless…

F3. If C and Z participate in a social practice, the fact that Z participates in one way rather than another gives C a reason to participate correspondingly in one way rather than another.

F3a. C's behavior with respect to Z may be a case of participating in two or more social practices simultaneously.

F3b. If C and Z participate in a social practice C may anticipate to some extent Z's choices among behavioral options on the basis of Z's personal characteristics and relationships to C and others.

F3c. Z may participate in one way rather than another (choose certain options rather than others) as a way of letting C know what kind of person Z is.

F4. If C has a given relationship to Z, C's behavior potential is different from what it otherwise would have been.

F4a. If Z has a greater behavior potential than P, it is likely that C would gain more behavior potential from a positive relationship with Z than with P.

F5. If C makes the first move in a social practice, that invites Z to continue the enactment of the practice by making the corresponding second move. (Move 1 invites Move 2.)

F6. If C makes the second move in a social practice, that makes it difficult for Z not to have already made the first move. (Move 2 preempts Move 1 ex post facto.)

F7. Z's positive or negative evaluation of C's behavior provides reasons for C to continue, discontinue, modify, or elaborate (etc.) such behavior.

F7a. If C chooses his behavior under the description "B1" and Z redescribes it as "B2" and C accepts the redescription and C appraises B2 differently from B1, then C will have an additional reason to engage in B1 or not to engage in B1, depending on the nature of the appraisal.

G. Person and Self

G1. A person is an individual whose history is, paradigmatically, a history of Deliberate Action.

G2. A person has a status in the real world.

G3. A person has a status in the world as an Actor, as an Observer, and as a Critic.

G4. A person has a status in the world as a possible Actor, as a possible Observer, and as a possible Critic.

G5. A person's statuses as Actor, Observer, and Critic each correspond to distinctive sorts of relationship to the world and/or parts of the world either simply or in their aspects.

G5a. A person acts as himself.

G5b. A person knows about himself.

G5c. A person knows about his relation to the world and his place in it.

G5d. A person evaluates his worth.

H. Limits, Constraints, and Limitations

H1. A person's personal characteristics correspond to reality constraints on the behaviors he can engage in.

H1a. B7) If the situation calls for a person to do something he can't do, he will do something he can do.

H1b. If the situation calls for a person to enact a behavior for which he lacks the requisite knowledge, he will enact some other behavior for which he has the requisite knowledge.

H1c. If the situation calls for a person to enact a behavior for which he lacks the requisite motivational priorities, he will enact some other behavior for which he has the requisite motivational priorities.

H2. A person's personal characteristics correspond to reality constraints on the ways in which he can acquire personal characteristics and relationships.

H2a. A person's personal characteristics correspond to reality constraints on which personal characteristics and relationships he can acquire.

H3. A person's world is made up of possibilities and nonpossibilities for behaving.

H4. A person's self-concept is a summary, and primarily intuitive (unreflective) formulation of his place in the scheme of things and his corresponding behavior potential.

H5. All the world's a stage.

H5a. Status takes precedence over fact.

H5b. Reality takes precedence over truth.

H6. (C2) A person will not choose less behavior potential over more.

H7. Behavior goes right, if it doesn't go wrong in one of the ways it can go wrong.

H8. A person always acts under conditions of uncertainty.

H9. A person always has enough information to act on.

I. Norms, Baselines, and Burdens of Proof

I1. A person takes it that things are as they seem, unless he has reason enough to think otherwise.

I2. (A9, D10) A person takes the world to be as he has found it to be.

I3. If a person has a given person characteristic and his behavior is an expression of it, that calls for no explanation, whereas if his behavior violates that person characteristic, that does call for an explanation.

I4. If a person has a given relationship and his behavior is an expression of it, that calls for no explanation, whereas if his behavior violates that relationship that does call for an explanation.

I5. If a person's relationships or personal characteristics change, that calls for an explanation.

I6. (H7) A person's behavior goes right, if it doesn't go wrong in one of the ways in which it can go wrong.

I7. A person takes it that a person who is a member of a group, class, or set of persons is a typical member except insofar as he knows or discovers otherwise.

I8. (E8) If a person makes nonnormative choices, that calls for an explanation.

I9. If a person engages in an intrinsic social practice, that calls for no further explanation.

Appendix Two: A Glossary of Descriptive Psychology Concepts Compiled by Clarke Stone

Descriptive Psychology
1. A set of concepts within which Person, Behavior, Language, and World can be described and understood.
2. A community that uses those concepts to actually describe and understand; and that uses such descriptions and understanding to deal effectively with all aspects of persons' activities.
3. A method of getting access to all the facts and all the possible facts about Persons and what they do.

Ability
1. A type of achievement or a class of achievements that I can be expected to succeed at under normal circumstances if I try.
2. To say that a person can (is able to) speak English is to imply that a certain kind of behavioral (i.e., nonaccidental) achievement of this kind is possible rather than impossible; thus a kind of Achievement Description.
3. One of the three Powers.

Achievement
1. The outcome aspect of behavior.
   $<B> = <I, W, K, KH, P, A, PC, S>$
2. Whatever is different in the world by virtue of the occurrence of the behavior in question.
3. Successful behavior achieves the wanted state of affairs.

Actor
The author of Behavior.
Notes:
As an Actor, I see the real world as the field of action, as the domain within which I live my life. In it are givens and possibilities; opportunities and nonopportunities; hindrances and facilitations for behavior. In it are reasons for acting one way rather than another. I am sensitized to behaviors that are available and ways of being that are available.

To a large extent, my possibilities are bound up in the objects, processes, events, and states of affairs in the world and in the human communities with their social practices and cultures, including, most importantly, my own community. However, the most important ingredient is me.

Attitude

1. Any type of behavior with a certain "object" (focus) that is in the value of the K parameter of that behavior.
2. Can be seen as a Trait with an "object" (focus).
3. One of the Dispositions.

Notes:

"Type of behavior" denotes one behavior rather than a variety (set) of behaviors, as with an Interest.

In this case, the word "object" is in quotes to separate it from the use of Object as one of the four basic reality concepts (OPESA). That is, it denotes a focus on something the person distinguishes (including objects). It does not require the person to focus on a material object and nothing else.

Appraisal

1. A description that carries motivational significance.
2. A status assignment that carries motivational significance.
3. A discrimination which tautologically carries motivational significance.

Notes:

The primary contrast is with the notion of a "mere description," which does not tautologically carry any motivational significance.

Capacity

1. The capacity for acquiring a given person characteristic is the potential for acquiring that person characteristic.
2. Whatever it takes to participate.
3. One of the Derivatives.

Notes:

Personal Characteristics (PCs) Formula: Capacity + Relevant History → PC.

Just as an Ability is always the ability to accomplish something, a Capacity is always the capacity to acquire some PC. Capacities are individuated by reference to:

1. The PC that would be the actualization of that potential.
2. The relevant history by means of which the potential could be actualized.

Thus a child who has the capacity to acquire the ability to do arithmetic as a result of individual tutoring over a 2-year period might not have the capacity to acquire that ability as a result of a single semester in a class in an urban public school. And a child who has the capacity to become a punctual person because her father always required it, might well not have the capacity to become a punctual person on the basis of the example provided by her mother (but she might also have the capacity to acquire that trait as a result of both parents not being punctual, etc.).

Circumstances

1. If we divide the world into three parts, i.e., the behavior, the person, and the rest of the world, "the rest of the world" is the circumstances.
2. This includes the history involved, especially a person's life history or learning history.
3. The situation.
4. The state of affairs.

Community

A community, <C>, is specified by six parameters:<M, S, Ct, L, P, W>, where:

M = Members (the historical individuals from whom the community is formed)

S = Statuses (the place anything is given in the practices of a community)

Ct = Concepts (the distinction between X and whatever is not X)

L = Locutions (the locutions reflecting Statuses, Concepts, Practices, and World of the community)

P = Practices (social practices) (the repertoire of behavior patterns which constitute "what there is for members to do")

W = World (beliefs, methodologies, ideologies, assumptions, presuppositions, and so on concerning "all that is")

Competence

1. Whatever rules out the possibility that the occurrence of a given behavior is simply a matter of luck, chance, accident, or coincidence.
2. The extent to which success can be attributed straightforwardly to the person rather than to favorable or accidental circumstances (but still short of complete chance or accident).
3. Any point on the "nonaccidental" dimension.
4. The degree to which success is purely and simply attributed to the individual rather than to the circumstances.

Notes:

Knowledge can be acquired by observation and thought, while competence requires in addition practice and experience.

Consider glass blowing. One can acquire what there is to know about glass blowing by reading books and visiting exhibits. But to acquire competence at glass blowing, an apprenticeship in a community of glass blowers is needed.

Concept

1. The distinction between X and some set of alternative non-Xs (which may be lumped together as "not X").
2. P uses concept C in engaging in behavior B.
3. P acts on concept C in engaging in behavior B.
4. An aspect of Behavior.

Notes:

The distinction X/not X is not binary.

"Not X" is a spectrum of things. For example, there is "facing due east" and "not facing due east." In most common terms, there are 359 other directions to face that would be "not facing due east" (one for each degree in a circle). Of course, 360 degrees in a circle is just a common convention. A circle can be divided much more finely than that; and we haven't even talked about facing up or down. "Not X" is a spectrum of possibilities and not de facto binary.

Critic

As a Critic, I first evaluate whether what is the case and what is happening now are satisfactory, making use of the Observer information.

1. If things are good enough or better than just good enough, that judgment is available to the Actor, and both Critic and Actor are free to enjoy that.
2. If things are not good enough, as a Critic, I formulate a "diagnosis," i.e., an account of what is wrong; and a "prescription," i.e., a specification of what to do differently to try to help matters. The "prescription" is the primary feedback to the Actor.

Notes:

In particular cases, I decide. I pass judgment. I decide whether an action or course of action is proceeding as it ought to. If I decide it is not, I also decide in what way it falls short and how such a situation ought to be treated so as to correct matters.

I also decide whether the action chosen was the one that ought to have been chosen in the circumstances. I also decide whether a given description of the behavior and, more generally, of the world, is accurate, coherent, complete, relevant, etc., and how it is to be treated if it is not.

Like a traditional judge, I do not create the standards I apply. I am not inherently creative. The standards I apply are community standards. This is why the judgments I make are objective. I speak for Us.

Deliberate Action

1. A case of behavior in which we know what we're doing and are doing it on purpose.
2. A form of behavior in which the individual behaving not merely knows what he is doing, but also chooses to do it.

3. The central concept of behavior—if there were no cases of this kind, there would be no cases of any kind.
4. A form of behavior in which the person:
   a. engages in an Intentional Action,
   b. knows what he is doing, and
   c. has chosen to do that.

Notes:
In Set-Theoretic Notation, this is shown as:
   <B> = <I, <B>, <B>, KH, P, A, PC, S>
   The Diamond Notation is shown in Chapter 3 (Fig. 3.1).

Derivatives
   One of the three major categories of person characteristics: Dispositions, Powers, and Derivatives.
   Dispositions and Powers are defined by their direct connection to behavior.
   Derivatives are defined by their direct connection to dispositions or powers and have only indirect connections to behavior. The three Derivatives are:

1. *States.* The kind of changes that may be quick, nonpersistent, and readily reversible.
2. *Capacities.* The power to acquire person characteristics.
3. *Embodiment.* The object form, the body, of the person.

Dispositions
   Dispositions are person characteristics identified by grouping behavior together by frequency patterns. In all cases, the frequency noted would be enough—or little enough—for "one of us" to call attention to it.
   There are four categories of Dispositions:

1. *Traits.* To have a given trait is to be disposed to engage (or fail to engage) in a certain kind of behavior.
2. *Attitudes.* Like a Trait, except the behavior is focused on an object, e.g., "She hates spiders," where spiders are the object.
3. *Interests.* Like an Attitude, behavior is focused on an object. Unlike Traits, Interests are not restricted to a certain kind of behavior. For example, if P is interested in chess, P will do many things related to chess.
4. *Style.* Not what you do, but how you do it.

Distinction
   A difference that makes a difference.

Drama
   A structured behavioral episode or series of episodes (including Social Practices) which makes sense to us.

Dramaturgical Pattern
1. The pattern of occurrence of a kind of behavior in the life history of a person.
2. A structured behavioral episode or series of episodes (including Social Practices) which makes sense to Us.
3. A drama.

Embodiment
The parameter where the object characteristics of persons are included. One of the three Derivatives.

Event
1. An event is a direct change from one state of affairs to another.
2. An event is a state of affairs having two states of affairs ("before" and "after") as immediate constituents.

Fact
1. How things are in the world.
2. A particular state of affairs.
3. A single item of information.
4. A situation without reference to context.

Notes:
In stating a fact, we are dividing the set of all possible worlds into two groups, i.e.:

- Those in which what the fact states is the case and those in which what the fact states is not the case.
- Those that fit the description and those that don't; and we are saying that the real world belongs to the first group and not the second.

Forms of Behavior Description
Given the following behavior:
<B> = <I, W, K, KH, P, A, PC, S>
and using a calculational system, it is possible to use substitution, deletion, and identity to generate various forms of behavior description. Below are listed the first-order descriptions.

- The substitution operation codifies recursive and reflexive aspects of behavior.
- The deletion operation provides behavior descriptions which are explicitly noncommittal in regard to aspects (parameters) of the behavior. In effect, they are forms of incomplete description where the incompleteness is systematically specified.

Identity (parameter)
1. Every behavior is someone's behavior, and the Identity parameter of behavior provides a place to specify that.

$<IA> = <B> = <Identity, W, K, KH, P, A, PC, S>$

2. An index to denote any particular person, such as a name, a driver's license number, or an SSN.
3. Not a synonym for personal identity, social identity, or self-concept.

Implementation

1. The converse of Significance.
2. A kind of Performance therefore the most easily visible part of Behavior.
3. In general, behavior has a multilevel structure involving:
   a. The behavior, which is "what the person is up to" or "what the person's really doing."
   b. One or more "implementation" behaviors, which is what observation reports of behavior generally describe.

Notes:
The Actor doesn't, in general, have a problem with significance, because Actors begin with that. Actors' problems lie mainly in creating implementations. In contrast, the Observer will begin with the Actor's implementations (since those are most readily observable), then encounter issues around "What is the Actor doing by doing that?"

Instrumental

1. A behavior is instrumental when there is a goal of some kind external to the behavior itself for the sake of which the behavior is engaged in.
2. A synonym for "ulteriorly motivated."
3. The opposite of "intrinsic" or "done for its own sake."

Notes:
Assuming all behavior is instrumental (is ulteriorly motivated, done to get something, etc.) causes an infinite regress, which is the sign of a false premise; therefore only some behavior is instrumental. The remaining behaviors are either intrinsic or simultaneously intrinsic and instrumental (as demonstrated by the ladder of significance).

Intentional Action (IA)

1. A primitive, general concept of Behavior ($<B>$).
2. A calculational system from which all further varieties of behavior can be generated.
3. A calculational system for generating forms of behavior description.
   $<IA> = <B> = <I, W, K, KH, P, A, PC, S>$

Interest

1. Any set of behaviors with a certain "object" (focus) that is in the value of the K parameter of that behavior.
2. In addition, Interests are intrinsic.
3. One of the Dispositions.

Notes:

There is no single type of behavior specified, partly because an interest in something is generally shown through a variety (set) of different behaviors involving the object of interest, and partly because the set of such behaviors will differ with different objects. For example, an interest in golf can be shown by playing golf, by joining the golf association, by reading books on golf, by designing ideal golf courses, by reading biographies of famous golfers, and so on.

In this case, the word "object" is in quotes to separate it from the use of Object as one of the four basic reality concepts (OPESA). That is, it denotes a focus on something the person distinguishes (including objects). It does not require the person to focus on a material object and nothing else.

Intrinsic

1. A behavior done for its own sake.
2. The opposite of instrumental.

Notes:

Intrinsic behavior is necessary. If behavior were only instrumental and nothing else, then any behavior that seemed like a reason to do X would be serving other behaviors which were the real reason to do X. Except those other behaviors (Y and Z) would also only be serving other behaviors ... and so on, an infinite regress; therefore we need intrinsic behaviors to stop the infinite regress inherent in an instrumental-only paradigm.

In addition, this principle of intrinsic behavior "stopping" instrumental behaviors "puts a cap" on the Ladder of Significance. That is, our observations must eventually reach an intrinsic behavior intrinsic enough to need no further explanation.

Judgment

1. A synonym for appraisal.
2. A synonym for status assignment.
3. The ability to show the proper sensitivity and make proper decisions in this or that domain, the decision that "one of us" would make.

Notes:

We normally speak of "good judgment" and "bad judgment." Good judgment is successful judgment therefore normal judgment; it does not need an explanation, and can be just "judgment." Bad judgment is a failure; it does need to be explained, so we note the failure by calling it "bad judgment."

Know (concept)

1. Acting on the distinction between X and some set of alternative non-X's (which may be lumped together as "not X").
2. Using concept C to engage in behavior B.
3. Acting on concept C to engage in behavior B.

Know (parameter)

1. The "cognitive" aspect of behavior.
   <B> = <I, W, Know, KH, P, A, PC, S>
2. The place to specify which distinctions (concepts) are being acted on in the given behavior.
3. This parameter includes some representation of the circumstances, state of affairs, or context in which the behavior takes place.

Know-How (parameter)

This parameter represents the "competence" aspect of the behavior in question, which in turn reflects the learning history of the person whose behavior is in question. The person's competence rules out the possibility that the occurrence of a given behavior is simply a matter of luck, chance, accident, or coincidence.

   <B> = <I, W, K, Know-How, P, A, PC, S>

Notes:

Know-How is used as a technical term in connection with Intentional Action. Rather than being anchored on a type of achievement, Know-How is anchored on a specific achievement, i.e., the value of the Performance parameter. Rather than identifying a kind of competence, which accounts for a certain kind of success, Know-How is an indefinite reference to a learning history, and to the corresponding competence, by virtue of which the occurrence of that performance was not a matter of luck, chance, accident, or coincidence.

Knowledge

1. 1.The set of facts and concepts a person has the competence to act on.
2. A person's cognitive repertoire.

Ladder of Significance

Significance is an Observer concept. As Observers, we can only see directly the Performance of a particular Behavior. We must investigate to find out what the Actor is implementing.

For example, if I see P "waving a hand" <B1>, I might decide "P was trying to say hello to Q" <B2>; thus there are two levels—the Performance of <B1> which was an implementation of <B2>.

Equivalently, <B2> is the significance of <B1>. Note, however, that P might have been "getting rid of a fly" <B3>. <B3> might have been the significance of <B1>. Since P is doing <B1> in both cases, and there's more than one possibility, we must observe, investigate, etc., to find out what's going on (what the real behavior is; what the top-level behavior is).

The result will always be at least two levels high, that is, there will always be "<B2> is the significance of <B1>" at a minimum; however, there's no necessary limit to the number of "steps" or "rungs" (behaviors) between the top-level behavior <B2> and the bottom-level behavior <B1>.

For example, P could be waving a hand <B1> to attract Q's attention <B1.1> to point out an oncoming truck <B1.2> so Q can avoid the danger <B2>. This "ladder of significance" has four rungs (<B1>, <B1.1>, <B1.2>, and <B2>).

Note also that we, as observers, need a stopping point for our quest for "what P was doing by doing that." That is, we need a point at which we know we have actually reached the top-level behavior and can say that's what the real behavior is. The cap on the ladder of significance will always be an intrinsic behavior of some sort. In the example above, we don't need to ask why P would want friend Q to avoid danger. What friend puts a friend in danger? Helping Q avoid danger is seen as an end in itself—intrinsic behavior—so it is the cap on that ladder of significance. That's what P was really doing: helping Q avoid danger.

Locution

A word, phrase, or sentence that is uttered.

Objects

1. An object is a state of affairs which has other, related objects as immediate constituents.
2. An object divides into related, smaller objects.
3. The "O" in "OPESA."

Notes:

An object that is not a state of affairs, i.e., it has no constituents, is an ultimate object.

As with all objects, what distinguishes one sort of ultimate object from another is the set of attributes (properties and relationships) such an object can have. The choice of an ultimate object sets strong limits to what there can be in the world that corresponds to that choice.

These limiting cases are familiar to us in phrases like "the world of baseball," "the world of physics," or "the world of Hollywood."

Observer-Describer.

As an Observer, I note:

1. What is the case now.
2. What is happening now.
3. What has happened in the past and what happens generally.
4. What is the case generally.
5. How things work.

Since the results of observation are available to the person doing the Observer job, they are available to the person in doing the Actor and Critic jobs, and similarly for Actor and Critic.

OPESA

1. The abbreviation for "objects, processes, events, and states of affairs," the four basic reality concepts.

Patterns of Behavior
In general, there are five patterns of behavior:
1. Individual.
   These are expressed by the Dispositions aspect of Person
   Characteristics and also by State. Dispositions are patterns relative to
   others. State is a pattern relative to self.
2. Social Practices.
   Social practices are what there is to do for the members of the society.
   A member's behavioral history (pattern) is the history of participating
   in these social practices.
3. Social Institutions.
   Social practices are ingredients of organized sets, or structures, of
   social practices. These larger units are "institutions." Raising a family,
   educating children, passing laws, farming, engaging in trade, and
   speaking a language are examples of institutions.
4. Way of Life.
   The ultimate unit of social behavior is a culture, or way of life. Note:
   ways of life are not built up out of institutions, social practices, and
   Deliberate Action. Rather, these latter are differentiated out from ways
   of living. (A game is not everywhere demarcated by its rules—or by its
   descriptions.)
5. Dramaturgical.
   A person's life does not consist of a random sequence of disparate
   Deliberate Actions or Social Practices. Such a life would not be
   a human life, nor would it make any sense. Nor would such
   an individual long survive if left to his own devices. Thus the
   dramaturgical pattern is the part a person plays in the scheme of
   things.

Paradigmatically
Regarded as representative or typical.
For example, a Person typically engages in Deliberate Action. Deliberate
Action is representative of what persons do; thus periods without deliber-
ate actions must be explained or accounted for.
For example, persons who are unconscious are not engaged in deliber-
ate action because they are unconscious.

Performance
1. The process, or procedural, aspect of behavior. Process aspects
   include:
   a. Having a beginning, end, and duration.
   b. Being interruptible.
   c. Occurring in some specific context of time and place.
   d. Starting with one state of affairs and ending with a different one.
2. An expression of the individual's acquired behavioral competence
   (Know How).

3. A behavioral attempt (P parameter of Behavior).
   \<B> = \<I, W, K, KH, Performance, A, PC, S>

Person

1. A Person is an individual whose history is, paradigmatically, a history of Deliberate Action in a Dramaturgical Pattern.
2. One of four perspectives on the Person Concept.

Person Characteristics

1. Every behavior reflects some of the characteristics of the person whose behavior it is. That is, if the person has certain characteristics instead of others, the behavior will be some certain behavior instead of some other. This parameter codifies that aspect of behavior.
2. The values of this parameter specify which person characteristics the behavior is an expression of.
   \<B> = \<I, W, K, KH, P, A, Personal Characteristic, S>
3. Sorting behavior according to these two criteria: which types of behaviors occur; their temporal patterns of occurrence.
   The possibilities can be grouped together as follows:
a Dispositions: Traits, Attitudes, Interests, and Style.
b Powers: Ability, Values, and Knowledge.
c Derivatives: States, Capacities, and Embodiment.

Person Concept

1. The ability people have that enables them to understand people is the ability to use, or act on, a certain concept. This concept is designated as "the Person concept" or, interchangeably, "the concept of the Person."
2. Mastery and use of this concept is universal among persons.
3. It is universal among persons because mastery of that concept and the routine spontaneous exercise of that mastery are what make a person a person.

Powers

1. The behaviors that are possible or not possible for a given person, codified in Ability, Values, and Knowledge.
2. Powers codify the possible values of the KH, W, and K parameters of the behaviors of a given person.

Notes:

Any behaviors for which the K, W, or KH values are not available are not possible for that person; it will not be in the person's behavioral repertoire; it will not be part of the person's behavior potential. All of this is at a given time, of course. These things change.

Process

1. A process is a sequential change from one state of affairs to another.
2. A process is a state of affairs which has other, related processes as immediate constituents.
3. A process divides into related, smaller processes.

Notes:

The process begins with some state of affairs, A, and ends with a different state of affairs, B. The change from A to B consists of at least two sequential changes, e.g., from A to Q and from Q to B. This implies that a process has duration.

Reality

Reality is the totality of all constraints on the deliberate actions of persons.

Notes:

The link between "reality" and "the real world" is the notion of our behavioral possibilities and impossibilities. Whatever else they do, our representations of "the real world" codify our possibilities/impossibilities for behavior. In contrast, the notion of "reality" is directly the notion of those possibilities/ impossibilities as such, with emphasis on the latter ("reality constraints").

Consider what can be done with a dog present. Those things are possible if a dog is present. They are part of the real world for you and me, provided a dog is present. But if dogs suddenly vanished from the universe, no dog-related possibility would be available to us or anyone else—no fetch, no walkies, no dog shows, no breeding, no nothing—except the various ways of bemoaning the loss of dogs. The absence of dogs would be reality or a reality constraint.

The collection of all such constraints is Reality.

"Really Doing"

1. What the person is "really doing" is given by the description with the highest level of Significance. The behaviors given by the other descriptions are there only as implementations, and if the circumstances were different, they would be replaced by behaviors which were responsive to those other circumstances.

Reason

A State of Affairs that has motivational relevance for behavior.

When we group reasons into family resemblance groups, we find four major groups, with one of them having three subgroups. The following are the kinds of reasons people ultimately have.

Notes:

1. Hedonic.
   Variations on pleasure, pain, noxiousness, and disgustingness.

2. Prudential.

Variations on my self-interest, what is good for me (or bad for me), what is to my advantage (or disadvantage).

3. Ethical.

Variations on what is right or wrong, good or bad, fair or unfair, just or unjust and with whether I have a duty or obligation.

4. Aesthetic.

Variations on the primitive notion of fittingness. Artistic: how things fit together. Social: what the situation calls for. Intellectual: what fits the facts of the matter.

Self-concept

1. The summary formulation of a person's status as a person.

2. A person's place "in the scheme of things."

Notes:

A summary formulation, that is, all of the statuses P has in all of P's communities plus P's status as a person who chooses which community to act from.

My place in the scheme of things is my status. My having that place, that status, is the same thing as my having the relationships I do with everything there is, singly and jointly.

Sensitive

Responsive to those states of affairs that do (or would) make a difference to "one of us."

Notes:

If I am a banker and doing my job as a banker, I will be approaching the world from the perspective of a banker and I will be sensitive and responsive to those states of affairs that make a difference to bankers. Furthermore, if I am doing the job of a banker in an ideal way, I will respond only to those states of affairs, and I will automatically, i.e., without necessarily any thought or decision, exclude from consideration any other states of affairs which are of interest only from the standpoint of another status (e.g., a mother, a Baptist, a Republican, a skier).

Significance

1. The "meaningful" or the "ulterior" aspects of behavior.

$<B> = <I, W, K, KH, P, A, PC, Significance>$

2. In general, behavior has a multilevel structure involving (a) the behavior which is "what the person is up to" or "what the person's really doing" and (b) one or more "implementation" behaviors, which is what observation reports of behavior generally describe.

3. What P is doing by doing that.

Notes:

Significance, the 8th parameter of Intentional Action ($<B>$), is an intentional action—the answer to the question, "What are you doing by doing that (the original $<B>$)?"

For example, by writing this commentary, I am trying to make clear a concept from Descriptive Psychology. By doing that I am trying to increase the behavior potential of readers who want to use Descriptive Psychology.

This "upward ladder of significance" is an important tool for describing the place the original behavior has in a person's life.

Situation

1. A particular state of affairs.
2. A complex of information.
3. A fact in context.
4. In identifying a situation, we demarcate a portion of the real world and are faced with the task of describing that portion.

Social Practice

1. Social practices are a society's patterns of behavior. In general, the patterns include more than one behavior, and most social practices involve behaviors on the part of more than one person.
2. As social patterns of behavior, social practices are learnable, teachable, doable, and paradigmatically, done. Every society at a given time has an organized set of social practices that constitute "what there is to do" for the members of the society.
3. A person's participation in a social practice is intrinsic if (a) the person is participating in that practice without an ulterior motive and without a further end in view and (b) the particular behavior is engaged in without an ulterior motive and without a further end in view other than those which are part of the practice itself.
4. Viewed as a process, social practices have stages, options, contingencies, and eligibilities. This process represents every Version of the social practice. Every social practice is done in one of the ways it can be done, that is, some version of the process takes place.

Notes:

In any community, Social Practices are "what there is to do."

Social practices are patterns of behavior. They are built up from Intentional Actions, and for a given community, they characterize what is to be done in that community. For example, within the farming community they would include: plowing, planting, fertilizing, irrigating, harvesting, etc.

Since an individual is a member of many communities, the totality of social practices of all her communities constitutes her behavioral repertoire.

A person may participate in more than one social practice simultaneously.

State of Affairs

1. A state of affairs is a totality of related objects and/or processes and/or events and/or states of affairs.
2. The circumstances.
3. The situation.
4. The SA in OPESA.

State

1. 1.The kind of change that may be quick, nonpersistent, and readily reversible.
2. In a particular state, there is a systematic difference in a person's powers or dispositions.
3. One of the Derivatives.

Notes:

Some of the states which we commonly distinguish are being tired, sleepy, asleep, in pain, intoxicated, anxious, angry, overjoyed, excited, sick, euphoric, in shock, depersonalized, confused, dizzy, weak, unconscious, exhausted, and depressed.

The consequences of such states are behavioral only via the differences in powers or dispositions. Thus if I am tired, that doesn't say there is a certain behavior I am likely to do. (If there is, it will be a reaction to being tired, not an expression of being tired. I drink coffee as a reaction to being tired, not to show I am tired.) If I am tired, things I can do quickly, easily, and accurately I now do less quickly, less easily, and less accurately (via a difference in abilities). Likewise, my trait of generosity, my attitude of enthusiastic appreciation of music, my interest in chess, and my energetic style are likely to be affected.

The more tired I am, the more likely they are to be affected. Some of the differences may, in turn, be expressed in what I do or don't do or in how I do what I do, but they need not be.

Status

1. A person's place in any domain; or if no domain is specified, in the scheme of things.
2. A way of talking about a person's behavior potential.
3. A way of talking about a set of relationships simultaneously.
4. A way of talking about how P is expected to treat X and how X is expected to treat P.

Notes:

Relationships in a given context can be replaced by talking about the place of things in that context. From the place of each thing, we can derive the relationships among them and vice versa.

Status Assignment

Giving something a place (status) in the scheme of things.

Notes:

The place that a thing has in the scheme of things is something that is decided, not merely discovered. This holds both for my scheme of things and for our scheme of things.

The "something" here is not restricted to persons, but may be anything—objects, processes, events, states of affairs, individuals, groups, heaps, sets, structures, happenings, absences, statements, actions, achievements, etc.

Style
1. How P does what P does.
2. A kind of Performance.
3. A kind of implementation.
4. One of the Dispositions.

Notes:
Style is used as a general person description. For example, we speak of a formal or informal style of speech; a sophisticated style of dress; a devious or straightforward interpersonal style; of a graceful or awkward or delicate style of movement; and so on.

"How P does what P does" refers to implementation, which corresponds to the Performance parameter. In giving a Style Description, we are saying that among the behaviors defined by the domain, we would expect to find more of those behaviors characterized by performances of the specified kind (more than we would expect from just anybody).

Trait
1. To have a given trait is to be disposed to engage in a certain kind of behavior.
2. Any behavior may be the basis for a trait description. Given a type of behavior, either a low-frequency pattern of occurrence or a high-frequency pattern of occurrence will generate trait descriptions. Low-X and high-X will be different traits.
3. Can be seen as an Interest without an "object" (focus).
4. One of the four Dispositions.

Notes:
A brave, generous, or hostile person is one in whose life history brave, generous, or hostile behaviors (respectively) occur with greater frequency than in the lives of other persons, other things being equal. How much "greater frequency" is enough? Well, (1) more than you would expect from just anyone in those same circumstances and (2) enough more to be worth commenting on. Ultimately, this is a community standard and will vary from community to community, as with most things.

Verbal Behavior
1. A Deliberate Action in which the primary Performance is a locution.
2. Behaviors, $<V>$, that can be denoted by specifying three parameters:
$<C, L, \{B\}>$
where:
$C = Concept$

(the concept being acted on, compared to C', all other concepts that might have been acted on).

L = Locution

(the word, phrase, or sentence uttered).

B = Behavior

(a set of behaviors that qualify as "acting on Concept C").

3. The sense in which verbal behavior is straightforwardly behavior shown via deletion and substitution as follows:

$$<IA> = <\theta, \theta, C, \theta, L, \theta, \theta, \theta>, \{B\}.$$

4. One of five perspectives on the Person Concept.

Notes:

To say that a behavior is a verbal behavior is to give an explicitly incomplete description of behavior rather than merely a vague one, since it makes a commitment to only two of the eight parameters of behavior. Recalling the use of the Deletion operation to generate systematically incomplete forms of behavior description, we could include "Verbal Behavior Description" in that category.

Want

1. The "motivation" aspect of behavior. This parameter of behavior provides a place to specify that.

   $$<B> = <I, Want, K, KH, P, A, PC, S>$$

2. Behaviors are partly different via a wanted state of affairs, and the Want parameter provides a place to specify what that state of affairs is.
3. Successful behavior consists of achieving the wanted state of affairs.

Notes:

Values of the Want parameter are necessarily also part of the values of the Know parameter, but not vice versa.

World

1. What you see when you look around you.
2. What you see depends on the place each thing has in your behavioral scheme, that is, its status. This is not "objective," because every community has different statuses for objects, processes, events, and states of affairs.
3. The real world.
4. Not a synonym for "reality."
5. One of five perspectives on the Person Concept.

References

Angier, N. (2009). When 'what animals do' doesn't seem to cover it. New York Times.

Anscombe, G. E. M. (1957/1966). *Intention*. Ithaca, NY: Cornell University Press.

Aristotle, Ross, W. D., & Brown, L. (2009). *The Nicomachean ethics*. Oxford: Oxford University Press.

Arnheim, R. (1969). *Visual thinking*. Berkeley: University of California Press.

Asimov, I. (1950). *I, Robot*. Greenwich, Conn: Fawcett Publications.

Auchincloss, E. L., Samberg, E., & American Psychoanalytic Association. (2012). *Psychoanalytic terms & concepts*. New York: American Psychoanalytic Association.

Austin, J. L. (1962). *How to do things with words*. Cambridge: Harvard University Press.

Barber, T. X. (1969). *Hypnosis: A scientific approach*. New York: Van Norstrand-Reinhold Co.

Bateson, G. (1972). *Steps to an ecology of mind: Collected essays in anthropology, psychiatry, evolution, and epistemology*. San Francisco: Chandler Pub. Co.

Bellow, S. (1964). *Herzog*. New York: Viking Press.

Benhabib, S. (1988). Judgment and the moral foundations of politics in Arendt's thought. *Political Theory, 16*(1).

Bergner, R. (2010). What is behavior? And so what? *New Ideas in Psychology*, https://doi.org/10.1016/j.newideapsych. 2010.08.001.

Bergner, R. (2000). Love and barriers to love: an analysis for psychotherapists and others. *American Journal of Psychotherapy, 54*(1), 1–17.

Bergner, R. (1997). What is psychopathology? And so what? *Clinical Psychology: Science and Practice, 4*, 235–248.

Bergner, R. M. (2013). All the world's a stage: a person-centered view of science. In K. E. Davis, R. M. Bergner, F. Lubuguin, & W. Schwartz (Eds.), *Vol. 10. Advances in Descriptive Psychology* (pp. 7–18). Ann Arbor, MI: Descriptive Psychology Press.

Bergner, R. (2015). Status dynamic psychotherapy. In E. Neukrig (Ed.), *The Sage encyclopedia of counseling and psychotherapy*. Los Angeles, CA: Sage Publications.

Bergner, R. (2016). What is behavior? And why is it not reducible to biological states of affairs? *Journal of Theoretical and Philosophical Psychology, 36*(1), 41–55.

Bergner, R. (1983). In K. Davis & R. Bergner (Eds.), *Vol. 3. Advances in Descriptive Psychology* (pp. 209–228). Greenwich, CT: JAI Press.

Bergner, R. (2003). Emotions: a relational view and its clinical applications. *American Journal of Psychotherapy, 57*, 471–490.

Bernfield, S. (1944). Freud's earliest theories and the school of Helmholtz. *Psychoanalytic Quarterly, 13*, 341–362.

Berne, E. (1964). *Games people play: The psychology of human relationships*. New York: Grove Press.

Bettelheim, B. (1983). *Freud and man's soul*. New York: A.A. Knopf.

Bowers, K. S. (1979). Time distortion and hypnotic ability: underestimating the duration of hypnosis. *Journal of Abnormal Psychology, 88*(4), 435–439.

Bruner, J. (1973). *Beyond the information given: Studies in the psychology of knowing*. New York: W. W. Norton & Company.

Buber, M. (1958). *I and thou*. New York: Scribner.

Bushe, G. R. (2013). The appreciative inquiry model. In E. H. Kessler (Ed.), *Vol. 1. Encyclopedia of management theory* (pp. 41–44). Sage Publications.

Caston, J. (2011). Agency as a psychoanalytic idea. *The Journal of the American Psychoanalytic Association, 59*(5), 907–938.

Cavell, S. (1969/2002). *Must we mean what we say?* Cambridge: Cambridge University Press.

Chalmers, D. (1995). Facing up to the problem of consciousness. *Journal of Consciousness Studies, 2,* 200–219.

Collingwood, R. D. (1945). *The idea of nature.* Oxford: The Claredon Press.

Csikszentmihályi, M. (1988). *Optimal experience: psychological studies of flow in consciousness.* Cambridge, UK: Cambridge University Press.

de Waal, F. (2016). *Are we smart enough to know how smart animals are?* New York: Norton.

du Couëdic, M. (1981). 1881—the electrical congress and universal exposition. *IEC Bulletin, 15*(3).

Davis, K., & Todd, M. (1982). Friendship and love relationships. In K. Davis & T. Mitchell (Eds.), *Vol. 2. Advances in Descriptive Psychology* (pp. 79–122). Greenwich, CT: JAI Press.

Douglas, M. (1966). *Purity and danger.* London: Routledge and Kegan Paul.

Edwards, P. (Ed.), (1967/2006). *The encyclopedia of philosophy.* New York: Macmillan.

Erickson, M. H. (1964). The confusion technique in hypnosis. *American Journal of Clinical Hypnosis, 6*(3), 183–207.

Ellenberger, H. F. (1970). *The discovery of the unconscious; the history and evolution of dynamic psychiatry.* New York: Basic Books.

Fonagy, P., Gergely, G., Jurist, E. L., & Target, M. (2002). *Affect regulation, mentalization and the development of the self.* New York: Other Press.

Fonagy, P., Gergely, G., & Target, M. (2008). Psychoanalytic constructs and attachment theory and research. In J. Cassidy & P. R. Shaver (Eds.), *Handbook of attachment: Theory, research, and clinical applications* (pp. 783–810). New York, NY: Guilford Press.

Frye, N. (1957/1967). *Anatomy of criticism.* New York: Athaneum.

Freud, S. (1912a). On the universal tendency to debasement in the sphere of love. In *The standard edition of the complete psychological works of Sigmund Freud.* London: Hogarth Press.

Freud, S. (1912b). The dynamics of transference. In *The standard edition of the complete psychological works of Sigmund Freud.* London: Hogarth Press.

Freud, S. (1917/1975). Mourning and melancholia. In *The standard edition of the complete psychological works of Sigmund Freud.* London: Hogarth Press.

Freud, S. (1925/1975). Some additional notes on dream-interpretation as a whole. In *The standard edition of the complete psychological works of Sigmund Freud.* London: Hogarth Press.

Garfinkel, H. (1956). Conditions of successful degradation ceremonies. *American Journal of Sociology, 61,* 420–424.

Gennep, A. (1909/1960). *The rites of passage.* Chicago: University of Chicago Press.

Gergen, K. (2015). From mirroring to world-making: Research as future forming. *Journal for the Theory of Social Behaviour, 45*(3), 287–310.

Gibson, J. J. (1979). *The ecological approach to visual perception.* Boston: Houghton Mifflin.

Gill, M. M., & Brenman, M. (1961). *Hypnosis and related states; psychoanalytic studies in regression, (Austen Riggs Center monograph).* Madison, CT: International Universities Press.

Godwin, S. (2015). Against parental rights. *Columbia Human Rights Law Review, 47*(1), 1–83.

Goffman, E. (1956/1990). *The presentation of self in everyday life.* London: Penguin.

Greenberg, R., Katz, H., Schwartz, W., & Pearlman, C. (1992). A research based reconsideration of the psychoanalytic theory or dreaming. *Journal of the American Psychoanalytic Association, 40,* 531–550.

Green, K. (1999). Was Wittgenstein Frege's Heir. *The Philosophical Quarterly, 49*(6), 289–308.

Hall, C. S., Lindzey, G., & Campbell, J. B. (1998). *Theories of personality.* New York: J. Wiley & Sons.

Harré, R. (1964). *Matter and method.* London: Macmillan.

Hobaiter and Byrne. (2014). The meanings of chimpanzee gestures, current biology. Accessed: https://doi.org/10.1016/j.cub.2014.05.066.

Harnsberger, B. (2015). *Status dynamics, through-lines, and the dramaturgical pattern of the recovering addict.* unpublished doctoral thesis Newton, MA: The Massachusetts School of Professional Psychology.

Hacker, P. M. S. (2015). Wittgenstein and forms of life. *Nordic Wittgenstein Review Special Issue,* 1–20.

Hacker, P. M. S. (2018). *The passions: A study of human nature.* Hoboken, NJ: John Wiley & Sons.

Hayes, S. C., Strosahl, K. D., & Wilson, K. G. (2012). *Acceptance and commitment therapy: The process and practice of mindful change* (2nd ed). New York, NY: The Guilford Press.

Hilgard, E. (1973). The domain of hypnosis. *American Psychologist, 28,* 972–982.

Holmes, J. (2013). *Depression doesn't always have to be depressing.* Pensacola, FL: Pelican Press.

Hutchinson, G. E. (1957). Concluding remarks. *Cold Spring Harbor Symposia on Quantitative Biology, 22*(2), 415–427.

Jahoda, G. (2005). Theodor Lipps and the shift from "sympathy" to "empathy". *Journal of the History of the Behavioral Sciences, 41,* 151–163.

Jeffrey, H. J. (1998a). Cognition without processes. In H. J. Jeffrey & R. Bergner (Eds.), *Vol. 7. Advances in Descriptive Psychology* (pp. 33–66). Ann Arbor, MI: Descriptive Psychology Press.

Jeffrey, H. J. (1998b). Consciousness, experience, and a person's world. In H. J. Jeffrey & R. Bergner (Eds.), *Vol. 7. Advances in Descriptive Psychology* (pp. 67–106). Ann Arbor, MI: Descriptive Psychology Press.

Jeffrey, H. J. (2010). Structure. In K. E. Davis, F. Lubuguin, & W. Schwartz (Eds.), *Vol. 9. Advances in Descriptive Psychology* (pp. 361–3407). Ann Arbor, MI: Descriptive Psychology Press.

Jeffrey, H. J., & Putman, A. O. (2013). The irrationality illusion: a new paradigm for economics and behavioral economics. *The Journal of Behavioral Finance, 14*(3), 161–194.

Jeffrey, H. J., & Putman, A. O. (2015). Subjective probability in behavioral economics and finance: a radical reformulation. *The Journal of Behavioral Finance, 16*(3), 231–249.

Kant, I., Guyer, P., & Wood, A. W. (1787/1998). *Critique of pure reason.* Cambridge: Cambridge University Press.

Kierkegaard, S., & Journalen JJ:167. (1843). *Søren Kierkegaards Skrifter. Vol. 18 (p. 306).* Copenhagen: Søren Kierkegaard Research Center. 1997.

Kirchenheim, C., & Persinger, M. (1991). Time distortion—a comparison of hypnotic induction and progressive relaxation procedures: a brief communication. *International Journal of Clinical and Experimental Hypnosis, 39,* 2.

Klein, G. (1976). *Psychoanalytic theory: An exploration of essentials.* Madison, CT: International Universities Press.

Kohut, H. (1984). *How does analysis cure?* Chicago: University of Chicago Press.

Kris, A. (1982). *Free association.* New Haven: Yale University Press.

Kret, M. E., Jaasma, L., Bionda, T., & Wijnen, J. G. (2016). Bonobos (*Pan paniscus*) show an attentional bias toward conspecifics' emotions. *Proceedings of the National Academy of Sciences of the United States of America, 113*(14), 3761–3766.

Kubrick, S., & Clarke, A. C. (1968). *2001: A space odyssey.* United States: Metro-Goldwyn-Mayer Corp.

Kuhn, T. S. (1970). *The structure of scientific revolutions.* Chicago: University of Chicago Press.

La Barre, W. (1954/1968). *The human animal.* Chicago: The University of Chicago Press.

Larkin, P., & Thwaite, A. (1993). *Collected poems: Larkin.* New York: Noonday Press.

Leary, T. (1961). *Drugs, set & suggestibility.* In *Paper presented at the annual meeting of the American Psychological Association, 6 September 1961.*

Lessing, G. E. (1967/1962). *Hamburg dramaturgy.* New York: Dover Press.

Lukes, S. (2005). *Power: A radical view.* New York: Palgrave Macmillan.

MacDougall, D. (1907). Hypothesis concerning soul substance together with experimental evidence of the existence of such a substance. *Journal of the American Society for Psychical Research, 1*(5), 237–244.

MacIntyre, A. C. (1958). *The unconscious: A conceptual analysis.* London: Routledge & Kegan Paul.

Malle, B. F., Moses, L. J., & Baldwin, D. A. (Eds.), (2001). *Intentions and intentionality: Foundations of social cognition.* Cambridge, MA: The MIT Press.

Maslow, A. H. (1943). A theory of human motivation. *Psychological Review, 50*(4), 370–396.

Maslow, A. H. (1968). *Toward a psychology of being.* New York: Van Nostrand Reinhold Co.

Meissner, W. (1991). *What is effective in psychoanalytic psychotherapy?* Northvale, NJ: Jason Aronson.

Morgan, A. H., & Hilgard, J. R. (1978-1979). The Stanford hypnotic clinical scale for adults. *American Journal of Clinical Hypnosis, 21*(2–3), 134–147.

Nagel, T. (2012). *Mind & Cosmos: Why the materialist neo-Darwinian conception of nature is almost certainly false.* Oxford: Oxford University Press.

Neisser, U. (1976). *Cognition and reality: Principles and implications of cognitive psychology.* New York: Freeman.

Orne, M. T. (1959). The nature of hypnosis: artifact and essence. *Journal of Abnormal and Social Psychology, 58,* 277–299.

Ossorio, P. G. (1966/1995). *Persons. The collected works of Peter G. Ossorio. Vol. I.* Ann Arbor, MI: Descriptive Psychology Press.

Ossorio, P. G. (1969/2010). *Meaning and Symbolism. The collected works of Peter G. Ossorio. Vol. VI.* Ann Arbor, MI: Descriptive Psychology Press.

Ossorio, P. G. (1973). Never smile at a crocodile. *Journal for the Theory of Social Behavior, 3,* 121–140.

Ossorio, P. G. (1977/2015). *Personality and Personality Theories. The collected works of Peter G. Ossorio. Vol. IX.* Ann Arbor, MI: Descriptive Psychology Press.

Ossorio, P. G. (1978/2005). *"What actually happens": The representation of real world phenomena. The collected works of Peter G. Ossorio. Vol. IV.* Ann Arbor, MI: Descriptive Psychology Press. Also published Columbia, SC: University of South Carolina Press, 1978.

Ossorio, P. G. (1981). Conceptual-notational devices: the PCF and related types. In K. Davis (Ed.), *Vol. 1. Advances in Descriptive Psychology.* Greenwich, CT: JAI Press.

Ossorio, P. G. (1983). A multicultural psychology. In K. E. Davis & R. M. Bergner (Eds.), *Vol. 3. Advances in Descriptive Psychology* (pp. 13–44). Greenwich, CN: JAI Press.

Ossorio, P. G. (1985). An overview of Descriptive Psychology. In K. Gergen & K. E. Davis (Eds.), *The Social Construction of the Person* (pp. 19–40). Rome, NY: Springer-Verlag.

Ossorio, P. G. (1986/1990). Appraisal. In A. O. Putman & K. E. Davis (Eds.), *Vol. 5. Advances in Descriptive Psychology* (pp. 155–171). Ann Arbor, MI: Descriptive Psychology Press [Original work published 1986 as LRI Report No. 37. Boulder, CO: Linguistic Research Institute.].

Ossorio, P. G. (1991). Naive baseball theory. *Psychological Inquiry, 2*(4), 352–355.

Ossorio, P. G. (1997). *1997 rap session with Peter Ossorio.* Society for Descriptive Psychology Web Site http://www.sdp.org/sdp/rap97/rap97.html.

Ossorio, P. G. (1998/2012). *Place. The collected works of Peter G. Ossorio. Vol. III.* Ann Arbor, MI: Descriptive Psychology Press.

Ossorio, P. G. (2000). *2000 rap session with Peter Ossorio.* Society for Descriptive Psychology Web Site http://www.sdp.org/sdp/rap00/rap00.html.

Ossorio, P. G. (2006a). Out of nowhere. In K. E. Davis & R. M. Bergner (Eds.), *Vol. 8. Advances in Descriptive Psychology* (pp. 108–143). Ann Arbor, MI: Descriptive Psychology Press.

Ossorio, P. G. (2006b). *The behavior of persons. The collected works of Peter G. Ossorio. Vol. V.* Ann Arbor, MI: Descriptive Psychology Press.

Papineau, D, "Naturalism", The Stanford Encyclopedia of Philosophy (Winter 2016 Edition), Edward N. Zalta (ed.), Retrieved from https://plato.stanford.edu/.

Pepper, S. (1942). *World hypotheses: A study in evidence.* Berkeley: University of California Press.

Peek, C. J. (2013). Integrated behavioral health and primary care: a common language. In Talen, & Valeras (Eds.), *Integrated behavioral health in primary care: Evaluating the evidence, identifying the essentials*. New York: Springer.

Peters, R. S. (1958). *The concept of motivation*. London: Routledge & Keegan Paul, London.

Phillips, A. (2014). *Becoming Freud: The making of a psychoanalyst*. New Haven: Yale University Press.

Pitkin, H. F. (1972). *Wittgenstein and justice: On the significance of Ludwig Wittgenstein for social and political thought*. Berkeley: University of California Press.

Plotkin, W., & Schwartz, W. (1982). A conceptualization of hypnosis: I. Exploring the place of appraisal and anomaly in behavior and experience. In K. Davis & T. Mitchell (Eds.), *Vol. 2. Advances in Descriptive Psychology* (pp. 139–194). Greenwich, CT: JAI Press.

Plotkin, W., & Schwartz, W. (1985). A conceptualization of hypnosis: II. Hypnotic induction procedures and manifestations of the hypnotic state. In K. Davis & T. Mitchell (Eds.), *Vol. 4. Advances in Descriptive Psychology* (pp. 75–98). Greenwich, CT: JAI Press.

Premack, D., & Woodruff, G. (1978). Does the chimpanzee have a theory of mind? *Behavioral and Brain Sciences, 1*(4), 515–526.

Proops, I, "Wittgenstein's logical atomism", The Stanford encyclopedia of philosophy (Winter 2017 Edition), Edward N. Zalta (ed.), Retrieved from https://plato.stanford.edu/.

Prosser, W. (1941). *Handbook of the Law of Torts*. St. Paul: West Publishing Company.

Pryor, K., Haag, R., & O'Reilly, J. (1969). The creative porpoise: training for novel behavior. *Journal of the Experimental Analysis of Behavior, 12*, 653–661.

Putman, A. (1981). Communities. In K. Davis (Ed.), *Vol. 1. Advances in Descriptive Psychology*. Greenwich, CT: JAI Press.

Putman, A. (1990). Organizations. In A. Putman & K. Davis (Eds.), *Vol. 5. Advances in Descriptive Psychology*. Ann Arbor, MI: Descriptive Psychology Press.

Putman, A. (1998). Being, becoming and belonging. In J. Jeffrey & R. Bergner (Eds.), *Vol. 7. Advances in Descriptive Psychology* (pp. 127–160). Ann Arbor, MI: Descriptive Psychology Press.

Putman, A. O. (2010). Ordinary magic: what Descriptive Psychology is, and why it matters. In K. E. Davis, F. Lubuguin, & W. Schwartz (Eds.), *Vol. 9. Advances in Descriptive Psychology* (pp. 9–39). Ann Arbor, MI: Descriptive Psychology Press.

Putman, A. O. (2013). When worlds collide: the source of intractable value problems. In K. E. Davis, R. M. Bergner, F. Lubuguin, & W. Schwartz (Eds.), *Vol. 10. Advances in Descriptive Psychology* (pp. 81–112). Ann Arbor, MI: Descriptive Psychology Press.

Putman, A. O. (2016). *Worlds and ultimate satisfaction*. Ann Arbor, MI: Descriptive Psychology Press.

Range, F., Horn, L., Viranyi, Z., & Huber, L. (2009). The absence of reward induces inequity aversion in dogs. *Proceedings of the National Academy of Sciences of the United States of America, 106*(1), 340–345.

Roberts, M. (1982). Men and women: partners, lovers, and friends. In K. Davis & T. Mitchell (Eds.), *Vol. 2. Advances in Descriptive Psychology* (pp. 57–78). Greenwich, CT: JAI Press.

Roberts, M. (1985). Worlds and world reconstruction. In K. Davis & T. Mitchell (Eds.), *Vol. 4. Advances in Descriptive Psychology* (pp. 17–52). Greenwich, CT: JAI Press.

Rogers, C. (1961). *On becoming a person*. Boston: Houghton Mifflin.

Royce, J. (1908). *The philosophy of loyalty*. New York: Macmillan.

Robison, M. K., Gath, K. I., & Unsworth, N. (2016). The neurotic wandering mind: an individual differences investigation of neuroticism, mind-wandering, and executive control. *The Quarterly Journal of Experimental Psychology, 70*(4), 649–663. https://doi.org/10.1080/17470218.2016.1145706.

Rizzolatti, G., & Craighero, L. (2004). The mirror–neuron system. *Annual Review of Neuroscience, 27*, 169–192.

Rogers, C. (1951). *Client-centered therapy: Its current practice, implications and theory*. London: Constable.

Rogers, C. (1975). Empathic: an unappreciated way of being. *The Counseling Psychologist, 5*(2), 1–10.

Romero, T., Konno, A., & Hasegawa, T. (2013). Familiarity bias and physiological responses in contagious yawning by dogs support link to empathy. *PLoS One, 8*(8).

Ryle, G. (1949/2002). *The concept of mind*. Chicago: University of Chicago Press.

Sarbin, T., & Coe, W. (1972). *Hypnosis: A social psychological analysis of influence communication*. New York: Holt, Rinehart, & Winston, Inc.

Sartre, J.-P. (1943/1966). *Being and nothingness: An essay on phenomenological ontology*. New York: Washington Square Press.

Savage-Rumbaugh, S., Rumbaugh, W., & Fields. (2009). Empirical Kanzi: The ape language controversy revisited. *Skeptic, 15*(1), 25–33.

Schafer, R. (1959). Generative empathy in the treatment situation. *Psychoanalytic Quarterly, 28*, 342–373.

Schafer, R. (1976). *A new language for psychoanalysis*. New Haven, CT: Yale University Press.

Schafer, R. (1983). *The analytic attitude*. New York: Basic Books.

Schofield, M. (2002). Leucippus, Democritus and the *ou mallon* principle: an examination of Theophrastus *Phys. Op.* Fr. 8. *Phronesis, 47*(3), 253–263.

Schwartz, W. (1978). Time and context during hypnotic involvement. *International Journal of Clinical and Experimental Hypnosis, 26*, 307–316.

Schwartz, W. (1979). Degradation, accreditation and rites of passage. *Psychiatry: Journal for the Study of Interpersonal Processes, 42*(2), 138–146.

Schwartz, W. (1980). Hypnosis and episodic memory. *International Journal of Clinical and Experimental Hypnosis, 28*, 375–385.

Schwartz, W. (1984). The two concepts of action and responsibility in psychoanalysis. *Journal of the American Psychoanalytic Association, 32*(3), 557–572.

Schwartz, W. (1988). What makes something psychoanalytic? *Psychiatry, 51*, 417–426.

Schwartz, W., & Godwyn, M. (1988). Action and representation in ordinary and lucid dreams. In J. Gackenback & S. La Barge (Eds.), *Lucid dreaming: New direction in consciousness during sleep*. New York: Plenum.

Schwartz, W. (1990). A psychoanalytic approach to dreamwork. In S. Krippner (Ed.), *Dreamtime and dreamwork*. Los Angles: Tarcher.

Schwartz, W. (1993a). The manifest problem as the psychoanalytic unit in the interpretation of dreams. *International Journal of Psychosomatics, 40*, 11–13.

Schwartz, W. (1993b). Problem representation in dreams. In J. Wotiz (Ed.), *The Kekule riddle: A problem for chemist and psychologists*. Vienna, IL: Cache River Press.

Schwartz, W. (2002). From passivity to competence: a conceptualization of knowledge, skill, tolerance, and empathy. *Psychiatry: Journal for the Study of Interpersonal Processes, 65*(4), 338–345.

Schwartz, W. (2013). The parameters of empathy: Core considerations for psychotherapy and supervision. In K. E. Davis, R. M. Bergner, F. Lubuguin, & W. Schwartz (Eds.), *Vol. 10. Advances in Descriptive Psychology* (pp. 197–212). Ann Arbor, MI: Descriptive Psychology Press.

Schwartz, W. (2014). What is a person and How can we be sure? A Paradigm Case Formulation. *Journal of Evolution and Technology, 24*(3).

Seligman, M. E. P. (1972). Learned helplessness. *Annual Review of Medicine, 23*(1), 407–412.

Shakespeare, W., & Furness, H. H. (1963). *As you like it*. New York: Dover Publications.

Shakespeare, W. (1992). In B. A. Mowat & P. Werstine (Eds.), *The Tragedy of Hamlet, Prince of Denmark*. New York: Washington Square-Pocket.

Shay, J. (2010). *Achilles in Vietnam: Combat trauma and the undoing of character*. New York: Simon and Schuster.

Shedler, J. (2010). The efficacy of psychodynamic psychotherapy. *The American Psychologist, 65*, 98–109.

Shideler, M. (1992). *Spirituality: An approach through Descriptive Psychology*. Ann Arbor: Descriptive Psychology Press.

Shor, R. E. (1959). Hypnosis and the concept of the generalized reality-orientation. *American Journal of Psychotherapy, 13*, 582–602.

Shor, R. E., & Orne, E. C. (1962). *The Harvard Group Scale of hypnotic susceptibility, Form A: An adaptation for group administration with self-report scoring of the Standard Hypnotic Susceptibility Scale, Form A*. Palo Alto, Calif.: Consulting Psychologists Press.

Singer, P. (2009). *Animal liberation*. New York: HarperCollins.

Skinner, B. F. (1971). *Beyond freedom and dignity*. New York: Knopf/Random House.

Smith, T. W. (2016). *The book of human emotions*. New York: Little, Brown.

Stanislavski, C. (1936/1989). *An actor prepares*. New York: Routledge.

Strawson, P. F. (1959). *Individuals*. London: Methuen & Co Ltd.

Sullivan, H. S. (1953). *The interpersonal theory of psychiatry*. New York: Norton.

Taylor, C. (1985). *Human agency and language*. Cambridge: Cambridge University Press.

Titchener, E. B. (1909). *Lectures on the experimental psychology of the thought-processes*. New York: The MacMillan Company.

Torres, W., & Bergner, R. (2010). Humiliation: its nature and consequences. *Journal of the American Academy of Psychiatry and Law, 38*(2), 195–204.

Wachtel, P. L. (1980). Transference, schema, and assimilation: the relevance of Piaget to the psychoanalytic theory of transference. *The Annual of Psychoanalysis, 8*, 59–76.

Wagenmakers, E.-J., Beek, T., Dijkhoff, L., & Gronau, Q. (2016). Registered replication report: Strack, Martin, & Stepper (1988). *Perspectives on Psychological Science, 11*(6), 917–928.

Wakefield, J. (1997). Normal inability versus pathological disability: why Ossorio's definition of mental disorder is not sufficient. *Clinical Psychology: Science and Practice, 4*, 249–258.

White, S. (2012). *Line of fire*. New York: Dutton.

Wincelberg, S. (Writer). (1966). Dagger or the mind [Television series episode]. In The Star Trek. New York, NY: NBC.

Winnicott, D. W. (1956/1984). Primary maternal preoccupation. In *Through paediatrics to psychoanalysis: Collected papers* (pp. 300–305). London: Karnac.

Winnicott, D. W. (1965). Ego distortion in terms of true and false self. In *The maturational process and the facilitating environment: Studies in the theory of emotional development* (pp. 140–157). New York: International Universities Press, Inc.

Winnicott, D. W. (1971). *Playing and reality*. London: Routledge.

Wise, S. (2000). *Rattling the cage: Toward legal rights for animals*. Cambridge, MA: Perseus Books.

Wittgenstein, L. (1953). *Philosophical investigations*. Oxford, UK: Wiley-Blackwell.

Wittgenstein, L. (1922). *Tractatus logico-philosophicus*. London: Routledge & Kegan Paul.

Wittgenstein, L. (1972). In G. E. M. Anscombe & G. H. Wright (Eds.), *On certainty*. New York: Harper & Row.

Yermish, A. (2010). *Cheetahs on the couch: Issues affecting the therapeutic working alliance with clients who are cognitively gifted*. Unpublished doctoral dissertation Newton, MA: The Massachusetts School of Professional Psychology.

Ziff, P. (1960). *Semantic analysis*. Ithaca, NY: Cornell University Press.

Index

Note: Page numbers followed by *f* indicate figures and *np* indicate footnotes.